ONE HUNDRED
AND ONE TREASURES

From the Collections of
The William L. Clements Library

ONE HUNDRED AND ONE TREASURES

From the Collections of
The William L. Clements Library

A Celebration of Seventy-five Years

1923–1998

Edited by
JOHN C. DANN

CLEMENTS LIBRARY
UNIVERSITY OF MICHIGAN
ANN ARBOR, MICHIGAN
1998

HALF TITLE, PAGE I:
The William L. Clements Library,
engraving by W. B. Shaw, 1930

Published in the United States of America by
The William L. Clements Library
The University of Michigan

Manufactured in the United States of America

ISBN 1-881606-01-5

THIS BOOK HAS BEEN PUBLISHED
WITH GENEROUS FUNDING
PROVIDED BY
THE MOSAIC FOUNDATION
OF RITA & PETER HEYDON
BASED IN ANN ARBOR

IN HELPING TO PROVIDE THIS GLIMPSE INTO THE
MAGNIFICENT COLLECTIONS OF THE CLEMENTS LIBRARY,
THE HEYDONS HOPE THAT THEIR GIFT WILL INSPIRE
OTHERS TO KNOW AND SUPPORT THIS REMARKABLE
INSTITUTION DURING ITS CELEBRATORY
SEVENTY-FIFTH YEAR.

TABLE OF CONTENTS

Introduction
11

Editor's Preface
15

LIST OF ENTRIES

INTRODUCTION

THIS IS A CELEBRATION — not a guide, not a catalogue. The dictionary defines the word as "to honor, to make publicly known." And these pages celebrate what is, in many different ways, one of the most remarkable storehouses of the treasures of history — the unique materials that made America and spread its influence and enchantment across the world. It is, in a sense, the story of the remarkable men and women who shaped the United States and a timely tribute to those who, over three quarters of a century, collected and preserved the records of their accomplishments.

"To make publicly known" is an important aspect of the Celebration, for — as we prepare to turn a new page on a new century — the keepers of these treasures plan to open their doors wider and share their bounty, in imaginative ways and a more accessible fashion, with scholars and schools, patriots and prospectors: everybody in fact who knows that history derives from the minds and memories, the hearts and courage of men and women of all races, colors, and creeds. The rich heritage of all America's peoples is contained and brought to life within the walls of the William L. Clements Library, and technology is rapidly making it available throughout the world. No matter how long dead, or even forgotten, men and women of the past can still become mentors for our present and future.

William Lawrence Clements, who lived through seventy-three years from 1861 to 1934, knew that very well. It is our good fortune that he was born in Ann Arbor, within the ambience of the University of Michigan which had been founded in 1837 and matured quickly as it expanded its disciplines. He graduated from its College of Engineering and went to work for his father who was a partner in a Bay City business that made hoists and cranes. An imaginative young man, he was awarded patents for improvements to cranes and steam shovels, some of which played a major part in the construction of the Panama Canal.

It is not surprising that a young man who was helping to build his country should be fascinated by those who had come before. By the 1890s, soon after his marriage, William Clements had enough money to pursue a private passion, and he began collecting rare books and Americana. He bought the *Columbus Letter* — the report to the King and Queen of Spain describing the first voyage to "discover" a world that did not then exist on any map — printed in Rome in 1493. He had Thomas Hariot's *A briefe and true report of Virginia* of 1588, one of only six copies in the world. He had John Smith's *True Relation of Virginia* of 1608 and Jefferson's *Notes* on the state a century and a half later. In letters and documents, he possessed the greatest gathering in America of information on the American Revolution in the papers of General Thomas Gage, Sir Henry Clinton, and General Nathanael Greene.

But history is often better illuminated by unconsidered trifles; sometimes household accounts can tell as much about a man as a battlefield, and it was the very diversity of Clements' collection that was its strength. For he also collected what passes for ephemera: broadsides and song sheets, newspapers and magazines, cookery books and sermons, school primers and slave documents, knowing that the ability to weave together such sources was to be given a much deeper insight into the meaning of America.

He was convinced that history comes more vividly into the present when it is "hands on"—when each new generation is able to hold in its own hands or at least see with its own eyes the books and papers of long ago—so he decided, in 1921, to give his collection to his *alma mater*. When it was accepted, he provided it with a suitable home, a handsome building designed in the style of the Italian Renaissance by Albert Kahn. He personally supervised contractors and architects. It cost him a little under $200,000, a large sum of money that would be counted in millions today and, for all his remaining years, during which he served as a Regent of the University of Michigan, he was the presiding spirit. And when the William L. Clements Library was dedicated on June 15, 1923, the extraordinary richness of his gift became more widely apparent.

Randolph G. Adams was appointed as the Library's first Director. Dr. Adams was succeeded by Howard H. Peckham in 1953 and he, in turn, by John C. Dann in 1977. These three men added wisely and selectively to the great benefaction of which they were custodians. It is a remarkable achievement for any institution to have had only three Directors in seventy-five years, but the Clements has a more notable reason for celebrating its succession than that. Randolph Adams worked with Mr. Clements for eleven years. Howard Peckham enjoyed ten years with Mr. Adams, and John Dann, who joined the Library in 1972, had the benefit of five years with Mr. Peckham before he settled comfortably in the chair. Each, therefore, had the inestimable advantage of belonging to a tradition and inheriting a single-minded view of the Library's role and purpose, and each kept the faith of the Founder.

Their continuing mission is evident and easily defined: to pursue and possess the primary sources of American history. They collected books and ephemera, not because such items were rare, not because they were pretty. The deciding factor was and is historical content and significance, and, unlike many other great libraries, the Clements has never stopped collecting. Indeed, its 75th birthday celebrations are significantly directed towards increasing the resources to enable the pursuit to continue. It has been lucky, too, in its friends. The Clements Library Associates—a group which commemorates its own fiftieth anniversary this year—has been vitally important in supporting collection growth.

As much out of curiosity as anything else, I asked John Dann to record information on when and how the Library had acquired each of the 101 treasures represented in these pages. This information will greatly interest those who appreciate the history and lore of the book trade, and we share it, in italics, with our readers. But it also brings out several important factors that help to explain the Library's successes over the years. One of these is that the Clements Directors have always understood that close, personal relationships of friendship and trust with book dealers have in large part made the Library what it is today. This level of respect is deep and mutual, and it always has been so, from the earliest days when William L. Clements relied so heavily on the wisdom and sage advice of Lathrop Harper, Joseph Sabin, Doctor Rosenbach, and the great British firms of Maggs Brothers, Henry Stevens, and Bernard Quaritch. Similar relationships with their successors in the book trade today have given the Clements Library many eyes and many devoted friends in searching out and securing its latest treasures, and William Clements intended it to be so. The record of sources also brings out the importance of donors of rare and important books and manuscripts throughout the Library's history. Could anyone imagine a finer permanent home for much-loved books or ancestral papers?

The handful of American libraries that can be considered in the same pantheon as the Clements are each unique in their way. Each has predominant interests. The Clements has become one of the world's four or five leading archives of American historical maps, and it has one of the very finest collections of visual images in America, some of which are two or three centuries older than the United States itself. It is rich in topographical drawings, engravings, and prints. Perhaps its greatest strength is in manuscripts. But the keepers of these treasures have always known as well that primary sources include playbills and manuals, diaries of ordinary people involved in extraordinary events, tickets of voyages, and restaurant menus.

Well over half of all the items in the Clements are unique and it requires a certain audacity even to attempt to represent its holdings with a mere 101 items. It took Scheherazade 1,001 nights to finish her fabulous recitation, but we would scarcely have dented the resources of the Clements even at that number. Still we make no apology for this taste of treasure, this sampler, this Celebration. Our aim is the opening of doors. With John Dann as mentor, and his staff as guides, we have made the selection like a weaver, choosing threads and colours to make a pattern — if you like, a Star Spangled Banner to highlight a Celebration of greatness and future promise.

Walter Hayes, *Chairman,*
75TH CELEBRATION COMMITTEE

EDITOR'S PREFACE

THE CLEMENTS LIBRARY has needed a publication of this sort for years. Walter Hayes, Chairman of the Library's seventy-fifth anniversary campaign, suggested such a project. We desired something which in words and in pictures could tell persons unfamiliar with the Clements a bit about what the Library is and what it does. We did not want a comprehensive list, an erudite bibliography, a scholarly exhibit catalogue, or a visitor's guide, but a book that could be enjoyable to read, even in small bites, and a selective visual feast of the Library's collections, if only a fraction of them. Its purpose would be to inform, to amuse, and to encourage more substantial contacts in the future. Emulating Scheherazade in a highly abbreviated format, we decided to present these treasures in the form of 101 illustrated stories. The purpose here would not be to keep the storyteller alive, but the reader awake!

The hard part was making the selections. Should the publication concentrate only on high spots, or should it attempt to be representative of the collections as a whole? How does one select 101 treasures, when the Library contains thousands of items of similar rarity, and importance, and interest?

The entire curatorial staff took part in the selection process, and the result was a congenial compromise between "greatest treasures" and a display of the breadth and diversity of the collections. We hope, in an enjoyable fashion, to remind scholars and the general public alike that one of the world's truly great historical libraries is at the University of Michigan, and then to give them some idea of the scope and type of materials it contains.

In the initial stage of writing textual descriptions, staff members Arlene Shy, Rob Cox, and Brian Dunnigan all cheerfully assisted. The editor wrote slightly more than half of the entries, and he rigorously edited the whole, although attempting to preserve the individuality of writing styles. Errors of any sort are his responsibility alone. These previously mentioned staff members, along with John Harriman, Joan Barth, and Rachel Onuf graciously proofread the manuscript. Shneen Coldiron assisted the semi-computer-illiterate editor to standardize camera-ready copy, and Arlene Shy and Laura Daniel oversaw the gathering of pictures. Paul Jaronski of the University's News and Information Service took most of the photographs. Paul Hoffmann of Stinehour Press, who has worked often with the Clements Library, brought his usual brilliance and patience to designing the volume and shepherding it through the production process.

Most of all, I want to thank Walter Hayes for inspiring and enthusiastically supporting the project at every turn, and Peter and Rita Heydon for the timely and generous financial support making its publication possible.

John C. Dann
LIBRARY DIRECTOR

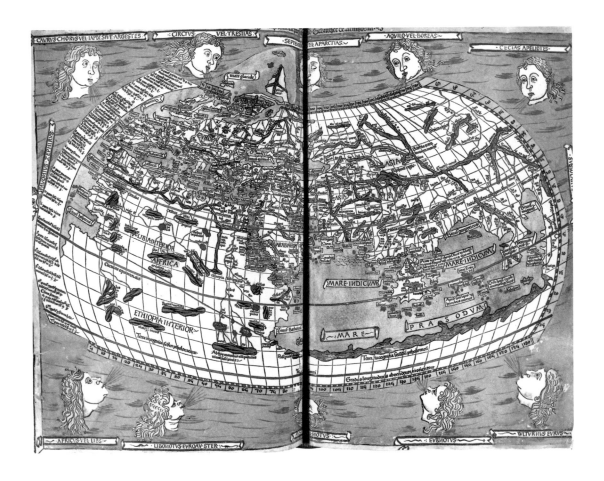

✑ 1 ✑

A WORLD WITHOUT AMERICA:
THE PTOLEMY MAP

ALL THE EARLY EUROPEAN VOYAGES of discovery, including that of Christopher Columbus, were based largely on geographical information that was even then more than a thousand years old. Ptolemy of Alexandria made astronomical observations between 121 and 150 A.D. His world, projected on a map in the late Middle Ages, extended from 20 degrees south to 65 degrees north and from a basic meridian through the Canary Islands to 180 degrees east. Drawn from the standpoint of an astronomer, it was intersected by curved lines of latitude and longitude. He left the map of the unknown world blank though he did assume the existence of a large continent south of the Equator.

Ptolemy's work was well known to Arab geographers but was not introduced into Western Europe until the fifteenth century. Publication of *Geographia* in 1475 marked a turning point in European knowledge of world geography which had advanced little during the Middle Ages. Two editions appeared in Ulm, Germany, in 1482 and 1486, both of which used essentially the same maps printed from wood blocks with hand-cut lettering. Twelve faces or windheads equating to the points of the compass surround the world map with each wind named to indicate its direction.

Although this is the most accurate and comprehensive of ancient maps and remained standard until "modern" times, it was wrong in many respects. The Mediterranean is much enlarged and the Indian Ocean is a large lake. The size of the Caspian Sea is exaggerated and Scandanavia is an island. There is no America, but Iceland is located and Ceylon is magnified fourteen times. It is nevertheless the father of all maps and the most important. It is, essentially, the world as Europeans knew it before Columbus, and it was a map he personally knew and used.

The copy of Ptolemy's *Geographia* (Ulm, 1486) in the Clements Library is the oldest of an outstanding collection of fifteenth- through nineteenth-century atlases. The Library is one of the world's noted resources for research on cartographic history.

Purchased from Goodspeed's, 1949.

⚜ 2 ⚜

"I DID NOT FIND ANY MONSTERS"

WHEN COLUMBUS RETURNED to Spain he told the story of his odyssey in a letter to the Royal Court. It is the first printed account of the New World, a document written in a modest, sensitive style, recording the awe and wonder of America's first visitors. The edition of Columbus' letter shown here was printed in Rome, in Latin, in 1493. Before the year 1500 at least seventeen editions were printed — in Barcelona, Valladolid, Strasbourg, Florence, Rome, Antwerp, Basel, and Paris.

The narrative, though brief, is entirely captivating, in particular in recording the kind and gentle nature of the natives. They "are exceedingly straightforward and trustworthy and most liberal with all they have; none of them denies to the asker anything that he possesses; on the contrary they themselves invite us to ask for it." They "persist in the belief that I leaped out of the skies . . . and they were the first to announce the fact wherever we landed, some of them calling out loudly to the others, 'Come, come, and you will see the men from heaven'." And he records, "I did not find any monsters among them, as many expected, but men of great dignity and kindliness." There is a promise in the letter to give "our invincible sovereigns as much

¶ Epistola Christofori Colom: cui etas nostra multū debet: de Insulis Indie supra Gangem nuper inuētis. Ad quas pergren/ das octauo antea mense auspiciis τ ere inuicti ssem oꝫ Fernādi τ Helisabet Hispaniaꝝ Regū missus fuerat: ad magnificum dñm Gabrielem Sanchis eorundē serenissimoꝝ Regum Thesaurariū missa: quā nobilis ac litteratus vir Leander de Cof o ab Hispa no idiomate in latinum cōuertit tertio ka's Maii· M·cccc·xciii Pontificatus Alexandri Sexti Anno primo·

Quoniam suscepte prouintie rem perfectam me psecutum fuisse gratum tibi fore scio: has constitui exarare: que te vniuscuiusꝗ rei in hoc nostro itinere geste inuentecꝗ ad/ moneant: Tricesimotertio die postꝗ Gadibus discessi in mare Indicū perueni: vbi plurimas insulas innumeris habitatas ho/ minibus repperi: quarum omnium pro feliciffimo Rege nostro preconio celebrato τ vexillis extensis contradicente nemine pos/ sessionem accepi: primecꝗ earum diui Saluatoris nomen impo/ sui: cuius fretus auxilio tam ad hanc: ꝗ ad ceteras alias perue/ nimus· Eam vo Indi Guanahanin vocant· Aliarū etiam vnam quanꝗ nouo nomine nuncupaui: quippe aliā insulam Sancte Marie Conceptionis· aliam Fernandinam· aliam Hysabellam· aliam Joanam·τ sic de reliquis appellari iussi· Cum primum in eam insulam quam dudum Joanam vocari dixi appulimus: iu xta eius littus occidentem versus aliquantulum processi: tamcꝗ eam magnam nullo reperto fine inueni: vt non insulā: sed conti nentem Chatai prouinciam esse crediderim: nulla tñ videns op pida municipiaue in maritimis sita confinib? preter aliquos vi/ cos τ predia rustica: cum quoꝗ incolis loqui nequibam· quare si mul ac nos videbant surripiebant fugam· progrediebar vltra: existimans aliquā me vrbem villasue inuenturū· Denicꝗ videns ꝗ longe admodum progressis nihil noui emergebat: τ bmōi via nos ad Septentrionem deferebat: ꝗ ipse fugere exoptabā: terris etenim regnabat bruma: ad Austrumcꝗ erat in voto cōtendere:

[18]

gold as they need, as much spices, cotton . . . as many slaves to serve as sailors . . . rhubarb and other kinds of spices." The outcome of his journey he described as "manifold and marvelous."

Columbus' accomplishment was remarkable in itself, but the modest pamphlet is what, in many ways, makes the feat of monumental world importance. Norse explorers had reached America before Columbus, and perhaps other intrepid fishermen had done so as well, but they sailed in an age before the invention of printing. It was the publication of Columbus' exploits that transformed an isolated occurrence into a major event, publicized to the world, and therefore capable of inspiring further explorations. These contemporary, printed accounts of exploratory voyages, of which the Library has such a remarkably complete collection, were avidly read by persons of all nationalities. Portuguese triumphs encouraged Italians and Spaniards and they, in turn, encouraged the French, the Dutch, and the English. The printed word ensured that the Age of Exploration would be a highly competitive, international epoch rather than a guarded exercise in nationalistic secrecy.

Purchased from B. F. Stevens & Brown, 1913. Gift of W. L. Clements, 1923.

❧ 3 ❧

FIRST ROUND-THE-WORLD TOURIST

PERHAPS NO ONE IN HISTORY has had quite such a story to tell as Antonio Pigafetta. Judged by any standard, *Le Voyage et Navagation facit par les Espaignolz es Isles de Mollucques* (Paris, 1525) is one of the most important books ever published.

Ferdinand Magellan was a battle-scarred veteran of more than fifteen years of service to his native Portugal. He had served in India and North Africa, been to China, and helped explore the Spice Islands from the East before being dismissed by King Manuel in 1513 for allegedly trading with the Moors. He became a naturalized citizen of Spain, and with the backing of the Spanish Crown and Dutch banking interests, Magellan put together a fleet which sailed from Seville on August 10, 1519. Of the five vessels and approximately 275 men aboard, only one vessel and thirty-five persons would eventually return to Spain, the others casualties to shipwreck, mutiny, disease, starvation, and hostile encounters with native people. Magellan did not survive the voyage, having fallen victim to local warfare in the Philippines, but Antonio Pigafetta did, and his narrative was largely responsible for proving that the world was round. Pigafetta's was not the only eyewitness account, but it was the first to get into print, the longest, and the most enjoyable to read.

Pigafetta was neither a navigator nor a scientific explorer, but an enthusiastic traveler who reveled in the strange sights and miraculous escapes while minimizing the controversies and hardships. He idolized Magellan, and took great pride in his courtly role as narrator of the enterprise to the aristocracy of Europe. Relatively little is known about Pigafetta, except that he was born of a prominent noble family of Vincente, Italy, and he appears to have become a Knight in the Order of Malta after returning home, writing his narrative, and sharing it with the King of Spain, the Pope, and other influential personages.

Considering the importance of the voyage — the first expedition to explore the southern shores

Le boyage et na,
uigation/faict par les Espaignolʒ es
Isles de Mollucques.des isles quilʒ
ont trouue audict boyage/des Roys
dicelles/de leur gouuernement ᴁ ma-
niere de biure/auec plusieurs aultres
choses.

Cum priuilegio,

❡ On les bend a Paris en la maison de
Simon de Colines/libraire iure de su
niuersite de Paris/demourāt en la rue
sainct Jehan de Beauluais/a lensei-
gne du Soleil Dor.

of South America, find a navigable passage around the American continent, sail the Pacific, discover the Philippine Islands, and circumnavigate the globe—it is surprising how obscure Pigafetta's narrative and the particulars of its survival have remained until fairly recently. It is now clear that he wrote his original account in Italian, accompanying the text with a series of maps. The original manuscript, now lost, was copied contemporaneously, and four manuscript versions exist, one in Italian and three in French. The narrative was first published, without the maps, in this French translation in Paris in 1525. Only nine copies are known to bibliographers. It was not until 1800 that an Italian edition, with reproductions of the original maps, would be published. The Library issued the first modern translation of the 1525 French printed edition in 1969.

In the sixteenth and seventeenth centuries, there developed an intense interest in narratives of exploration and travel. Pigafetta's account was first republished in the various editions of collected voyages edited by Ramusio between the 1530s and 1560s. An abbreviated English translation appeared in Richard Eden's *The Decades of the New Worlde* (London, 1555, 1577) and a full text in Samuel Purchas' *Hakluytus Posthumus* (London, 1625). All of these editions are to be found in the Library.

Streeter Sale purchase by Carnegie Bookshop, 1966. Gift of Clements Library Associates.

☙ 4 ☙

FIRST PICTURES OF AMERICA

THE NEW WORLD presented challenges to the understanding of even its most erudite conquerors. Geographically new, the cultures were also new, sometimes startlingly so, as were the fauna, flora, and profusion of languages. To understand this world required a translator, a person who could render unfamiliar sights and experiences in terms familiar to Europeans. Gonzalo Fernández de Oviedo y Valdes (1478–1557) was among the first Spaniards to attempt to create order from this profusion of new life and was the first European colonist to attempt a systematic documentation of the New World's natural riches.

Oviedo spent an unhappy youth watching his loved ones die around him and hearing reports of exciting discoveries over the seas made by his acquaintance Christopher Columbus. After serving his King for many years, and approaching middle age, Oviedo surrendered to the lure of the New World and obtained an appointment as supervisor of mining in Tierra Firme, the area now comprising most of the Caribbean coast from Colombia to Nicaragua. "Discovered" in 1503, during Columbus' fourth and final voyage, Tierra Firme was a major source for gold and silver prior to the conquest of Peru, and the appointment placed Oviedo in the beating heart of Spanish America.

Joining Pedrarias Dávila's expedition that sailed on April 11, 1514, Oviedo made his way to Santa María del Antigua, near the present-day border between Colombia and Panama, where he was welcomed by Vasco Núñez de Balboa. Over the next forty years, Oviedo crossed and recrossed the Atlantic at least a dozen times, frequently butting heads with Pedrarias and the redoubtable Dominican friar Bartolomé de las Casas, and becoming intimately familiar with the natural history of Colombia, Panama, and Hispaniola.

During one of his sojourns in Spain in 1519, Oviedo was commissioned by Emperor Charles V to write a history of the New World. The results, slow to appear, were published in two remarkable volumes, *De la natural hystoria* (Toledo, 1526) and *La historia general de las Indias* (Seville, 1535). Although not a true scholar, not even fluent in Latin, Oviedo displayed a clear ability to catalogue and describe the varied riches of the New World, from plants useful for food and medicines, to the animals, people, and mineral riches. Familiar enough with classical sources to allude to Pliny, he was also observant and original enough to recognize that New World animals differed from those familiar in the Old, even distinguishing European pigs from New World peccaries, and he was generally careful to record the native names alongside the closest Spanish equivalent. In vivid language, Oviedo did his best to describe animals as new and varied as the anteater, armadillo, and sloth ("the stupidest animal that can be found in the world"), and plants such as the avocado, papaya, and soursop.

With his professional interest in mines, Oviedo was a particularly careful observer of the Indian mining operations in Castilla del Oro, the western region of Tierra Firme. He described their ingenious methods for panning gold from alluvial deposits or diverting streams to collect the residue that settled among the rocks and crevices of the stream bottom, techniques that served miners well in California over three centuries later. The illustration, showing distinctly non-European gold miners, is the first accurate vision Europeans had of what Native Americans looked like. Oviedo wrote down a number of Indian words that have since become incorporated into European languages, such as hurricane, canoe, barbeque, and hammock. Untrained though he was as naturalist, geologist, ethnographer, or linguist, Oviedo was sincerely interested in the people of the New World and in describing their ways for an eager European audience.

Purchased from Lathrop C. Harper, 1918. Gift of W. L. Clements, 1923.

✿ 5 ✿

PATHFINDER OF THE SOUTHWEST

IN MAY 1536 a band of ragged Spaniards straggled into the frontier town of Sinaloa, Mexico, and encountered a party of soldiers in search of slaves. The leader of the band, Alvar Núñez Cabeza

de Vaca and his companions, Andrés Dorantes de Carrança, Alonzo Castillo de Maldonado, and Estéban, a slave, had endured eight years of privation and traversed thousands of miles of ocean, swamp, mountain, and desert en route to Sinaloa. Along the way this group of men became the first Europeans to visit the deep South and American Southwest.

Of noble Andalusian blood, and the grandson of the conqueror of the Grand Canary, Cabeza de Vaca chose to engage in the epic pursuit of his generation, the transmutation of New World grants into gold. Fortune beckoned when he was appointed treasurer of an expedition led by Pánfilo de Narvaez to assist in the subjugation and colonization of the coast from central Florida to eastern Mexico. Having witnessed the ease with which Spanish arms dismantled the powerful Aztec empire, he and his compatriots were confident that Narvaez's army of 600 soldiers and colonists would more than suffice to conquer the entire region and in the process, drench themselves in riches and fame.

Setting sail in June 1527, the expedition ran into a series of disasters at sea, including wrecked ships and a violent hurricane, before being driven to a landfall near present-day Tampa Bay in

April 1528. His force already reduced to half its original number, Narvaez led the survivors on a blind march northward to Apalachee Bay, where he constructed boats and headed to sea. Under different circumstances, Narvaez's decision to take to the water might have possessed a certain logic, but in the absence of shipwrights and proper materials, the five rickety vessels were scattered as soon as they met the swift currents at the mouth of the Mississippi River, and a monumental storm arose to dash any hopes of reuniting and reaching "civilization." On November 6, 1528, two boats, including Cabeza de Vaca's, were tossed ashore on an island off the Texas coast, where disease and violence at the hands of the native inhabitants soon reduced the eighty that landed to fifteen.

Taking matters into his own hands, Cabeza de Vaca headed inland, and for five years he was held against his will by Indians he called the Mariames. During this captivity, he earned a degree of respect by learning to practice Mariame medicine, and he became a trader of shells, beads, and other goods, traveling great distances inland. When he at last came into contact with some of his lost comrades, who had also been held captive, they concocted an arduous escape that took them across the deserts of the Southwest back to Mexico. Ironically, having escaped "enslavement" by the Indians, they were liberated by soldiers in search of Indians to enslave.

The *Relacion* contain no alluring tales of gold or silver, but Cabeza de Vaca shows a sufficient willingness to accept the humanity of the native inhabitants to make his book to some degree objective in describing the indigenous peoples of the South as they were when encountered for the first time by a European. The Clements copy of the narrative, which was first published in 1545, is the second edition of 1555.

Purchased from Lathrop C. Harper, 1913. Gift of W. L. Clements, 1923.

꙯ 6 ꙯

AMERICA'S FIRST PRINTED BOOK

THE CATHOLIC CHURCH in Mexico, from the earliest days of the Spanish conquest, made missionary work and education of the native population the highest priority. The first Bishop of Mexico, Don Fray Juan Zumáraga, produced a catechism, translated into the Nahuatl language, which was sent to Juan Cromberger of Seville, Spain's premier printer. To avoid the practical problems of sending proofs back and forth across the Atlantic, Cromberger forwarded a printing press, supplies, and a printer! The printer's name was Juan Pablos. The printing shop was established in 1538–39, next to the Bishop's residence in Tenochtitlan, present-day Mexico City.

The *Doctrina Breve*, the earliest complete book printed in America, illustrated on the following page, was written by Bishop Zumáraga and published in 1543–44. It was issued sixty years before Jamestown and seventy-five years before the Pilgrims set foot on Plymouth Rock. The book serves as a reminder that South and Central America developed mature cultures, part native, part European, long before the very beginnings of British North America.

Purchased from Lathrop C. Harper, 1927.

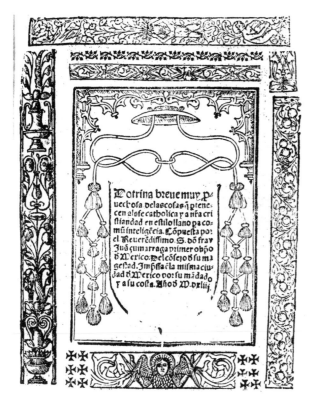

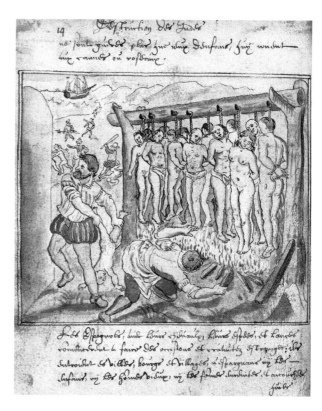

No. 6 Doctrina Breve (1543–44)

No. 7 Casas Ms. Relacion (1582)

❧ 7 ❧

CRUELTY, GRAPHICALLY DISPLAYED

IT IS ESTIMATED that within a century of the European conquest of the New World, more than 80 percent of the native population of the Americas had been annihilated through disease, enslavement, warfare, and murder. As appalling as these figures are, we would be mistaken in assuming that the conquest proceeded without criticism. In Spain there was a vigorous protest against the brutality, if not the propriety, of colonization and conversion. The opposition was spearheaded by the Dominican friar, Bartolomé de las Casas (1474–1566).

Scholarly and diligent, he was a former student of the University of Salamanca. Casas seems an unlikely *conquistador*, yet only a decade after Columbus' first voyage, he followed his father and uncle to the New World in search of fortune. Although ordained in the Dominican order in Hispaniola, Casas was not initially motivated by spiritual concerns. It was gold, not souls, he sought in the New World. He accepted orders, it seems, primarily to secure advantage in the spoliation of Cuba. All of this changed in 1514, when the massacre of Indians at Caonao and other atrocities committed by "those who go by the name of Christian" stirred Casas into some penetrating soul searching. From that year, he dedicated his life to the "defense" of the Indians, vociferously arguing for their humanity, for a moderation of the worst abuses of the conquest, and for conversion. Casas remains a popular hero in contemporary Latin America and among oppressed people of all nationalities.

Casas returned to Spain for the first of many times in 1515, to take his campaign on behalf of the native people directly to the Court. Through arduous debates with foes, including Gonzalo Fernández de Oviedo y Valdes, the learned cleric eventually attracted the attention and support of Emperor Charles V. His moral vision, however, was not spotless. In arguing for the prohibition of the enslavement of Indians (which he won in 1546), he advocated instead the enslavement of Africans to fill the labor demands of the New World.

Casas was the author of numerous historical and polemical works, but only eight "tracts" were actually printed during his lifetime, an additional title shortly after his death. The best known and most influential of his works was the first of the tracts, entitled *Brevissima Relacion de la Destruction de las Indias* (Seville, 1552). The work laid out, in excruciating detail, the cruelties inflicted upon the native population by Spanish explorers and colonizers. He sometimes resorted to exaggeration to bolster his polemics, but he had observed, firsthand, much of what he recorded and he personally knew and interviewed most of the people involved in the conquest. He was a meticulous historian of the entire colonization effort, a collector of source materials, and his documentation was hard to contradict. Casas' views were highly controversial during his lifetime, and because the *Relacion* was critical of the Spanish establishment, it was picked up and used by the enemies of Spain and Catholicism in ways never intended by the author.

The *Relacion* became a staple text, quoted and reprinted by other European nations to further their colonial agendas and to gain moral leverage in colonial conflicts with the Spanish. In the process, Casas' work helped create the "Black Legend" of the Americas, attributing a harshness to the Spanish treatment of indigenous Americans while tacitly excusing the "milder" colonialism of other nationalities. The book was translated and published frequently in the Netherlands during their wars with Spain, in Paris in 1579 and 1621, in Germany in 1598, and in England in 1583, 1656, and 1699. The title of the 1656 English edition was: *The Tears of the Indians: Being An Historical and true Account Of the Cruel Massacres and Slaughters of above Twenty Millions of innocent People.* The 1689 edition added: *Popery Truly Display'd in its Bloody Colours.*

The French edition of 1579, translated by Jacques Miggrode as the *Tyrannie et Cruautez des Espagnols*, was equally pointed. In 1582 a second edition of this translation was being prepared for publication in Paris, supplemented with lurid watercolor illustrations. A change in the political and religious climate in France, from Protestant to Catholic, made publication impolitic, and the edition was scrapped. The illustrated manuscript survived in the unique copy shown here, and the pictures, whether from this copy or some other source which has been lost, became the basis for Theodor de Bry's engravings in a Latin edition published in Frankfort in 1598. In addition to this prize, the Clements Library collections contain a bound volume of the rare original Casas tracts and numerous later editions.

Phillips Ms. 18228. Purchased from George D. Smith Estate, 1920. Gift of W. L. Clements, 1923.

THE LOST COLONY HIGHLY PRAISED

THOMAS HARIOT (1560–1621), mathematician and astronomer, was tutor to Sir Walter Raleigh who sent him in 1585, under Sir Richard Grenville, to survey Virginia. His *A briefe and true report of the new found land of Virginia* is the earliest English book to describe the first English colony in America, and it is a book which many regard with the kind of reverence accorded to Shakespeare's First Folio.

❧❧A briefe and true re-
port of the new found land of Virginia: of
the commodities there found and to be rayfed, as well mar-
chantable, as others for victuall, building and other necessa-
rie vfes for thofe that are and fhalbe the planters there; and of the na-
ture and manners of the naturall inhabitants : Difcouered by the
Englifh Colony there feated by Sir Richard Greinuile *Knight in the*
yeere 1585. which remained vnder the gouernment of Rafe Lane Efqui-
er, one of her Maiefties Equires, during the fpace of twelue monethes : at
the fpeciall charge and direction of the Honourable SIR
WALTER RALEIGH Knight, Lord Warden of
the ftanneries ; who therein hath beene fauou-
red and authorifed by her Maieftie and
her letters patents:

Directed to the Aduenturers, Fauourers,
andWelwillers of the action, for the inhabi-
ting and planting there:

By *Thomas Hariot*; feruant to the abouenamed
Sir Walter, a member of the Colony, and
there imployed in difcouering.

Imprinted at London 1588.

Hariot was writing with a purpose. He was cross with a handful of people who had returned from Virginia after the first Roanoke voyage of 1584 and were disdainful of the colony's promise. "There have been diverse and variable reports with some slanderous and shameful speeches bruited abroad," he declaimed. He pointed out that this first group had been there for only six weeks, while he had stayed a year. Except for twenty days, he and his companions had lived by drinking the local water and by "the victuall of the countrey." They had slept on the ground in the open air, and yet of the 108 who made the journey, only four died and three of those were "feeble, weake and sickly persons before ever they came thither."

Hariot addresses his *true report* "To the Adventureres, Favourers, and Welwillers of the enterprise for the inhabiting and planting in Virginia," and in spite of the note of irritation with the timidity of the first colonists, his basic tone is one of excitement and great promise which this richly endowed and beautiful land had for Englishmen and women who were willing to labor. Hariot was intoxicated with the natural bounty of the country, and no more forthright declaration of confidence in the future of America exists. "We found the soyle to be fatter; the trees greater and to growe thinner; the ground more firme and deeper mould; finer grasse and as good as ever we saw any in England . . . more plentie of their fruites; more abundance of beastes; the more inhabited with people, and of grater pollicie and larger dominions, with greater townes and houses." The people were naked but for deerskin and mantles and aprons but, "they beleeve also the immortalitie of the soule," in heaven and a hell which they called *Popogusso*. Hariot was enchanted.

Hariot's *Virginia* was published in quarto in 1588 and there are only six known copies. The one held by the Clements is one of three in the United States.

Purchased from Bernard Quaritch, 1913. Gift of W. L. Clements, 1923.

OUR EARLIEST SETTLEMENT PORTRAYED

THE ACCOMPANYING ENGRAVING, apparently executed by Baptista Boazio, an Italian artist living in London, is the first map of settlement in the bounds of the present United States. It is a view
of St. Augustine, founded by the Spanish in 1565, and the print depicts the attack on the weakly-
defended outpost by Sir Francis Drake in 1585. It is one of four large, finely-engraved plates—the
others depicting Santiago, Santo Domingo, and Cartegena—all Spanish cities which Drake attacked in the course of the war between Britain and Spain, 1585–86. These plates were issued with
a brief narrative, largely written by Walter Bigges, one of the ship captains who lost his life in the
course of the campaign. There were several editions of this work and each of them is rare. The Library has an exceptionally fine copy of the first edition, published in Leiden in 1588.

One of the endless fascinations of closely studying the earliest periods of the discovery and exploration of North America is the connecting links and associations between one event or one expedition and another. The Drake Expedition raised antagonism between the British and the
Spanish in the New World to new heights and probably set back English colonization by almost

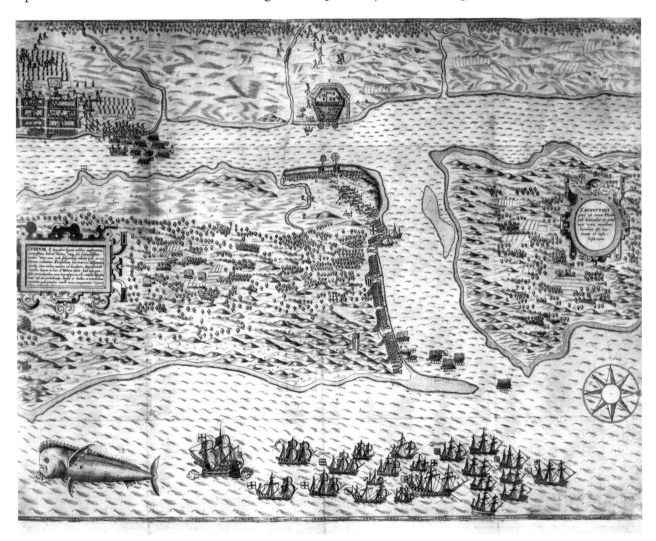

two decades. But incidentally, from a pictorial and historical perspective, the same expedition provided much of what we know visually about Native American culture and early European settlement at Roanoke. On his return voyage to England, after sacking settlements in the Spanish Caribbean, Drake and his fleet put in at present-day North Carolina and brought most of the early Roanoke colonists home. Among them were Thomas Hariot and John White, narrator and artist of the colony. The dolphin and other wildlife shown in the Drake expedition engravings are very possibly the work of John White himself.

As ironic as it may seem, had Roanoke not weakened to the point that colonists such as Hariot and White wished to return to England, we probably would not have this invaluable documentation. The St. Augustine view and the White drawings remain the only authentic pictorial record of the earliest period of European-American contact and settlement in what is now the United States.

Purchased from Lathrop C. Harper, 1919. Gift of W. L. Clements, 1923.

⤫ 10 ⤬

COFFEE TABLE TRAVEL BOOKS OF THE SIXTEENTH CENTURY

WHILE THE "QUARTO" EDITION of Thomas Hariot's *A briefe and true report of the new found land of Virginia* (London, 1588) will always remain the premier, and single most desirable published volume on British settlement in the United States, the illustrated 1590 edition of the same work, in English, is as rare and visually far more important.

Thomas Hariot was a skilled mathematician and surveyor. John White, member of the same 1586 colonizing expedition, was a draftsman and artist, and the two of them worked together closely, exploring Pamlico and Albemarle Sounds, making surveys, taking extensive notes, and producing sketches. On their return to England, Hariot published the narrative, and White finished a series of watercolors providing an invaluable record of the natural history and the native population. At some point in 1588, Richard Hakluyt, the great promoter of English exploration and colonization, convinced a German engraver, Theodor De Bry, who was visiting London on business, that he should produce a new edition of Hariot's work, illustrated with both a map and White's drawings. The original drawings survive to this day at the British Library.

The result was the first part of what eventually would be the grandest and most complicated set of illustrated travel narratives. There was a tremendous interest throughout Europe in learning about the strange and wonderful new lands and peoples being discovered in the late sixteenth and the seventeenth centuries, and the De Bry firm, situated in Frankfurt, would publish twenty-seven different travel narratives in fourteen "Parts," and numerous variant editions over the course of forty-four years (1590–1634). Part I, which contained the Hariot narrative and the White drawings, was published in Latin, German, French, and English, the latter two being exceedingly rare.

Collecting every possible edition and variant of the entire series became a passionate enthusiasm of William L. Clements.

The particular engraving shown here is of Secotan, a typical Indian village. The original John White watercolor exists, showing that the engraver took slight liberties, although probably with the assistance of Hariot and White themselves, in order to make it more informative to the reader. Three dwellings and additional Indians were added, and areas of cultivation were made more specific, with tobacco, corn, and sunflowers distinctly drawn and particularly identified.

Public interest in travel narratives resulted in publication of a number of collected works, similar to the De Brys. William Clements pursued all of them in his collecting. The Library has superb copies of the various collected voyages of Hakluyt, Purchas, Monobaldo, Hulsius, Ramusio, Thévenot, and later editors. They contain many of the texts of notable explorations which never were printed separately.

Purchased at Sotheby's by Henry Stevens, Son & Stiles, 1920. Gift of W. L. Clements, 1923.

❧ 11 ❧

NEW FRANCE, EXPLORED AND DISPLAYED

WELL BEFORE THE FIRST ENGLISH COLONISTS arrived in Massachusetts, French explorers had become intimately familiar with much of Nova Scotia, the St. Lawrence, and Lake Champlain and had already made their way into parts of the Great Lakes. The French had the particular good fortune to penetrate North America by way of the St. Lawrence River and to establish early and generally amicable trading contacts with the native peoples. This permitted a rapid entrée to the interior and the accretion of vast amounts of geographical information.

Equally fortuitous was the leadership of Samuel de Champlain, who first explored the St. Lawrence in 1603, founded Quebec in 1608, and directed the growth of New France until his death in 1635. He is deservedly considered the founder of Canada. Not only was Champlain an energetic and ambitious explorer, he was also a skilled artist and cartographer who recorded his discoveries and ensured their timely publication. Champlain produced four books, describing his North American voyages, between 1612 and 1632, and a remarkable series of maps and illustrations. Through his pen, the nature of New France and its waterways rapidly unfolded. By the time of his last book and map in 1632, Champlain had identified the major Indian nations, defined the basic form of the Great Lakes, and laid open the northern route into the heart of the continent.

Samuel de Champlain's exploratory efforts focused on the St. Lawrence valley and the routes radiating from it. In 1609 he visited the lake that bears his name. By 1613 he had explored the Ottawa River and turned his attention to the Huron country of modern Ontario. Two years later, the explorer saw Georgian Bay, crossed the eastern end of Lake Ontario, and entered the Iroquois country near Oneida Lake. Not only did he record his own observations, but he also absorbed Indian accounts of lands, rivers, and lakes far to the West, incorporating all these data into his maps and texts.

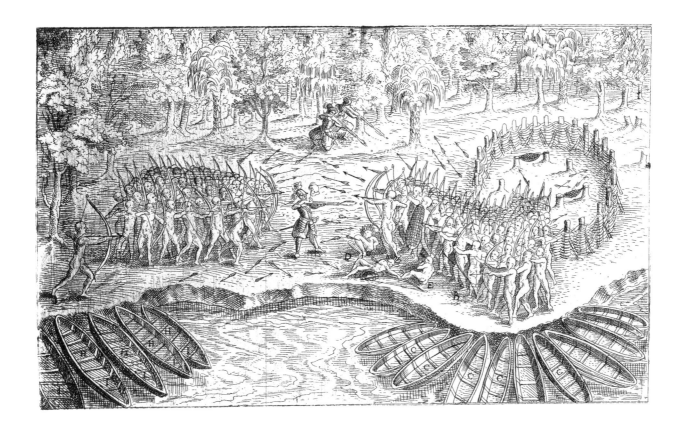

But, even as Champlain revealed vast areas of North America to European eyes, he helped draw lines of conflict that would distinguish the history of New France. The explorer encountered ancient rivalries between the native inhabitants of the St. Lawrence-Great Lakes region and the five Iroquois nations of what is today New York. Anxious to cement relations with his new Algonquin, Huron, and Montagnais allies, Champlain was drawn into their traditional warfare against the Iroquois. When faced with this sudden shift in the balance of power, the Iroquois turned to Dutch traders for the weapons and trade goods needed to combat their enemies. The English would later take the place of the Dutch in New York, but the northern front of future colonial wars had been defined. This animosity deeply influenced Champlain's explorations and mapping. Although he recorded surprising detail for the northern parts of the Great Lakes, southern Lake Huron, Lake Erie, and the connection with Lake Ontario remained poorly known at the time of his death. He had been able to explore and record what was accessible via the St. Lawrence and Ottawa rivers, but the areas under Iroquois control remained unfamiliar to the French until mid-century.

Two early encounters between Champlain and the Iroquois set the stage for a century of warfare that would cause wholesale displacement of many of France's trading partners and stunt the growth of the colony itself. The first came during his 1609 voyage up Lake Champlain. Then, in 1615, Champlain and a Huron war party invaded the heart of Iroquoia and lay siege to an enemy village. Both incidents were drawn by Champlain and included, respectively, as illustrations in his *Voyages* of 1613 and 1619.

The encounter of 1609, pictured in the 1613 volume displayed here, offers an especially dramatic view of the clash of Native American and European military technologies. On July 29, near Ticonderoga, Champlain with two French companions and allied Indians confronted a party of Iroquois. Stepping forward unexpectedly from his mass of warriors, the armored Frenchman leveled and fired his cumbersome matchlock arquebus, killing two Iroquois chiefs. Unaccustomed to firearms, the Iroquois fled. The father of New France thus helped ignite a century of wilderness conflict that would more than once threaten the very existence of his colony. The accounts of his exploits are preserved at the Library in superb copies of his 1613, 1627, and 1632 volumes, the latter being a compendium of all his published works.

Purchased from Lathrop C. Harper, 1913. Gift of W. L. Clements, 1923.

FIRST ACCOUNT OF THE JAMESTOWN SETTLEMENT

THERE IS A CONSIDERABLE AMOUNT of documentation on the first two decades of colonization efforts in Virginia, but the first public news of actual events and conditions in the colony was provided by *A True Relation of such occurrences and accidents of noateas hath hapned in Virginia* (London,

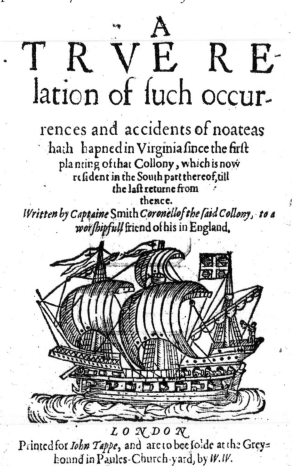

1608). It was John Smith's premier appearance in print, and it was the first account of the Jamestown colony.

John Smith apparently wrote it in the form of a lengthy personal letter, which he sent home in the care of Captain Francis Nelson, who sailed to England in early June 1608. The Virginia Company siezed upon it as useful for encouraging future colonization, and without Smith's knowledge they turned it over to an editor, John Healey, who probably omitted material which would discourage either investment or settlement. The edition illustrated here is the first which acknowledged the pamphlet's true authorship.

In spite of its limitations, *A True Relation* is an exciting glimpse of the beginnings of United States history, because the reader knows, as the author of course did not, that this was the first permanent English settlement. It describes the voyage from London to the West Indies, the first sighting of the mainland, the unfortunate selection of Jamestown as a spot to build the first fortified town, and the first fourteen months of actual life in the colony. Smith was a tough, fairly

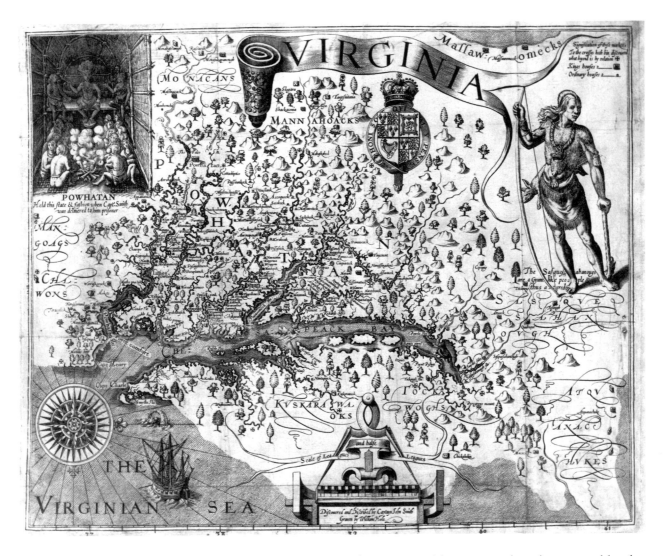

uncouth character, but he was fearless, had unlimited energy, and he emerged as the natural leader while his social betters gradually died off from disease. For anyone who knows the geography of the James-York Peninsula, it is fascinating to read about Smith's explorations and see in print for the first time such place names as the Chickahominy, Rappahannock, or Pamunkey Rivers. There is even a reference to the country of "Apamatica," a place which would become all too familiar to Robert E. Lee and many of the descendants of Jamestown's first settlers two and a half centuries later. The Library has made a particular effort to acquire these first, eyewitness accounts of the American landscape by its earliest explorers and settlers, and its collection, encompassing the region from Newfoundland to Florida, is virtually complete.

John Smith's map, also illustrated here, was published five years later, in 1613, as part of another promotional pamphlet of the Virginia Colony. Philip L. Barbour, John Smith's meticulous twentieth-century biographer and editor, makes a fairly convincing case that the general geographical outlines of the map were based upon a now-lost Spanish chart available to Smith in England in 1612 when he was composing the work for Oxford University Press. Smith was an intrepid explorer, and he obviously made careful notes and sketches of land features and native settlements. In 1614 he applied these same skills to surveying New England, and his map, published in 1616, guided the Pilgrims to Plymouth four years later. These two maps stand on their own merits as among the finest and most remarkable cartographic accomplishments of the seventeenth century. Smith prided himself on being an expert on native place names. Whether or not he recorded them correctly, many of these, and additional English place names which he affixed to his maps, remain with us today.

Book purchased from George D. Smith, 1919. Map purchased from Stevens, 1920.

Gift of W. L. Clements, 1923.

⤳ 13 ⤳

AMERICA'S PILGRIMS: EYEWITNESS AT PLYMOUTH

A Relation or Journall of the beginning . . . of the English Plantation . . . at Plimouth (London, 1622) is to the Pilgrim settlement what John Smith's *True Relation* (1608) was to Jamestown—the first published eyewitness account of the colony's founding and earliest history. It is quite a substantial pamphlet, 72 pages in length, and was published for a variety of purposes: to provide relatives and friends at home a description of the colony and its apparent success after a first difficult winter, a justification for having settled in Massachusetts, an explanation of why the colony would be slow in repaying investors, a reason to expect greater prosperity in the coming years, and advice to new settlers on what to bring and what to leave behind.

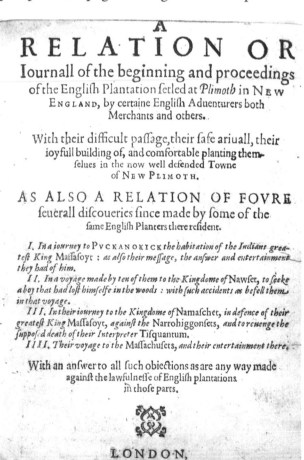

There has always been a mystery as to this pamphlet's authorship. It is known as Mourt's Relation, because the introduction is signed "Thy friend, G. Mourt." There was no one of that name among the passengers on the *Mayflower*, but Mourt is presumably George Morton, one of the Pilgrims who did not immigrate until 1623, but who assisted in getting the book published in England while the author remained in the New World. It was probably written by Edward Winslow, who was the acknowledged author of a supplementary narrative published in 1624. George Morton later published a history (1664) of the Plymouth Colony himself, and that volume, along with Mourt and the Winslow supplement, remained the basic historical information on the settlement until the middle of the nineteenth century, when the diary of Governor Bradford, stolen in Boston during the occupation by British troops in the American Revolution, was found among the books in the library of the Bishop of London and published. The Bradford diary itself was given by Britain to the state of Massachusetts as an act of friendship in 1897. While that diary is far more complete in its record of Pilgrim beginnings, Mourt's *Relation* remains a very important and highly readable source of information.

In retrospect, it seems quite remarkable that such a small and relatively unimportant colony as that established by the Pilgrims at Plymouth has received such extraordinary fame and attention since. Many far more ambitious colonizing experiments are largely forgotten. The answer probably lies in the fact that Plymouth Colony, where relative economic equality, ethnic homogeneity, and a spirit of religious tolerance prevailed, was a closer model of the image that Americans traditionally have had of themselves than Jamestown or Massachusetts Bay. The Pilgrims had a particular talent for producing large families, and descendants, many of them ardent members of the Mayflower Society, do a commendable job in preserving the history of the colony "Mourt" first told the world about in 1622.

Purchased at Sotheby's by Stevens, 1921. Gift of W. L. Clements, 1923.

❧ 14 ❧

FIRST PRINTING IN THE ENGLISH COLONIES

A *Platform of Church Discipline* (1649) is the earliest book printed in the present United States that is in the Clements Library. The Cambridge press was brought to America in 1638, and approximately two dozen books, pamphlets, and broadsides are known to have been printed between 1639 and 1649, eleven or twelve of which have survived in at least a single copy. The press was located in close proximity to Harvard University from its founding until its demise in 1692, when Boston became the center of the colony's printing trade. The quality of printing at the Cambridge press, particularly in the first decade, was decidedly amateurish. The majority of works published by New Englanders, at least through the 1660s, was done in England.

A local press served an important purpose in any frontier community, particularly in seventeenth-century New England, where a highly literate clergy felt a strong responsibility to define and promote their religious beliefs. The Cambridge Platform of 1649 seems a noncontroversial description of the nature, the forms, and the procedures of church government, but in fact it represented an uneasy compromise between Independency and Presbyterianism, between very exclusive and more inclusive concepts of church membership, and differing viewpoints on the relationship between church and state. Massachusetts Bay, in 1630 the great experiment in English Puritanism, was by 1649 being left behind by the events of the English Civil War. The Cambridge Platform was partly an attempt to establish a model for British emulation, in part an effort to preserve and codify the old New England ways before they were overwhelmed by new ideas, new immigrants, and a rising generation, ignorant of its Puritan heritage.

Although modified in later years, the Cambridge Platform remains the fundamental basis of Congregationalism in the United States. The formal Congregational Church, as a separate de-

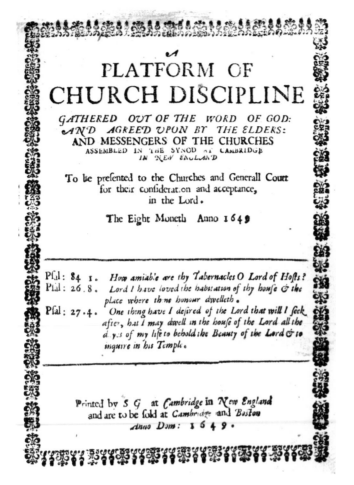

nomination, would lose many of its churches and members in later years to the Unitarians, Baptists, and Presbyterians. But the Congregational forms of church government, emphasizing a degree of independence on the parish level and a distinct separation between church and state, would influence all denominations as they adapted to the American environment.

The Library has a fine collection of seventeenth- and eighteenth-century American imprints, with emphasis upon those of more general, significant content. The majority are particularly fresh, complete copies. Of the Cambridge Press of the seventeenth century, the Library has twenty imprints, including the two Eliot Bibles, the 1672 laws, the first printed election sermons for Massachusetts and Connecticut, and Nathaniel Morton's *New Englands Memorial* (1669), the first serious historical work published in this country, documenting largely the early history of Plymouth Colony. The Library also has an extensive holding of the more numerous seventeenth-century English imprints of American authorship.

Gift of the McGregor Fund, per desire of Tracy W. McGregor, Detroit, 1938.

❧ 15 ❧

NEW ENGLAND'S FIRST MUSE

Brought to the shores of the New World when her beloved husband enlisted in the Puritan holy experiment, Anne Bradstreet (1612–1672) faced her own new world. From the cultured and cultivated heart of Old England, she was exiled into the wild and untamed periphery of New England, facing, as she phrased it, "new manners at which my heart rose." Her faith and poetry allowed her to cope with the transition and eventually to thrive. "After I was convinced it was the way of God," she wrote, "I submitted to it."

Raised in the religious hothouse of Laudian England, Bradstreet was privy to the highest nonconformist social circles, enjoying a thorough religious education and a bracing social and intellectual environment. Her father, Thomas Dudley, steward to the Earl of Lincoln, provided Anne with the best private tutors and easy access to the Earl's library, encouraging her intellectual aspirations. At sixteen she married the Earl's promising protegé, Simon Bradstreet, and two years later the couple boarded the *Arbella,* bound for New England with John Winthrop. Their social status was not diminished by the move. Anne's father was appointed deputy governor of the Massachusetts Bay Company, of which Simon was already an assistant, and Simon later became one of the colony's most important statesmen and twice its governor.

Settling first at Ipswich, and later in North Andover, Anne began to write poetry and shared it with members of her family on both sides of the Atlantic. Without her consent, or even knowledge, her brother-in-law, John Woodbridge, arranged to have a collection of her poetry published in London as *The Tenth Muse, Lately sprung up in America* (London, 1650). Coming from a woman, and a colonist, *The Tenth Muse* was quite a curiosity, the first book of poetry ever published by a New Englander. Its novelty was highlighted by the addition of eight poetic, prefatory remarks incorporating fulsome praise from sage men testifying to the

THE
TENTH MUSE
Lately fprung up in AMERICA.
OR
Severall Poems, compiled
with great variety of VVit
and Learning, full of delight.
Wherein efpecially is contained a compleat difcourfe and defcription of

The Four — Elements,
Conftitutions,
Ages of Man,
Seafons of the Year.

Together with an Exact Epitomie of the Four Monarchies, viz.

The — Affyrian,
Perfian,
Grecian,
Roman.

Alfo a Dialogue between Old *England* and New, concerning the late troubles.
With divers other pleafant and ferious Poems.

By a Gentlewoman in thofe parts.

Printed at London for *Stephen Bowtell* at the figne of the Bible in Popes Head-Alley. 1650.

quality of the writing and to its authorship by a woman. C.B., for instance, described the work as a "Master-peice of Poetry," which could "surpasse, or parallel, the best of man." Bradstreet dealt more pointedly, and openly, with the issue of female authorship. In dedicating the book to her father, she concluded, "I am obnoxious to each carping tongue, who sayes, my hand a needle better fits, a poets pen, all scorne, I should thus wrong, for such despight they cast on female wits: If what I doe prove well, it wo'nt advance, They'l say its stolne, or else, it was by chance."

The Tenth Muse makes it obvious that the author was well read in the theology, literature, and poetry of the period, and she possessed the self-confidence to deal with serious social, historical, and political issues. Her poems "The four elements, constitutions, ages of man and seasons of the year" and "An exact epitome of the four monarchies" include a whirlwind tour of physical science and human history. Only the third major poem in the collection, "A dialogue between Old England and New, concerning the late troubles," even hints at her life in New England. These appealed to the taste of her generation, winning favorable comments from Nathaniel Ward and Cotton Mather among others.

Although she never again published in her lifetime, Bradstreet continued to write and revise, and in the process, her poetical works grew increasingly personal in nature, increasingly introspective. She died in North Andover in 1672. The printed volume is of the greatest rarity.

Purchased from Lathrop C. Harper, 1912. Gift of W. L. Clements, 1923.

VIRGINIA'S FIRST STEPS WESTWARD

BY 1650, there were approximately 12,000 inhabitants in Virginia settled in the vicinity of the James and York Rivers. The population was stable and rapidly expanding, but the soil was beginning to show the effects of overplanting. London merchants and their colonial partners were increasingly interested in expanding the highly lucrative trade with the Indians for furs and skins, and Virginians began eyeing, covetously, the "uninhabited" lands of Carolina to the south and west, anxious that Englishmen rather than Spaniards fill this gap in European settlement.

Three pamphlets and two maps were published between 1649 and 1671 which provide important documentation on this earliest phase of westward expansion, all of them present in the Library in particularly fine copies. Edward Williams' *Virginia: More Especially the South Part Thereof Richly and Truly Valued* (London, 1649) was essentially a promotional tract, looking toward the Carolinas. The other two works, Edward Bland's *The Discovery of New Brittaine* (London, 1651) and *The Discoveries of John Lederer* (London, 1671), were accounts of actual explorations.

Edward Bland's and Abraham Wood's journey, which is recorded in the work illustrated here, seems to have been motivated more by an interest in establishing future land claims and fur trading posts than actual exploration of the unknown. The group, six Englishmen and one Indian guide, traveled more to the south than the west. Modern scholarship suggests that present-day

THE
DISCOVERY
OF
Nevv Brittaine.
Began *August* 27. *Anno Dom.* 1650.

By {*Edward Bland*, Merchant.
Abraham Woode, Captaine.
Sackford Brewster, } Gentlemen.
Elias Pennant, }

From Fort *Henry*, at the head of *Appamattuck* River in *Virginia*, to the Fals of *Blandina*, firft River in *New Brittaine*, which runneth Weft; being 120. Mile South-weft, between 35. & 37. degrees, (a pleafant Country,) of temperate Ayre, and fertile Soyle.

LONDON,
Printed by *Thomas Harper* for *John Stephenson*, at the Sun below Ludgate. *M.DC.LI.*

Weldon, North Carolina, on the Roanoke River, was the farthest destination reached by the party, well east of the mountains and far distant from any river flowing west, as claimed. But it was an important first step.

John Lederer, an intrepid German, conducted three expeditions in 1670 which were true missions of exploration. The first went as far as Charlottesville and the Blue Ridge; the second, as far southwestward as South Carolina; the third to the mountains beyond the source of the Rappahannock. Lederer was disappointed in not finding a route through the mountains, but his travel account, edited and published by Sir William Talbot, and his map not only outlined routes for profitable trade with distant Indian tribes, but suggested that the American continent was a far larger entity than previously envisioned.

The Clements' copy of Bland's *Discovery of New Brittaine* (1651) includes John Farrar's 1651 map, also reproduced here. The map exists in several different states and is found in Bland's account as well as later, post-1651 editions of Williams' *Virginia*, although directly illustrating the text of neither volume. It is a particularly engaging bit of cartography by a longtime Virginia Company employee, and important, not for its accuracy, but for graphically illustrating the continued belief that riches of some sort—in this case an easy route to China by way of the South Seas—lay almost within grasp. English and French explorations of the early eighteenth century would quickly dispel the myth of a close water route to the Orient. But restless American colonists and European investors always came up with a new image on which to base their dreams of wealth and encourage exploration in the direction of the setting sun: a Northwest Passage, a fur trade empire in the Middle West, fertile lands untouched by the plow, grazing lands, timber, and mineral wealth. The Farrar map illustrates what became an inherent part of the American Dream — the idea that anyone always had the option of pulling up stakes and heading a bit farther west, where some sort of fortune awaited those willing to take a chance and work for it.

Purchased from Bernard Quaritch, 1920. Gift of W. L. Clements, 1923.

ᘓ 17 ᘓ

THE CAROLINAS EXPLORED

THE FAILURE of Britain's first North American colonization effort at Roanoke and the proximity to Spanish St. Augustine seem to have dampened English enthusiasm for settling the Carolinas in the first half of the seventeenth century. A number of land grants associated with Virginia were made, but it was not until after the restoration of the monarchy in 1660, when Britain was broadening its presence in the West Indies, that serious efforts were made to plug this gap, protecting Virginia and the colonies northward and isolating St. Augustine.

In March 1663, Charles II granted present-day North and South Carolina to eight of the most prominent political figures in England who had strongly supported the Restoration three years earlier. The Earl of Clarendon, Duke of Albemarle, Lord Craven, Lord Berkeley, Lord Ashley, Sir John Carteret, Sir William Berkeley, and Sir John Colleton are largely remembered today for geographical features to which their names have been affixed.

Shortly after the Carolina grant was made, in 1663, Captain William Hilton of Barbados was sent to explore the coasts of both North and South Carolina, and the following year a group of Barbadians formed the first settlement at Charles Town (Cape Fear) in present North Carolina. It was not an ideal site, and the proprietors suggested explorations southward, to ascertain whether conditions were more favorable. Lieutenant Colonel Robert Sandford was placed in command of the expedition which set sail from Charles Town on June 14, 1666, and returned on July 12 after exploring the territory as far as the southern coastal limits of South Carolina. His fleet consisted of two small vessels, a sloop of fifteen tons burden, and a shallop of three tons.

The basic sources for the earliest exploration and settlement of North Carolina consist of two scarce pamphlets, both at the Clements Library, and a manuscript report: William Hilton's *A Relation of a Discovery lately made on the Coast of Florida* (London, 1664); *A Brief Description of the Province of Carolina, On the Coasts of Florida, and More particularly of a New Plantation begun by the English at Cape-Feare . . . .* (London, 1666), which includes a map; and Sandford's handwritten account of the 1666 exploring expedition. The Sandford manuscript was found in the papers of the Earl of Shaftesbury and is now at the Public Record Office. It has been available to scholars for decades and has been published several times.

The Library was surprised and delighted, recently, to obtain another, previously unknown manuscript account of early British efforts in the Carolinas—a detailed, six-page journal of Lieu-

A Discovery of the Coasts Islands Rivers Sounds & Creeks
of that part the province of Carolina betweene
Cape Romano and Port Royall vizt.

Saterday June the 16: 1666 Wee set sayle in the ship Rebecca and
with the shallop speedwell. from the mouth of Charles River and
Sunday the 17th in the afternoone wee discried a large opening against
which wee came to an anckor: and sent the shallop in to sound the
channell. but shee could not get in by reason of Creeks and Shoulds yt
lay out, that Eueninge the wind blowing fresh from Sea wee weighed and
stood of, On tensday the 19th wee lost the shallop by ffoule weather
Thursday the 21t afternoone wee discryed a very fayre opening and
stood of that night till ffriday the 22th at which tyme wee stood in &
Sounding as wee went in had not lesse in the narrowest place then
2 fadome, and then 3. 4. 5. 7. 8. fadome water. wee ran vp with our
ship about 4 miles from the Rivers mouth, on both Sydes the River
is great store of Oyster Banks and good Creeks that run to the Mayne
land about an hower after wee came to an Anckor 2 Indians came
aboard vs who told vs wee were in the River Grandee and that that
Cuntry was called Eddistan, presently after there came seuerall
other Indians with venison Corne Bread fish amongst whome was
two of those Indians, that were at Barbados Sateday the 23d some
of vs went on shoare to get fresh water but could find none neere
the River Syde, but the Indians taking our Caske carried them about
halfe a mile into the woods to a large Pond where was water
enough. the Land is generally very choice, and Good the Mould is
mellow and blacke about a foot deepe, and vnder a red Marly land.
It beares Large Oake Walnutt and few pines vnlesse Sprule pines
the woods afford very good pasture for Cattle beeing richly laden with
English Grasse, for ffowle and fish it affords like that of
Charles River. there is turtle in aboundance the Same afternoon
wee went a Mile Eastward from our ship and landed in a dry
Marsh where wee found an Indian Path which wee kept and it
led vs through many fields of Corne ready to gather alsoe other
Corne, pease & Beanes which had bin latter planted there the

Rose

tenant James Woory, who accompanied Sandford on the exploring expedition of June-July, 1666. Sandford's narrative is longer and more comprehensive, but Woory's provides a variety of new details, such as the names of the vessels (*Speedwell* and *Rebecca*) and a somewhat different perspective on the adventure. While Woory's handwritten account apparently was not sent by Sandford to the colony's patron, the Earl of Shaftesbury, a copy, along with a manuscript copy of Sandford's report, did manage to get into the hands of Sir Edmund Andros, who in 1666 was an army officer in the West Indies. Andros had a financial interest in the Carolinas in the early 1670s before becoming governor of New York in 1674. The Andros Papers were sold and dispersed on the market in the present century.

One of the most fascinating aspects of Woory's account is the description of the natives and their extensive settlements and farms. He describes acres of cornfields and bountiful crops of squash, melons, peas, and beans. The natives seemed exceptionally friendly, urging the Europeans to settle among them. The irony of the narrative is that, after describing these native settlements, Woory ended his letter with the comment that "it is great Pitty, that such brave places should Lye unpeopled and abundance of our Nation want Land." The native population of America had good reason to mistrust newcomers who could look at them, accept their hospitality, and not see them as human beings.

Purchased from William Reese, 1994. Gift of Clements Library Associates.

❧ 18 ☙

EXPLORING THE GREAT LAKES

LARGEST AND MOST DISTANT, deepest and most mysterious of the Great Lakes, Superior was, surprisingly, also the first to be mapped with accuracy. This was an achievement not of military or commercial explorers but rather seekers of souls. During the last third of the seventeenth century, Jesuit missionaries directed renewed attention to the northern reaches of the Great Lakes for many of the same reasons that had influenced Champlain's mapping—the more southerly regions were dominated by Iroquois warriors hostile to French encroachment.

When Samuel de Champlain died at Quebec in 1635, members of the Society of Jesus had already labored in Canada for a decade. They came for the purpose of gathering converts from among the peoples with whom the French traded in furs, but they also made lasting contributions to the exploration and understanding of the interior regions. Deeply dedicated to their purpose and particularly well educated, the Jesuits were keen observers. They recorded their progress in a series of reports, known as the Jesuit *Relations*, which were published in France on a nearly annual basis for the Canadian missions between 1634 and 1673. They are small, unimpressive volumes in appearance, but they are the single most important source historians and anthropologists have for not only the activities of the missionaries, but Native American culture of Canada and midwestern America. They were printed in limited editions and are extremely rare. William L. Clements was able to put together a complete set, including the significant variant editions.

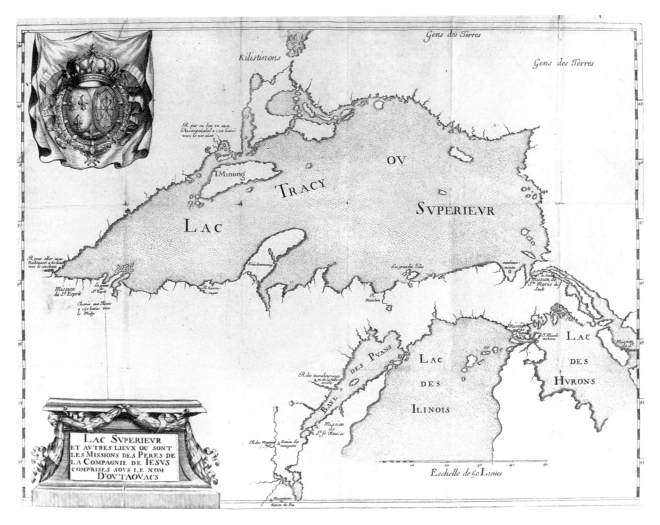

Jesuit missionaries had taken quickly to Huronia, present-day central and western Ontario, where Champlain also found his most cooperative trading partners and informants about unknown regions to the west. The Huron were a people under stress due to commercial rivalry with their cousins, the Five Nations of the Iroquois. Disaster befell the Huron between 1641 and 1649, when Iroquois warriors erupted from their homelands south of Lake Ontario to destroy their villages. In 1649 most of the Huron and other nearby peoples of the Great Lakes, notably the Ottawa, fled westward beyond Lake Michigan and Lake Superior.

It was not until 1665 that the Jesuits began to reassemble the scattered western remnants of their Huron flock. Father Claude-Jean Allouez arrived on Lake Superior in that year and, after an arduous journey to the southwestern end of the lake, established the mission of St. Esprit at La Pointe on Chequamegon Bay. He spent the next four years traveling and ministering on Lake Superior, accumulating as he went a comprehensive understanding of that massive body of water. Father Claude Dablon joined Allouez in 1669. The Iroquois tide receded in the 1660s, and the displaced Huron and Ottawa began to drift back toward the east. By 1670, large concentrations of these refugees were to be found at St. Esprit and at Green Bay, the Straits of Mackinac, and Sault Ste. Marie. Trading posts were established among them, and Jesuit missions as well. Even the official attention of France was attracted when, in May 1671, Simon-François de Saint-Lusson took formal possession of the region at Sault Ste. Marie.

The Jesuit *Relations* of 1670–71 had much to celebrate. Father Dablon could report the establishment of new missions at the Sault, Green Bay, and Michilimackinac. His account was illustrated by "a Map showing the regions, with their lakes and rivers, in which the Missions of that country are situated." He added that it had been "drawn by two Fathers of considerable intelligence, much given to research, and very exact, who determined to set down nothing that they had not seen with their own eyes." The "Jesuit Map" of Lake Superior was issued a second time in the *Relation* of 1671–72 "to satisfy the curiosity of those who have not seen it."

The anonymous priests, almost certainly Allouez and Dablon, were indeed exact and produced a map of great accuracy, not significantly improved upon until the nineteenth century. The shapes of Lake Superior and Lake Michigan, from Green Bay north, were correctly rendered for the first time, and the relationship between the three upper lakes was properly defined.

The Clements Library copy of this map, recorded as having been removed from the *Relation* of 1670–71, was acquired separately from the printed volume.

Purchased from Lathrop C. Harper, 1920. Gift of W. L. Clements, 1923.

❧ 19 ❧

IN COLD BLOOD, 1680

The Vain Prodigal Life, and Tragical Penitent Death of Thomas Hellier (London, 1680) is not only a very rare and historically significant pamphlet relating to colonial Virginia, but the first of a non-fictional literary genre which, along with the Indian captivity narrative, became immensely popular in the eighteenth and nineteenth centuries, and remains so to this day in the form of "true crime" narratives.

Thomas Hellier did not really seem to be a bad sort. He was smart, well-spoken, and charming when he wanted to be. He came from a good family but was spoiled by his parents and a grandfather. They were a bit afraid of him when ill-tempered, and overlooked or covered up youthful falsehoods and misbehavior. He was given every educational opportunity — a good basic schooling, apprenticeships to learn the trades of barber-surgeon and stationer — and he had a high opinion of his talents and abilities. He was also lazy and completely self-centered. He believed that the world owed him a living, and a very good one.

Dissipation and false friends led him to lose an inheritance, a wife and child, and his reputation. To avoid debtors' prison he agreed to be transported to Virginia and serve as a tutor in a wealthy family. On arriving in the colony, he was in fact sold to a planter as a farm laborer and was expected to hoe corn and tobacco and cut timber from sunup to sunset. He felt that he had been cheated, that the work was beneath him, and adding insult to injury, his mistress was unceasing in her demands and criticism. He ran away, but was captured and brought back to his intolerable labors. On May 24, 1678, without any careful planning of the crime, he rather casually axe-murdered his master, his mistress, and a servant girl who witnessed the crime. He was captured the following day, tried, convicted, and sentenced to death.

Although never directly identified, the author of the pamphlet would appear to have been the

Reverend Mr. Williams of Westover Parish. Struck that this was not the typical criminal, Williams conducted frequent interviews with the prisoner and attempted, in partnership with Hellier himself, to understand why someone of his background, educational advantages, and intelligence could commit such a terrible act. The condemned man thoroughly enjoyed the opportunity to talk about himself. For its day, this was quite a remarkable and objective piece of research into the criminal mind, and the pamphlet, which includes a narrative of the crime, an autobiography of the prisoner, a well-reasoned analysis by Williams, and a warning to others by Hellier, was sent to England, with Hellier's approval, to be printed. Hellier was clearly psychopathic, created by forces in his personal background all too familiar in today's world. The murderer was executed on August 5, 1678, and his decomposing body "hanged up in chains" at Windmill Point on the James, to provide a more graphic warning of the wages of sin to local inhabitants and vessels going up and down the river.

Due in large part to the purchase of the lifetime accumulation of James V. Medler, the Library has one of the most extensive collections of "true crime" literature — almost half of all murders described in print — dating from the colonial period to the early twentieth century. These printed records of lethal human frailty include penny broadsides, sensational pamphlets, verbatim court records, and highly scientific studies, and they provide unique documentation on society and everyday life as well as crime itself. *The Vain Prodigal Life* is not only an important "first" as crime literature but a rare commentary on indentured servitude and some of the problems associated with the system.

Purchased from Thomas T. Moebs, 1981.

∽ 20 ∽

THE BEGINNING OF TOWN PLANNING

WILLIAM PENN received a Royal patent for Pennsylvania in 1681. No other colonial proprietor took such an active personal interest in promoting his colony's affairs, and among other concerns, he was particularly anxious that Pennsylvania have a prosperous, healthful, and beautiful capital city.

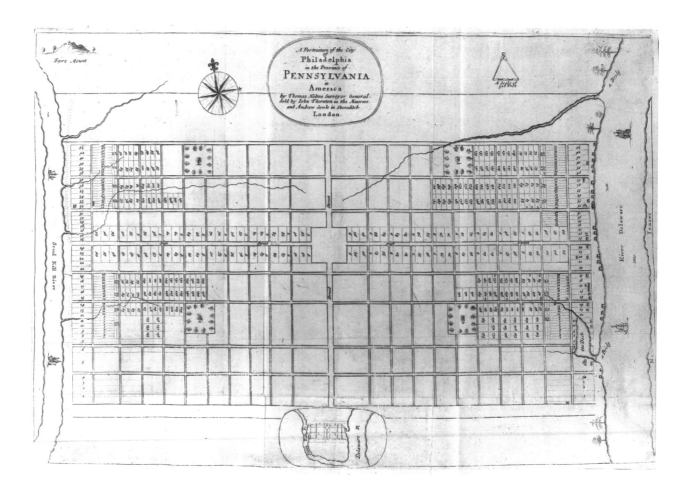

At some point in the spring of 1682 a location for Philadelphia was chosen, and Captain Thomas Holme was appointed as the colony's first Surveyor General. He carefully examined and surveyed the forested site that year, and a map was issued as part of the colony's promotional literature the following year. This was the first published city plan for any English settlement in America. The Library's copy, which is the earliest printing of the map, was bound into *A Letter from William Penn . . . to the Committee of the Free Society of Traders* (London, 1683).

Much has been claimed of this plan that is not quite true. It was not the first city in the world to have a grid system of straight streets, nor was the proprietor's plan rigorously followed in every detail. The perpendicular, main thoroughfare, present-day Broad Street, was actually moved two blocks to the west. The city squares, intended as pleasant, open spaces for the benefit of the public at large, were not respected in the eighteenth century, although they were largely restored in the century thereafter. Although Penn had envisioned the city as one of rural residences on large, garden-like plots stretching from the Delaware to the Schuylkill River, actual construction concentrated on the Delaware River side of town, with houses built in compact rows on fairly narrow lots. Numerous small streets and alleys were added to the plan.

In spite of the alterations, the essential plan—right-angled streets, with at least a central square—became the model for other towns not only in Pennsylvania but westward in central Ohio and the middle west. The symmetry of the system made for an attractive site plan for town promoters and developers. They could produce a nicely engraved plan for distant investors, similar to Holme's 1683 map, before a single street had been laid out or home constructed. Lots could be projected and sold in equal, known dimensions, minimizing property line disputes. We tend to remember William Penn as one of the father's of religious toleration and for his fairness to the Indians. He deserves, as well, to be considered as one of the country's first great land developers and real estate promoters — and a pretty slick one at that!

Purchased from Rosenbach Co., 1919. Gift of W. L. Clements, 1923.

☙ 21 ☙

THE PIRATE ATLAS

IN 1680, A MOTLEY CREW of pirates crossed the Isthmus of Panama, looting Spanish settlements along the way. They captured several vessels on the Pacific side, one of which was named the *Trinity* and which they made the flagship of the expedition. Since the voyage of Sir Francis Drake a century before and a few brief visits by Dutch ships earlier in the seventeenth century, no non-Spaniard had sailed in American Pacific coastal waters, and the Spanish settlements were entirely unprepared to defend themselves.

For more than a year, squabbling among themselves much of the time, the pirates explored and raided settlements and shipping up and down the coast from Acapulco to Chile, finally sailing around Cape Horn and back to the Caribbean where they divided their spoils. Twenty-two of the pirates associated with the voyage then took passage to England on two different ships, arriving in

March 1682, where they created a diplomatic crisis between England and Spain. At the urging of the Spanish ambassador, several were tried for piracy and murder, but all were acquitted. They brought back sufficient treasure to pay handsomely for the voyage, but the real prize of the expedition was a set of sea charts captured on July 29, 1681.

There are five first-person accounts of the expedition, all of which exist in manuscript copies and were in print before the end of the seventeenth century. The Library has all of these printed narratives. Some of the charts were added to manuscript copies of the various pirates' narratives and were also engraved for printed versions, but they are found in their most complete and glorious form in a series of manuscript atlases, eleven of them drawn by William Hack, a London chart maker whose work has a particularly distinctive style. Each of the "Hack Atlases" was drawn either for the King or for a prominent British statesman, and they were intended for reference use in the private libraries of the great and powerful men of the era. There exist other, less beautiful examples, which appear to have been made for actual shipboard use.

The Clements' Hack Atlas is a large folio volume in a contemporary, full red leather binding, which belonged in the mid-eighteenth century to Lord Grenville, better known in the United States as Prime Minister during the Stamp Act Crisis. It contains 184 maps, drawn not only from the captured Spanish charts, but other sources for the charts of the Straits of Magellan, the Galapagos Islands, and the island of Juan Fernandez. Those copied from the Spanish sources retain the three-dimensional, pictorial character common to Spanish and Portuguese sea charts of the era. They are visual rather than measured records of coastlines, perfectly adequate to the needs of local navigators on shorelines dominated by distinctive mountain ranges. The alignment of peaks and valleys with marked locations of shoals, islands, and inlets made it possible to get from harbor to harbor without advanced navigational equipment. The Dutch, French, and English natives, who came from and also tended to colonize lands which lacked these elevated topographical features, had to develop more sophisticated navigational charts, providing accurate positions of longitude and latitude. The data contained on the charts captured by the *Trinity*, although a wealth of new information, were not easily transposed to the scientific navigational maps being produced in the Netherlands, France, or England at the end of the seventeenth century. It was not until the early nineteenth century, when Portugal and Brazil became essentially client states of Britain, that detailed, modern maps and charts of South America became generally available.

Houghton Sale purchase by H. P. Kraus, 1979. Gift of Clements Library Associates.

∽ 22 ∾

ARRESTING WITCHES

IN FEBRUARY 1692 A GROUP of young girls of Salem, Massachusetts, including the daughter of Samuel Parris, the town's clergyman, began experiencing inexplicable fits, thrashing, shrieking, and painful pricks in their flesh. Left grasping for an explanation, the authorities repeatedly interrogated the "afflicted girls," who eventually confessed that they were diabolically tormented. As the interrogation continued, accusations flowed freely against members of the community, and the conclusion became inescapable: Satan had reaped a bountiful harvest of souls in the once-righteous Puritan colony.

At first, accusations were aimed only at marginal members of the community, the poor and elderly, the contentious and litigious. The great majority of the accused (and accusers) were women. The magistrates — including John Hathorne, Nathaniel Hawthorne's great-grandfather — permitted the use of spectral evidence. Arrests grew into indictments and convictions. In July, a scant month after the first trials were held, eighteen convicted witches were hanged; another, who refused to testify, was crushed under a weight of stones.

At the height of the accusations in July, two witches were identified in Haverhill. The warrant for their arrest is illustrated here. The accused, Hannah Bromage and Mary Green, were married to longtime residents of the town, a husbandman and weaver respectively. Haverhill was a small frontier town north of Salem, on the border with New Hampshire. This settlement would achieve fame in 1697 as home to the "heroine" Hannah Duston, who responded to being abducted by Indians by butchering ten of them as they slept, including six children, and bringing their scalps back to town as proof!

Shortly after the arrest, Bromage and Green were clapped in irons. Green was shackled to Sarah Towne Cloyce and Mary Towne Esty, who along with their third sister, Rebecca Towne Nurse, were focal points of the early accusations. Both Esty and Nurse were executed. Proving as wily as Hannah Duston was a few years later, Mary Green managed to escape from prison on August 2, and again on August 23, though in both cases she was apprehended. The delays she caused may have saved her life. In early October, worried about the escalating scale of accusations and the increasing prominence of those being accused, the provincial government suspended the trials. In November, Green was one of nine women who petitioned from the Ipswich jail to protest her innocence of all charges and to request release on bail. She insisted, probably rightly, that she feared no trial. With new, tighter rules of evidence, forty-nine of fifty-two prisoners were acquitted in the court session for January, with the remainder discharged later in the spring.

In trying to understand why Mary Green and Hannah Bromage were accused, it is necessary to know their accusers. Two of the them, Ann Putnam (1680–1716) and Mary Walcott, are instantly familiar to students of the Salem witch trials as "afflicted girls." Their families were among the most ardent supporters of the ministry of Samuel Parris and were representatives of the old agrarian and communalistic economic order of New England coming under assault by a newly emerging commercial order.

Timothy Swan, the third accuser, may be less familiar. At twenty-eight he was older than most, and he was male. It seems likely that Timothy was the linchpin in this particular pair of accusations, since the Swans, Bromages, and Greens were all long-standing members of the Haverhill community and all intimately acquainted. At this point, one can only guess at the patterns of hostility and mutual suspicion that shot through that village and can only imagine the fear and uncertainties in life that stalked a frontier town prone to Indian attack and imminent crop failure. Just as important, it is possible to imagine the resentment that some men felt toward a strong-minded, active woman like Mary Green. Under these conditions, accusations of witchcraft grew in the rocky soils of Puritan Haverhill as naturally as any tree.

On August 25, 1706, a troubled Ann Putnam reflected on her role in the Salem trials when applying for full membership in the church: "[I was] an instrument," she wrote, "for the accusing of several persons of a grievous crime, whereby their lives were taken away from them, whom now I have just grounds and good reason to believe they were innocent persons; and that it was a great delusion of Satan that deceived me in that sad time. . . . I desire to lie in the dust and to be humbled for it, in that I was a cause, with others, of so sad a calamity to them and their families."

Purchased from Carnegie Book Shop, 1983.

ᔆ 23 ᔆ

UNCOMMON BOOK OF PRAYER IN MOHAWK

THE CONVERSION of the native population to Christianity was the stated aim of every one of the early North American colonization projects. Various arguments were put forward, including the belief that the Bible foretold that conversion of the world's heathen was a preliminary step toward the Second Coming of Christ. A number of European and American scholars believed the Indians of America to be one of the Lost Tribes of Israel, deserving of special efforts to bring them back into the fold. If native people could be converted to Christianity, they could also be "civilized," taught to abandon their nomadic habits for farming, and perhaps come to live in peaceful coexistence with European settlers. As Europeans gained an ever larger hold on the North American continent, missionary efforts became nationalistic and even denominational, with Protestant clergymen vying with Catholic priests for the souls and political loyalties of Indian tribes on the frontiers.

Considerable missionary and educational efforts were made throughout the colonial period, and the Library is full of source materials on these efforts. Roger Williams published *A Key into the Language of America* (London, 1643), and John Eliot translated the Scriptures in their entirety into a phonetic native tongue. Eliot's Bible was published in Cambridge, Massachusetts, in two editions. Dartmouth College had its origins in John Wheelock's Indian School, and his efforts are documented in a series of pamphlets. The Library has all of these works and numerous sermons,

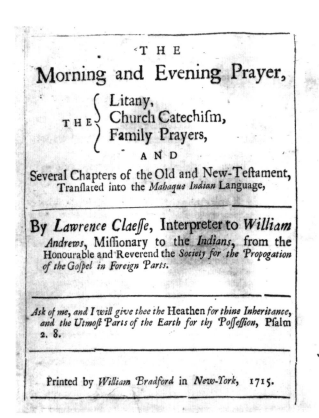 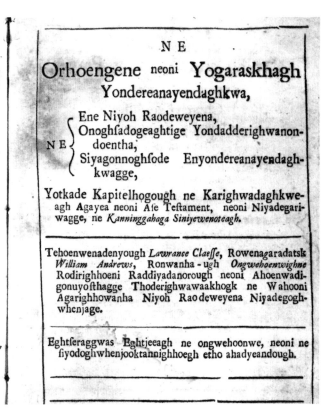

reports, and manuscripts documenting well-meaning but largely ineffectual efforts of Europeans and Americans to Christianize the natives.

Just as Indian missionary efforts resulted in publication of the first Bible, they also resulted in the first American publication of the Book of Common Prayer, illustrated here. Beginning in 1704, the Society for the Propagation of the Gospel in Foreign Parts, one of several London-based societies inspired by the Reverend Thomas Bray, who had been a missionary Anglican clergyman in Maryland, sent missionaries to work with the Mohawk Indians of New York. A Reverend Mr. Moor, at Schenectady, began the work of translating the Gospels and prayers into Mohawk. In 1712, the Reverend William Andrews took up the efforts, and in conjunction with Lawrence Claesse, a local interpreter, he produced the finished manuscript of the abbreviated Anglican Book of Common Prayer. William Bradford published it in 1715. The volume is considerably rarer than the Eliot Bible, and like it, preceded the publication of an English edition of the same work by decades.

Gift of Lathrop C. Harper, New York, 1944.

⤫ 24 ⤫

THE INDIAN CHIEF WHO MET THE KING

ENGLAND'S SUCCESS in establishing Georgia on its southern colonial frontier in 1733 can be attributed in part to the remarkable friendship between an English reformer and a Creek chieftain. James Oglethorpe and Tomochichi were both men of uncommon vision.

Years of service in Parliament and the British army had convinced James Oglethorpe that England must expand its trading empire. A believer in religious toleration, a crusader against impressment and the slave trade, Oglethorpe's humanitarian instincts had led him to study the appalling effects of debtor's prisons on London's poor. He transformed his ideas on penal reform and imperial expansion into a bold plan, one that would create a new American colony, a refuge for unemployed debtors. Oglethorpe argued that his colony would provide a defensive buffer against raids from the Spanish in Florida as well as open new sources for raw materials and opportunities for trade. In 1732, Oglethorpe and nineteen associates were granted a charter as Trustees for Establishing the Colony of Georgia in America.

Little is known about Tomochichi's early life, only that he was born among the Lower Creeks, on the west bank of the Chatta-

Tomo Chachi Mico
oder König Von Yamacran und Tooanahowi seines
Bruders des Mico oder Königes Von Etichitas Sohn.
nach dem Londischen Original in Augspurg nachgestochen von
foh: Jacob Kleinschmidt.

hoochee River opposite present-day Columbus, Georgia. Sometime after 1721, he and a group of Creeks and Yamassee settled at Yamacraw on the Savannah River. Tomochichi was there when Oglethorpe, with the first Georgia colonists, arrived in 1733 and began the settlement of Savannah, four miles downstream. Oglethorpe and Tomochichi, through an interpreter, Mary Musgrove, the half-breed wife of a Carolina trader, quickly negotiated a treaty which granted land to the colonists for the Savannah site. Through Tomochichi's diplomacy, Oglethorpe was able to make similar treaties with neighboring tribes. Tomochichi's willingness to extend friendship and secure the goodwill of his kinsmen provided the peace essential to Georgia's survival as a colony.

Oglethorpe, reporting back to London, marveled at the native's civility. Conversations with Tomochichi convinced him the Creeks could be easily converted if someone would translate their language well enough "to explain the mysteries of religion; as to the moral part of Christianity, they understand and assent to it." They "abhor" adultery, incest, and murder (killing enemies excepted) and in conducting tribal affairs, they "reason together with great temper and modesty." Only drunkenness, learned from traders, and their "passion for revenge, which they call honour," prevent them from being true Christians. In May 1734 Oglethorpe sailed for London, taking with him Tomochichi, his wife Senauki, their young nephew Tooanahowi, and several tribesmen.

As Oglethorpe hoped, their arrival in late June created a sensation in London. Immediately, Tomochichi and his entourage, their faces "beautifully painted after their custom," dressed in "Moorish fashion, in crimson and gold," were taken by royal carriage to Kensington Palace. Tomochichi presented George II with eagle feathers as a sign of "everlasting peace." The King replied with his assurance of England's friendship. Three days later the triumphal tour was cut short. Tomochichi's brother-in-law was stricken with smallpox. His death and burial were so deeply distressing that Oglethorpe took the grieving party to his country estate where they could mourn in private. By August, Tomochichi and his companions were again seen in public, everywhere attracting crowds as they made the tourist circuit—Windsor Castle, the Tower, Hampton Court, Greenwich Hospital, Eton College. The Archbishop of Canterbury sent his barge to bring Tomochichi's retinue to Lambeth Palace where, according to an exuberant press, they were received "with the utmost kindness and tenderness."

At last Oglethorpe presented his now-famous guests to the Georgia Trustees. A portrait was commissioned to hang in the boardroom. Artist William Verelst, who twenty years earlier had done portraits of the four Iroquois kings whose visit then thrilled London, painted Tomochichi with his young nephew at his side. Oglethorpe was not the only one to recognize Tomochichi's value in promoting the new colony. Samuel Urlsperger, who was recruiting Salzburgers for Georgia, had it engraved by Johann Jacob Kleinschmidt as a frontispiece (displayed here) to his *Ausführliche Nachricht von den Saltzburgischen Emigranten*. This series of books, consisting of detailed reports from immigrant pastors, remains one of the most important sources for the earliest history of Georgia, including information about the Creeks and their first encounter with English and German settlers.

With Tomochichi's support, Oglethorpe had convinced the Trustees to make policy decisions that he hoped would strengthen Georgia: slavery and the sale of rum were prohibited; relations between natives and traders were improved by establishing licenses, standardized prices, and measurements for peltry.

Tomochichi and his companions sailed from Gravesend in October 1734, accompanied by 52 new Salzburger emigrants and gifts for the natives valued at £400. An ode commemorating Tomochichi soon appeared in London bookshops. Four years later *Gentleman's Magazine* carried Tomochichi's obituary. He died, aged 97, "sensible to the last." His body was brought by water to be buried, as he requested, "amongst the English in the Town of Savannah."

Purchased from George S. MacManus & Co., 1983.

⤫ 25 ⤫

FUR TRADER'S PASSPORT TO DETROIT

BOLDLY WRITTEN ACROSS THE TOP of this document, in large and ornate script, is the name of the most powerful man in New France. Charles Beauharnois de La Boische, Marquis de Beauharnois, served as governor-general and representative of King Louis XV in his Canadian colony. Upon Beauharnois fell responsibility for the security of that colony and, to a large extent, the commercial well-being of its inhabitants. His attention was directed to most affairs in Canada, even a matter so seemingly minute as the 1737 departure of a single canoe for the post of Detroit.

Charles M.ᵈᵉ de Beauharnois

Commandeur de l'ordre Royal et militaire de S.ᵗ Louis

gouverneur et Lieutenant général pour le Roy En toute La

Nouvelle france Et province de la Loüisianne

Nous avons permis aux S.ʳˢ Beaubien Et Germain de

partir de cette ville avec un canot Equipé de quatre hommes

dont ils Nous ont donné les Noms Et demeures pour Se

vendre au poste du Détroit et d'Embarquer dans led. canot

les Effets Et marchandises propres pour la traitte aud.

poste Et en outre les vivres Et provisions necessaires dont

ils auront besoin pour leur Subsistance et celle de leur

Engagé pendant le Voyage

Deffendons aux d. S.ʳˢ Beaubien et germain de

prendre d'autre Route que celle du nord du Lac ontario

ny de faire aucune traitte ou Commerce avec les Sauvages

ny autres ailleurs q'aud. Poste et Ses dependances Sous les

peines portées par les ordonnances du Roy

Enjoignons aud. Engagez d'avoir chacun leur

quittant En montant qu'en descendant Sansqu'ils puissent

Trade with the Indians was the foundation of eighteenth-century New France and of great interest to its administrators. The fur trade had attracted the French to Canada and encouraged exploration of the lakes and rivers of the West. It had also created endless administrative difficulties. Official attempts to control the trade ultimately placed the French at a disadvantage in the struggle for empire with their English rivals.

The late seventeenth century had been a time of chaos in the upper country. Hundreds of illegal traders set out from the thinly populated settlements of the St. Lawrence to barter for pelts. Their methods were unrestricted, often unscrupulous, and they frequently involved liquor. Beginning in 1681, to place some controls on the traders, limited numbers of *congés*, or licenses, were issued by the governor. The license system was abolished and reestablished several times over the next seventy years. In 1728, not long after the appointment of Beauharnois as governor, the *congés* were revived.

Under the new regulations, Beauharnois was allowed to issue twenty-five licenses annually at a set fee. In fact, he sold them for what the market would bear, and in some years as many as fifty were issued. Many of the successful bidders were military officers or traders in partnership with post commandants. The profitability of the trade made licenses a powerful bit of patronage at the disposal of the governor. The *congé* system was again abolished in 1742, under much protest from interested parties. Trade concessions at posts were thereafter to be auctioned to the highest bidders. When this too encouraged abuses, *congés* were restored in 1749 and remained in use until the British conquest.

It was under the *congé* system of 1728 that two Detroit traders, Messrs. Beaubien and Germain, were allowed to leave Montreal with a canoe of goods. Both had been associated with Detroit since the first decade of its existence. Like most traders, they hired four *engagés* to convey their cargo. Governor-General Beauharnois signed their license on August 17, 1737, and it was legally registered in Montreal two days later. The traders were then free to depart for Detroit where the "effects and merchandise for trading" stowed in their canoe would be bartered for furs during the winter. If all went well, Beaubien and Germain would garner a handsome profit in 1738.

The carefully worded document expresses all the concerns of the government about trade in the *pays d'en haut* (the upper country), and the holders of this *congé* were closely regulated. Beaubien and Germain were required to take the route along the north shore of Lake Ontario, thus removing them from the temptations of English traders at Oswego. They could trade nowhere but at Detroit. Only the "proper effects and merchandise for trading" and food for the voyage could be stowed in their canoe. The officials were not entirely without compassion. Each *engagé* was allowed four *pots* (roughly two gallons) of *eau de vie* for personal use. The names and addresses of the *engagés* were recorded, and they were forbidden to barter any of their equipment with the Indians. If any of them deserted, it was the responsibility of Beaubien and Germain to report them to the commandant of the first French post.

Listed at the bottom are the names of the men who would do the work of paddling and portaging to Detroit. The document provides an interesting look at the diversity of personnel employed in this rigorous trade. Pierre Chicot hailed from Boucherville; Louis Clairemont was returning to his home town of Detroit; the man named Bouron was from Montreal. The last of the four was "Pierre Panis de Nation" from Boucherville, probably an Indian slave or *panis*.

The document comes from the papers of the Riopelle family, early settlers of Detroit. While the Clements Library defers to the excellent Bentley Library of the University of Michigan in collecting general materials on Michigan history, the Clements collections do contain significant resources on the colonial and frontier periods.

Gift of Mrs. Sydney F. Heavenrich, Detroit, 1942.

⚚ 26 ⚚

THE SINGING SCHOOL: ANTIDOTE
TO DISHARMONY

MUSIC WAS AN INTEGRAL PART of Puritan life, a cherished form of worship that the first generations of New Englanders fostered through the most difficult times. Yet, as good Calvinists of their day, they were deeply mistrustful of musical elaboration, instrumental accompaniment, and professional leadership. Musical literacy in New England Congregational churches deteriorated during the course of the seventeenth century, and along with it, the quality of singing. The "Old Way" or "common way" of singing that predominated in New England was always unaccompanied and performed at a languid pace, with members of the congregation singing individually, as they saw fit. Critics jibed that the sounds emanating from New England meeting houses were "like the braying of asses." Beginning around 1700, a group of clergymen in Britain and the colonies, including Cotton Mather, Thomas Symmes, and Nathaniel Chauncey, encouraged psalmodic reform, arguing that the discordant Old Way was not conducive to worship.

The spearhead for reform was the singing school, in which a small number of the faithful gathered under the tutelage of a skilled musician to learn the rudiments of vocal technique and tuneful singing. After two or three months of training, it was hoped that these students would provide a beneficial influence on other members of the congregation, providing a sort of musical inoculation. The result would be "regular" singing with all the parts fitting together. The earliest known singing school in the American colonies was operating in Virginia prior to December 1710, and in Boston instruction in psalm singing was advertised as early as April 1714. Singing schools caught on rapidly, encouraged partly by musically talented entrepreneurs who saw in them the means of earning extra income. "Where would be the difficulty," Thomas Symmes asked in his *The Reasonableness of Regular Singing* (1720), "if People that want Skill in Singing, would procure a Skillful Person to Instruct them, and meet Two or Three Evenings in the Week . . . ? Would not this be an innocent and profitable Recreation[?]"

Samuel Holbrook was one of many musicians contracted to conduct a school. Once a week he gathered his nine pupils at the house of Samuel Pitcher to learn "the Rules of Psalmody." Holbrook's identity is elusive, though he may have been the younger brother of Abiah Holbrook, a writing master in Boston who was conducting a school as early as 1717. A Samuel Holbrook worked as usher in his brother's school at a salary of £50 per annum, and he is recorded as having

Articals of Agreement

WE whose Names Are under Written do Mutualy Agree to
Abide by Comply with and Cyforme Our Selves in Every
Respect to the Articals within Mentioned

First — We do Agree to put Our Selves Under the tuishion and Instruction
of Mr Sam'l Holbrook to be by him Instructed in the Rules of Psalmody.

2ly — We Do agree (in Order to be taught the Above Rules) to mett
Once a week At the house of Mr Sam'l Pitcher And we do Appoint
the time for this Quarter to be thereof at Seven a Clock in
the Eueninge and so to Alter the time Each Quarter as the Company
shall thinke Proper

3ly — That if Aney One of us is Absent After said Hour
he shall forfit the sum of One Shilling Old tenor

4ly — We do Agree to Chuse a Clark to Receive such fines as may be
as Afor'd and Render an Acct of the same and of Other Money that
he shall Receive of the Company for the Maintainance of the Society
Once Every three Months.

5ly — We do Agree Not to sing After the hour of Nine and then that Who
Ever is so minded may withdraw and that if Aney are Inclined to
Stay Longer thay may Not Exceede the hour of tenn

6ly — We do agree that No person be Inuited or Admitted as a Member
with Oute the Consent of the Maj'r part of the Sosiaty

7ly — We Do agree that Every Person Upon his Entrance Shall
pay to the Clarke tenn Shill. Old tennor that so the Stock
is Keept good

8ly — We Do Agree to Conforme Our Selves with Regard to all the
Causes of Each of the Above Articals to the Maj'r Vote of y'e Com'y

	Sam'll Pitcher	
	Will'm Bracinster	
	Thac'le Tyffeler	
	John Math'w Lee	
	Joseph Lawronil	
	Caleb Eddy	
	Nathl Colton	
	Nathenial Wilkes	
	Thomas Baker	

established his own school by 1746. Since the selectmen of Boston granted permission for brother Abiah to keep a singing school in 1744, it seems not unlikely that the younger Samuel may have followed suit. This document is the only extant pre-Revolutionary contract for the establishment of a singing school.

Purchased from Ken Leach, 1995.

❧ 27 ❧
AMERICA'S FIRST WOMAN SCIENTIST

RAISED IN THE RESPLENDENCE of Coldengham, her father's country estate near Newburgh, New York, and educated entirely at home, Jane Colden (1724–1766) was a pioneer in the field of systematic botany and was the first American woman to earn an international reputation as a scientist. She was the fifth daughter of Cadwallader Colden, physician, scientist, and lieutenant governor of New York. Her father's substantial wealth, political influence, and his family and scholarly connections turned Coldengham into a bustling center of intellectual activity. It became a

regular stop on any botanical tour of America, and through its doors passed such luminaries as the roving Swede, Peter Kalm, and the self-taught American Quaker botanist, John Bartram. The circle was widened further by her father's correspondence with men such as Alexander Garden and Benjamin Franklin in America, Peter Collinson, John Fothergill, and Johannes Gronovius in Europe, and the brilliant Swedish naturalist, Carl Linnaeus.

Jane's father initiated her into the arcana of scientific botany while she was still in her twenties, and by her thirty-first birthday she had progressed so far that he began to share her work with his colleagues. Cadwallader admitted to Gronovius, in the letter displayed here, that he had long thought of botany as "an amusement which might be made agreeable to the Ladies, who are often at a loss to fill up time." Why to ladies? "Their natural curiosity," he answered, "& the pleasure they take in the beauty & variety of colours & dress seems to fit them for it." Botany, in other words, was in their nature. Yet Latin, an essential ingredient, was not, nor were the texts that were "so filled with Technical words" that women tired of the study long before they derived any pleasure. Although Jane did not know Latin, her father could still boast that she had "an inclination to reading, & a curiosity for natural history, with a sufficient capacity for obtaining a competent knowledge in botany," and would therefore acquit herself well.

Jane's "sufficient capacity" soon allowed her to surpass her father in botanical skills, and she became an important American proponent of the revolutionary Linnaean system. This system represented a fundamentally new way of looking at the natural world, a recognition of the systematic ordering of life that proved so powerful that a century later it would weather the storm of Darwinism. In 1755, when the letter enclosing these illustrations was written, Jane's collection of almost 400 plants was among the few in America to be meticulously described and arranged in strict adherence to the Linnaean system, demonstrating a sophisticated understanding of botanical theory and practice. In many cases, her specimens were illustrated with ingenious ink transfers. After she married William Farquhar in 1759, she transferred her energies to other spheres, never returning to the science for which she is remembered today.

Gift to the University of Michigan of Harley H. Bartlett, Ann Arbor. Transferred to Clements Library, 1978.

OUR FIRST RECOGNIZABLE AMERICAN CELEBRITY

WE LIVE TODAY IN AN AGE of pictures. Photography, and then the ability to print photographs in magazines and newspapers, perfected in the 1890s, created a public that expected its news to be presented graphically as well as in print. With the advent of moving pictures, television, video, and now digital imaging, pictures have gained ascendancy over the printed word.

The eighteenth century was a far different world. Drawings and paintings, woodcuts and copper engravings, and silhouettes cut out of paper were the means available of copying reality in pictorial form, and Americans were not, as a rule, very good at any of these artistic endeavors. Thanks to a few gifted artists such as Copley, Hesselius, Peale, Stuart, Trumbull, and the Sharpless, we

B. Franklin of Philadelphia

have respectable oil and pastel portraits of many of the leaders of the Revolutionary era available to us in museums or printed reproductions. But these were not widely available to their contemporaries. Average Americans of 1775 probably had some idea of the appearance of George III or other European monarchs from their coins, or frequently-pictured political figures such as John Wilkes or William Pitt from popular British magazines, but they could have no true idea of what even George Washington looked like unless they had seen him personally.

The one native-born American whose appearance was fairly well known, both in America and Europe, was Benjamin Franklin, who was not only a genius of many parts but a very willing partner in promoting his own fame. In Philadelphia of the 1720s to the 1750s, he was the most enterprising printer and the driving force behind innumerable public improvements: founder of the hospital, the first circulating library, the scientific group which developed into the American Philosophical Society, and the academy which developed into the University of Pennsylvania. Franklin's satirical writing and the homespun practical wisdom of *Poor Richard's Almanac* were reprinted in newspapers throughout the colonies and Britain. His real fame rested on his scientific experiments and publications. His book on more efficient stoves was published in 1744 and his first work on electricity in 1751. The latter earned him great fame throughout Europe, and when he came to London in 1757 as agent for the Pennsylvania Assembly, staying for most of seventeen years, he was already a celebrity.

Fine oil portraits and mezzotint engravings based on the paintings were commonplace in eighteenth-century London, and Franklin was an obvious subject. Two fine portraits were done in the 1760s, by Benjamin Wilson and by David Martin, and a variety of excellent engravings were made from them which were circulated as separate prints or magazine reproductions throughout the Anglo-American world. The likeness shown here, based on Wilson's portrait, was engraved by James McArdell in 1761 and was the first issued. Benjamin Franklin was our first famous American, and thanks to the fact that he went to England at the height of his fame, not only historians but his contemporaries had an accurate picture of what he looked like.

Purchased from the Old Print Gallery, 1991.

MAPPING FRENCH CANADA

THE BRITISH OFFICERS WHO LED the assault on New France during the Seven Years War fought their way into poorly known territory. To mariners, the St. Lawrence River was a dangerous and forbidding avenue to the heart of the French colony. For soldiers, the only practical routes followed rivers and a few difficult roads, and the extent and distribution of civilian settlement were poorly understood. It is not surprising, therefore, that General James Murray, first British military governor of Quebec, sought current cartographic information about the region. Still uncertain, during the winter of 1760–61, whether New France would be relinquished by Britain when peace came, Murray realized that better maps would at least provide an important advantage if it again became necessary to fight the French for Canada. If, on the other hand, the territory was retained, the maps would be useful in governing the colony.

Murray set in motion one of the most ambitious British surveys of his time. Utilizing the services of a group of talented military engineers, the developed part of the colony — from the Cedars in the southwest down the St. Lawrence to Isle au Coudres below Quebec — was minutely surveyed. The settlements of the Richelieu River were included as was the rugged overland route via the Chaudiere River from Quebec to New England. Captain Samuel Holland, Lieutenant John

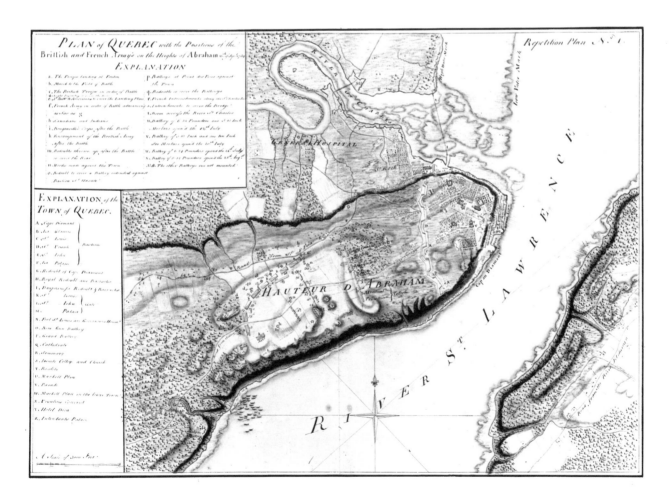

Montresor, Lieutenant Joseph Peach, and Lieutenant Lewis Fusier completed their surveys before the end of 1761 in the best style of eighteenth-century military engineering. Showing elevations, vegetation, cities, and details as small as individual farms, the finished maps also included marginal information about the numbers of families and *habitants* able to bear arms in each parish.

Murray's maps were intended for a select audience. Seven manuscript sets were produced, and recipients included King George III, Prime Minister William Pitt, the Board of Ordnance, North American commander in chief Sir Jeffery Amherst, governor of Montreal Thomas Gage, and probably Murray himself. Five copies are known to survive today.

The set of the Murray maps in the Library is the only one known today outside the major public institutions of Canada and Great Britain. It is possible that the Clements copy was prepared for General Gage. It includes three extra plans of Quebec and the surrounding area, illustrating in great detail the decisive battle of September 13, 1759 (which gained for Britain the capital city of Quebec), that of April 28, 1760 (the Battle of St. Foy, which nearly cost the invaders their foothold in Canada), and the unsuccessful siege of May 1760 (when France's last chance of regaining the colony was defeated by the fortuitous arrival of British warships). All 68 individual maps in the Clements' copy of the Murray atlas are beautifully colored. This multi-sheet map is one of the crowning achievements of the engineering corps of the eighteenth-century British Army, whose work is so well represented in the Library's collections.

Acquired by trade with Otto O. Fisher, 1957.

⤜ 30 ⤛

SHORTCUT THROUGH THE WILDERNESS

THE FATEFUL CONFRONTATION between Britain and France in 1753, which started the Seven Years War, occurred at a spot in North America far from the capitals of their respective colonies. Deep in the forests of what would become Pennsylvania, at a previously unknown place called Fort Le Boeuf, a young Virginia officer delivered a formal summons to an elderly Canadian captain. The events put into motion by Legardeur de Saint-Pierre's rejection of George Washington's message would eventually start a war in Europe and decide which nation would gain control of the northern half of North America.

Fort Le Boeuf rose to sudden prominence because of its location. It was the spear point of a French attempt to deny the Ohio valley to Britain. To effectively control the area, the French had to establish an efficient and defensible line of communication between Canada and the West. They had previously depended upon the St. Lawrence-Lake Ontario-Niagara Portage route to Detroit, the upper Great Lakes, and south to Louisiana by way of the Mississippi. The Allegheny River–Ohio River route would provide an invaluable shortcut to not only the Ohio country but Louisiana and the entire Mississippi River basin. In the spring of 1753, Canada's governor-general set out to gain control of this route by dispatching an expedition to fortify the portage to the Ohio. Despite terrible hardships, the Canadian troops built a fort at Presqu'Isle (Erie, Pennsylvania) and laboriously carved a road across escarpment and through swamps to the upper reaches of French

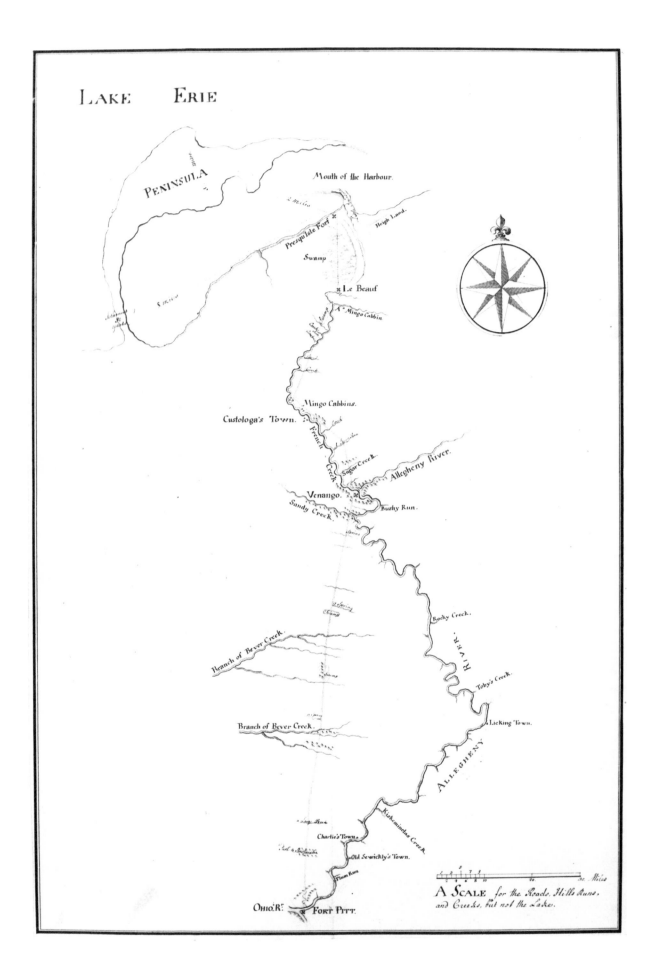

LAKE ERIE

PENINSULA

Mouth of the Harbour.

Presqu'Isle Fort

Heigh Land

Swamp

Le Beauf

A Mingo Cabbin.

Mingo Cabbins.

Custologa's Town.

French Creek

Sugar Creek.

Allegheny River.

Venango.

Bushy Run.

Sandy Creek.

Rocky Creek.

Branch of Bever Creek

RIVER.

Toby's Creek.

Branch of Bever Creek.

Licking Town.

ALLEGHENY

Kiskeminetas Creek.

Chartie's Town.

Old Sewickly's Town.

Plum Run.

OHIO R:

FORT PITT.

A SCALE for the Roads, Hills, Runs, and Creeks, but not the Lake.

Creek, which flowed south. There, navigation could resume whenever the water was high enough. Fort Le Boeuf rose on the site before winter ended the campaign.

Nowhere in the history of colonial America was the significance of water transportation routes and their connecting portages more apparent than at the carrying place between Lake Erie and the Allegheny River. It was France's last chance to confine the populous British colonies to the Atlantic seaboard. They won the race to the junction of the Allegheny and Monongahela rivers, where they placed Fort Duquesne in 1754, and they defeated General Braddock in 1755, but it was too little, too late. The British and Americans had vast numerical superiority, and the French lost the forks of the Ohio in 1758 and the portage to Lake Erie a year later. The route, in reverse, gave the British an important avenue to the Great Lakes.

Thomas Hutchins, one of the most proficient engineers of the British, and later the American Army during the Revolution, mapped the route between Pittsburgh and Presqu'Isle in 1762. It was then of particular interest to General Amherst in determining how the newly-occupied posts on the Great Lakes could best be supplied. In the end, the old French route through Lake Ontario and Niagara was considered more practical. The small posts on the portage to the Ohio —Presqu'Isle, Le Boeuf and Venango—remained in use only for another year. In 1763, they all succumbed to Indian attacks during Pontiac's War, and they were not needed afterwards.

This particular map, once in the possession of Sir Jeffery Amherst, is typical of hundreds of others at the Clements Library from the papers of General Thomas Gage, Sir Henry Clinton, Lord Shelburne, Lord Germain, and other sources.

Amherst Sale purchase at Sotheby's by Stevens, 1967.

❧ 31 ❧

NATIVE RIGHTS RESERVED

Largely forgotten in the history of the United States, the Proclamation of 1763, dated October 7 of that year, continues to be thought of in Canada as a notable constitutional document. In its original broadside form, with the British coat-of-arms at the top, it must have seemed important when posted in public places during the winter of 1763–64. If it shares some of the impressive appearance of the Declaration of Independence, the *Proclamation* lacks Jefferson's eloquent prose. The text, in fact, has many of the "pork-barrel" qualities of a modern Congressional bill, dealing with subject matter that is quite diverse.

The first sections of the *Proclamation* formalized British rule in former French territories, created three new Royal colonies (Quebec, East Florida, and West Florida), and defined the boundaries of Grenada, Nova Scotia, and Georgia. The northeastern fisheries were placed under the control of Newfoundland. A second section provided land grants for veterans of the Seven Years War who had served in regular forces in America or on ships in American waters. The remainder of the document dealt with Native Americans. All land beyond the Allegheny Mountains was reserved by the Crown for the Indians. Settlement of whites was prohibited, and squatters were to be re-

By the KING,

A PROCLAMATION.

GEORGE R.

WHEREAS We have taken into Our Royal Conſideration the extenſive and valuable Acquiſitions in *America*, ſecured to Our Crown by the late Definitive Treaty of Peace, concluded at *Paris* the Tenth Day of *February* laſt; and being deſirous, that all Our loving Subjects, as well of Our Kingdoms as of Our Colonies in *America*, may avail themſelves, with all convenient Speed, of the great Benefits and Advantages which muſt accrue therefrom to their Commerce, Manufactures, and Navigation; We have thought fit, with the Advice of Our Privy Council, to iſſue this Our Royal Proclamation, hereby to publiſh and declare to all Our loving Subjects, that We have, with the Advice of Our ſaid Privy Council, granted Our Letters Patent under Our Great Seal of *Great Britain*, to erect within the Countries and Iſlands ceded and confirmed to Us by the ſaid Treaty, Four diſtinct and ſeparate Governments, ſtiled and called by the Names of *Quebec*, *Eaſt Florida*, *Weſt Florida*, and *Grenada*, and limited and bounded as follows; *viz.*

Firſt. The Government of *Quebec*, bounded on the *Labrador* Coaſt by the River *St. John*, and from thence by a Line drawn from the Head of that River through the Lake *St. John* to the South End of the Lake nigh *Piſſin*; from whence the ſaid Line croſſing the River *St. Lawrence* and the Lake *Champlain* in Forty five Degrees of North Latitude, paſſes along the High Lands which divide the Rivers that empty themſelves into the ſaid River *St. Lawrence*, from thoſe which fall into the Sea; and alſo along the North Coaſt of the *Baye des Chaleurs*, and the Coaſt of the Gulph of *St. Lawrence* to Cape *Roſieres*, and from thence croſſing the Mouth of the River *St. Lawrence* by the Weſt End of the Iſland of *Anticoſti*, terminates at the aforeſaid River of *St. John*.

Secondly. The Government of *Eaſt Florida*, bounded to the Weſtward by the Gulph of *Mexico*, and the *Apalachicola* River; to the Northward, by a Line drawn from that Part of the ſaid River where the *Chatahouchee* and *Flint* Rivers meet, to the Source of *St. Mary's* River, and by the Courſe of the ſaid River to the *Atlantick* Ocean; and to the Eaſtward and Southward, by the *Atlantick* Ocean, and the Gulph of *Florida*, including all Iſlands within Six Leagues of the Sea Coaſt.

Thirdly. The Government of *Weſt Florida*, bounded to the Southward by the Gulph of *Mexico*, including all Iſlands within Six Leagues of the Coaſt from the River *Apalachicola* to Lake *Pontchartrain*; to the Weſtward by the ſaid Lake, the Lake *Maurepas*, and the River *Miſſiſippi*; to the Northward, by a Line drawn due Eaſt from that Part of the River *Miſſiſippi* which lies in Thirty one Degrees North Latitude, to the River *Apalachicola* or *Chatahouchee*; and to the Eaſtward by the ſaid River.

Fourthly. The Government of *Grenada*, comprehending the Iſland of that Name, together with the *Grenadines*, and the Iſlands of *Dominico*, *St. Vincents*, and *Tobago*.

And, to the End that the open and free Fiſhery of Our Subjects may be extended to and carried on upon the Coaſt of *Labrador* and the adjacent Iſlands, We have thought fit, with the Advice of Our ſaid Privy Council, to put all that Coaſt, from the River *St. John*'s to *Hudſon's Streights*, together with the Iſlands of *Anticoſti* and *Madelaine*, and all other ſmaller Iſlands lying upon the ſaid Coaſt, under the Care and Inſpection of Our Governor of *Newfoundland*.

We have alſo, with the Advice of Our Privy Council, thought fit to annex the Iſlands of *St. John's*, and *Cape Breton* or *Iſle Royale*, with the leſſer Iſlands adjacent thereto, to Our Government of *Nova Scotia*.

We have alſo, with the Advice of Our Privy Council aforeſaid, annexed to Our Province of *Georgia* all the Lands lying between the Rivers *Attamaha* and *St. Mary*'s.

And whereas it will greatly contribute to the ſpeedy ſettling Our ſaid new Governments, that Our loving Subjects ſhould be informed of Our Paternal Care for the Security of the Liberties and Properties of thoſe who are and ſhall become Inhabitants thereof; We have thought fit to publiſh and declare, by this Our Proclamation, that We have, in the Letters Patent under Our Great Seal of *Great Britain*, by which the ſaid Governments are conſtituted, given expreſs Power and Direction to Our Governors of Our ſaid Colonies reſpectively, that ſo ſoon as the State and Circumſtances of the ſaid Colonies will admit thereof, they ſhall, with the Advice and Conſent of the Members of Our Council, ſummon and call General Aſſemblies within the ſaid Governments reſpectively, in ſuch Manner and Form as is uſed and directed in thoſe Colonies and Provinces in *America*, which are under Our immediate Government; and We have alſo given Power to the ſaid Governors, with the Conſent of Our ſaid Councils, and the Repreſentatives of the People, ſo to be ſummoned as aforeſaid, to make, conſtitute, and ordain Laws, Statutes, and Ordinances for the Publick Peace, Welfare, and Good Government of Our ſaid Colonies, and of the People and Inhabitants thereof, as near as may be agreeable to the Laws of *England*, and under ſuch Regulations and Reſtrictions as are uſed in other Colonies: And in the mean Time, and until ſuch Aſſemblies can be called as aforeſaid, all Perſons inhabiting in, or reſorting to Our ſaid Colonies, may confide in Our Royal Protection for the Enjoyment of the Benefit of the Laws of Our Realm of *England*; for which Purpoſe, We have given Power under Our Great Seal to the Governors of Our ſaid Colonies reſpectively, to erect and conſtitute, with the Advice of Our ſaid Councils reſpectively, Courts of Judicature and Publick Juſtice, within Our ſaid Colonies, for the hearing and determining all Cauſes, as well Criminal as Civil, according to Law and Equity, and as near as may be agreeable to the Laws of *England*, with Liberty to all Perſons who may think themſelves aggrieved by the Sentences of ſuch Courts, in all Civil Caſes, to appeal, under the uſual Limitations and Reſtrictions, to Us in Our Privy Council.

We have alſo thought fit, with the Advice of Our Privy Council as aforeſaid, to give unto the Governors and Councils of Our ſaid Three New Colonies upon the Continent, full Power and Authority to ſettle and agree with the Inhabitants of Our ſaid New Colonies, or with any other Perſons who ſhall reſort thereto, for ſuch Lands, Tenements, and Hereditaments, as are now, or hereafter ſhall be in Our Power to diſpoſe of, and them to grant to any ſuch Perſon or Perſons, upon ſuch Terms, and under ſuch moderate Quit-Rents, Services, and Acknowledgements as have been appointed and ſettled in Our other Colonies, and under ſuch other Conditions as ſhall appear to Us to be neceſſary and expedient for the Advantage of the Grantees, and the Improvement and Settlement of Our ſaid Colonies.

And whereas We are deſirous, upon all Occaſions, to teſtify Our Royal Senſe and Approbation of the Conduct and Bravery of the Officers and Soldiers of Our Armies, and to reward the ſame, We do hereby command and impower Our Governors of Our ſaid Three New Colonies, and all other Our Governors of Our ſeveral Provinces on the Continent of *North America*, to grant, without Fee or Reward, to ſuch Reduced Officers as have ſerved in *North America* during the late War, and to ſuch Private Soldiers as have been or ſhall be diſbanded in *America*, and are actually reſiding there, and ſhall perſonally apply for the ſame, the following Quantities of Lands, ſubject at the Expiration of Ten Years to the ſame Quit-Rents as other Lands are ſubject to in the Province within which they are granted, as alſo ſubject to the ſame Conditions of Cultivation and Improvement; *viz.*

To every Perſon having the Rank of a Field Officer, Five thouſand Acres.—To every Captain, Three thouſand Acres.—To every Subaltern or Staff Officer, Two thouſand Acres.—To every Non-Commiſſion Officer, Two hundred Acres.—To every Private Man, Fifty Acres.

We do likewiſe authorize and require the Governors and Commanders in Chief of all Our ſaid Colonies upon the Continent of *North America*, to grant the like Quantities of Land, and upon the ſame Conditions, to ſuch Reduced Officers of Our Navy, of like Rank, as ſerved on Board Our Ships of War in *North America* at the Times of the Reduction of *Louiſbourg* and *Quebec* in the late War, and who ſhall perſonally apply to Our repective Governors for ſuch Grants.

And whereas it is juſt and reaſonable, and eſſential to Our Intereſt and the Security of Our Colonies, that the ſeveral Nations or Tribes of *Indians*, with whom We are connected, and who live under Our Protection, ſhould not be moleſted or diſturbed in the Poſſeſſion of ſuch Parts of Our Dominions and Territories as, not having been ceded to, or purchaſed by Us, are reſerved to them, or any of them, as their Hunting Grounds; We do therefore, with the Advice of Our Privy Council, declare it to be Our Royal Will and Pleaſure, that no Governor or Commander in Chief in any of Our Colonies of *Quebec*, *Eaſt Florida*, or *Weſt Florida*, do preſume, upon any Pretence whatever, to grant Warrants of Survey, or paſs any Patents for Lands beyond the Bounds of their reſpective Governments, as deſcribed in their Commiſſions; as alſo, that no Governor or Commander in Chief in any of Our other Colonies or Plantations in *America*, do preſume, for the preſent, and until Our further Pleaſure be known, to grant Warrants of Survey, or paſs Patents for any Lands beyond the Heads or Sources of any of the Rivers which fall into the *Atlantick* Ocean from the Weſt and North Weſt, or upon any Lands whatever, which, not having been ceded to, or purchaſed by Us as aforeſaid, are reſerved to the ſaid *Indians*, or any of them.

And We do further declare it to be Our Royal Will and Pleaſure, for the preſent as aforeſaid, to reſerve under Our Sovereignty, Protection, and Dominion, for the Uſe of the ſaid *Indians*, all the Lands and Territories not included within the Limits of Our ſaid Three New Governments, or within the Limits of the Territory granted to the *Hudſon's Bay* Company, as alſo all the Lands and Territories lying to the Weſtward of the Sources of the Rivers which fall into the Sea from the Weſt and North Weſt, as aforeſaid; and We do hereby ſtrictly forbid, on Pain of Our Diſpleaſure, all Our loving Subjects from making any Purchaſes or Settlements whatever, or taking Poſſeſſion of any of the Lands above reſerved, without Our eſpecial Leave and Licence for that Purpoſe firſt obtained.

And We do further ſtrictly enjoin and require all Perſons whatever, who have either wilfully or inadvertently ſeated themſelves upon any Lands within the Countries above deſcribed, or upon any other Lands, which, not having been ceded to, or purchaſed by Us, are ſtill reſerved to the ſaid *Indians* as aforeſaid, forthwith to remove themſelves from ſuch Settlements.

And whereas great Frauds and Abuſes have been committed in the purchaſing Lands of the *Indians*, to the great Prejudice of Our Intereſts, and to the great Diſſatisfaction of the ſaid *Indians*; in order therefore to prevent ſuch Irregularities for the future, and to the End that the *Indians* may be convinced of Our Juſtice, and determined Reſolution to remove all reaſonable Cauſe of Diſcontent, We do, with the Advice of Our Privy Council, ſtrictly enjoin and require, that no private Perſon do preſume to make any Purchaſe from the ſaid *Indians* of any Lands reſerved to the ſaid *Indians*, within thoſe Parts of Our Colonies where We have thought proper to allow Settlement; but that if, at any Time, any of the ſaid *Indians* ſhould be inclined to diſpoſe of the ſaid Lands, the ſame ſhall be purchaſed only for Us, in Our Name, at ſome Publick Meeting or Aſſembly of the ſaid *Indians* to be held for that Purpoſe by the Governor or Commander in Chief of Our Colonies reſpectively, within which they ſhall lie; and in caſe they ſhall lie within the Limits of any Proprietary Government, they ſhall be purchaſed only for the Uſe and in the Name of ſuch Proprietaries, conformable to ſuch Directions and Inſtructions as We or they ſhall think proper to give for that Purpoſe: And We do, by the Advice of Our Privy Council, declare and enjoin, that the Trade with the ſaid *Indians* ſhall be free and open to all Our Subjects whatever; provided that every Perſon, who may incline to trade with the ſaid *Indians*, do take out a Licence for carrying on ſuch Trade from the Governor or Commander in Chief of any of Our Colonies reſpectively, where ſuch Perſon ſhall reſide; and alſo give Security to obſerve ſuch Regulations as We ſhall at any Time think fit, by Ourſelves or by Our Commiſſaries to be appointed for this Purpoſe, to direct and appoint for the Benefit of the ſaid Trade; and We do hereby authorize, enjoin, and require the Governors and Commanders in Chief of all Our Colonies reſpectively, as well Thoſe under Our immediate Government as Thoſe under the Government and Direction of Proprietaries, to grant ſuch Licences without Fee or Reward, taking eſpecial Care to inſert therein a Condition, that ſuch Licence ſhall be void, and the Security forfeited, in caſe the Perſon, to whom the ſame is granted, ſhall refuſe or neglect to obſerve ſuch Regulations as We ſhall think proper to preſcribe as aforeſaid.

And We do further expreſly enjoin and require all Officers whatever, as well Military as Thoſe employed in the Management and Direction of *Indian* Affairs within the Territories reſerved, as aforeſaid for the Uſe of the ſaid *Indians*, to ſeize and apprehend all Perſons whatever, who, ſtanding charged with Treaſons, Miſpriſions of Treaſon, Murders, or other Felonies or Miſdemeanors, ſhall fly from Juſtice, and take Refuge in the ſaid Territory, and to ſend them under a proper Guard to the Colony where the Crime was committed of which they ſtand accuſed, in order to take their Tryal for the ſame.

Given at Our Court at *Saint James*'s, the Seventh Day of *October*, One thouſand ſeven hundred and ſixty three, in the Third Year of Our Reign.

GOD ſave the KING.

LONDON:
Printed by *Mark Baskett*, Printer to the King's moſt Excellent Majeſty; and by the Aſſigns of *Robert Baskett*. 1763.

moved. Neither private individuals nor colonial governors were permitted to make treaties or land grants in this territory — that right being reserved for the King and his representatives alone. Even within the boundaries of existing colonies, individuals were prohibited from purchasing land from the Indians, and colonial governors were allowed to make treaties only when the Crown was party to the transactions. All Indian traders were required to secure licenses.

Almost before the ink was dry on the *Proclamation*, the British government itself began ignoring many of the provisions, but the principles established by this document would have a major impact on Indian policy, in both Canada and the United States, up to the present day. In essence, the *Proclamation of 1763* recognized the sovereign rights of Native American tribes, above the laws of any particular colony or state, and it recognized their ownership of lands not formally and correctly ceded to the central government. To this day, on their own reservation lands, Indians are not technically required to obey state laws unless they have agreed to do so by direct negotiation with the federal government. It is a result of the *Proclamation of 1763* that native tribes, on reservations, can operate gambling establishments, sell tax-free cigarettes, and ignore state fishing and hunting regulations. For Native Americans, within the bounds of reservation lands, the *Proclamation of 1763* has far more tangible significance that the Declaration of Independence.

Over the course of the colonial period, the British Crown issued approximately one hundred Royal proclamations affecting America. Printed in broadside form by the Royal printer, they were forwarded to governors and officials in the colonies. Although hundreds of each were printed, even single copies of the broadside printings of many of them no longer exist. The *Proclamation of 1763* is perhaps the most important, and it is very scarce.

Gage Papers, purchased from Lord Gage, 1929, and from Clements Estate, 1937.

❧ 32 ❧

GLORIOUS AND SHORT-LIVED PEACE, CELEBRATED IN THE PULPIT

WHEN NEWS ARRIVED in the summer of 1763 that France had formally relinquished all former territorial claims on the mainland of North America, the colonies, from New Hampshire to Georgia, went a bit wild. It was almost too good to be true. In each of the previous colonial wars between France and Britain, colonial troops had taken part in expeditions that had captured Nova Scotia, New Brunswick, and even Louisbourg, only to see their hard-fought gains returned at the peace table. This time, the victory was decisive. Canada, including the outposts on the Great Lakes and the territory east of the Mississippi, became British. Louisiana, west of the Mississippi, was turned over to the Spanish. It seemed as if the British Empire, with the American colonies a prominent part of it, had entered a new golden age.

Upon the PEACE.

A

SERMON.

Preach'd at the Church of PETSWORTH,

In the County of GLOUCESTER,

On AUGUST the 25th,

The Day Appointed by AUTHORITY

FOR THE

Obfervance of that Solemnity.

By the Reverend JAMES HORROCKS, *A. M.*
Fellow of TRINITY College, CAMBRIDGE, and Mafter
of the GRAMMAR SCHOOL in WILLIAM and MARY College.

WILLIAMSBURG:
Printed by JOSEPH ROYLE, MDCCLXIII.

The Library has dozens of celebratory sermons and addresses which document this outpouring of patriotic fervor. A particularly rare one, known in but two surviving copies, is illustrated here. The Reverend James Horrocks was a graduate and fellow of Trinity College, Cambridge, before immigrating to Virginia in 1761. He was appointed master of the grammar school at the College of William and Mary in Virginia in 1763. He was obviously a man of some talents, and in 1764 he became rector of Bruton Parish in Williamsburg as well as president of the college. He became the Bishop of London's Commissary for Virginia in 1768 and served as a member of the governor's council. He died on a return trip to England in 1772.

Few people today would choose to read sermons by choice, but it was a favorite pastime in the eighteenth and early nineteenth centuries. Oratorical skill and logical argument were highly prized talents. The thousands of sermons and addresses which make up the vast majority of printed titles before 1800 allow us to gain insight into the attitudes of the different eras and different segments of the population. Election sermons, delivered year after year in each of the New England colonies, provide a rich portrait of changing ideas about government. Funeral sermons preserve attitudes about death, marriage, disease, and disaster. There are artillery sermons, ordination sermons, missionary sermons, and all sorts of addresses on special occasions. There are several hundred of these publications relating to the colonial wars, the Stamp Act, the Boston Massacre, and the American Revolution. New Englanders were the most likely to publish sermons, but there are enough surviving examples from the middle and southern colonies and states to provide similar insights.

The Reverend John Horrocks' sermon is not, actually, a religious address at all, but a discussion of moral behavior. He gently suggests that gambling, dissipation, extravagance, slavery, enthusiasm, and indebtedness might be counterproductive to happiness on Earth. He doesn't go so far as to call them sins, or even hint that "the great and good God" might consider wreaking vengeance—one suspects that Horrocks' God didn't do that sort of thing. It was the kind of message Virginians wanted to hear, and it tells us a great deal about mid-eighteenth-century Anglican and Virginia attitudes, so sharply different from those of Presbyterians or Congregationalists in the North.

Purchased at Harris Auction by MacManus, 1983.

THE COMPLETE EDUCATION

IN TODAY'S SOCIETY, which stretches out formal education over two decades between pre-school and graduate work, early American school books are something of a shock. With one small volume, and perhaps in no more than a few months' time, illiterate students were expected to master the intricacies of English grammar, punctuation, pronunciation, and the ability to read the Scriptures and words of up to six syllables. The *New England Primer* was the classic textbook of colonial America, but there were a few rival textbooks which are less well known. *The British Instructor* (London, 1763), shown here, is an intriguing example. According to the book's preface, the compiler "hath been employed, with renewed pleasure, for several years past in procuring for his friends Bibles, Testaments, and other good books, for the use of the poor Negroes and others abroad, especially in *Virginia* and *South Carolina*." Somewhat dissatisfied with existing books, he has put this one together himself, and while most copies would be sent to the colonies, he is also offering it to the British public. The book itself does not give enough hints to be certain of authorship,

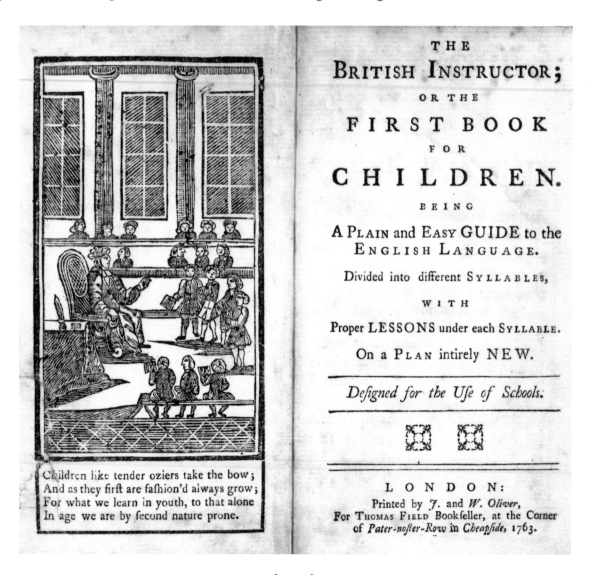

Children like tender oziers take the bow;
And as they firft are fashion'd always grow;
For what we learn in youth, to that alone
In age we are by fecond nature prone.

THE
BRITISH INSTRUCTOR;
OR THE
FIRST BOOK
FOR
CHILDREN.
BEING
A PLAIN and EASY GUIDE to the
ENGLISH LANGUAGE.

Divided into different SYLLABLES,

WITH

Proper LESSONS under each SYLLABLE.

On a PLAN intirely NEW.

Defigned for the Ufe of Schools.

LONDON:
Printed by *J.* and *W. Oliver*,
For THOMAS FIELD Bookfeller, at the Corner
of *Pater-nofter-Row* in *Cheapfide*, 1763.

but it probably was written by someone associated with the Thomas Bray Associates. That organization, particularly concerned with the education of African Americans, launched a special campaign in the early 1760s.

There seems to be no record of other copies of this book, which would be remarkable, except that there is a similar scarcity of most "cheap, practical" imprints of this sort. There were dozens of known printings of the *New England Primer* in the seventeenth and eighteenth centuries of which no copy survives. School books, almanacs, and cook books are publications that wear out with use. Fortunately, at least one copy of this title never got into the hands of a student!

Gift of John C. Dann, Ann Arbor, 1979.

ɷ 34 ɷ

"A GENTLEMAN WELL SKILL'D IN BOTANY AND NATURAL HISTORY"

MEN AND WOMEN OF EDUCATION in the eighteenth century had an insatiable curiosity about the natural world, a desire to explore its wonders, to collect and study specimens of plants and animals, and systematically to describe and classify all that was found. This, they optimistically believed, would allow them to understand the natural laws underlying the physical world. By mid-century, an international circle of scientists devoted to the study of natural history had developed—Linnaeus in Sweden, Gronovius in Leyden, Franklin and the Bartrams in America, and the Royal Society in London. England became the leader, her expanding colonial trade providing the incentive and wealth to finance investigation in the natural sciences. Also, England had a tradition of gardens—ornamental gardens developed by the wealthy and medical gardens connected with universities and hospitals—that encouraged botanical study.

In 1722 the Royal Society began plans to publish a natural history of British America. The members of the organization had been impressed by the work of Mark Catesby, a brilliant English naturalist who had previously traveled through tidewater Virginia and the West Indies and provided the Society with fine plant specimens, drawings, and descriptions. Catesby was chosen to further their American project with an expedition to Carolina. For three years, he traveled from Carolina to Florida, enduring the dangers and discomforts of the southern wilderness, collecting plants and animals, and making accurate drawings of all he found. Shipping specimens—finding suitable containers, getting cooperation from ship captains and reliable help from crews, who often consumed the alcohol used as a preservative—was a difficult business. He succeeded in sending an amazing variety of plants and seeds to his colleagues in London and, in return, they sent him exotic plants for his Carolina friends' gardens.

In 1726, Catesby returned to London with a superb collection of field drawings. The Royal Society "approved of his Labours" and was "pleased to think them worth Publishing," but the organization was not willing to make any further investment in his work. Catesby had hoped to have the drawings engraved by experts in Paris, but he now faced the daunting task of teaching himself to

engrave with acid on copper. He turned to Joseph Goupy, a French watercolorist and engraver, who gave him "kind Advice and Instructions." Peter Collinson, a leading London Quaker merchant and member of the Royal Society, lent Catesby money for support and publication of his work. Botanist William Sherard supplied Latin names for his plants. Catesby spent the next twenty years in intense, solitary labor, transferring his field drawings to copper plates. He personally hand-colored each engraving, using superior paper and pigments. They are today as breathtaking as they were when created over two hundred years ago.

Catesby's reputation as a naturalist soared with the publication of his first volume in 1731, and he labored twelve more years to produce the second volume. The Royal Society made him a Fellow, and *The Natural History of Carolina, Florida, and the Bahama Islands* (London, 1731–43) remains the outstanding natural history of colonial America.

During the years he was writing *The Natural History*, Catesby continued to work with London nurserymen on the domestication of American plants. In 1737, Christopher Gray, whose Fulham garden Catesby frequently visited, published *A Catalogue of American Trees and Shrubs That Will Endure the Climate of England*. Printed on a single sheet, it was illustrated by Catesby's drawing of the *Magnolia altissima* from *The Natural History* and listed plants with reference to pages in Catesby's work. This became the basis for a second work, *Hortus Britanno-Americanus*, which occupied him until his death in 1749. It was not published until 1763, and although not as grand, it is far more scarce than the two-volume work. The Clements Library has a beautiful set of *The Natural History* and one of ten known copies of *Hortus Britanno-Americanus*. The magnolia, illustrated here, is from the 1763 volume.

Purchased at Swann Auction by Carnegie Book Shop, 1979. Gift of Mrs. Emma Alexander, Ann Arbor.

ᨒ 35 ᨒ

A CARTOON THAT
MADE BENJAMIN FRANKLIN LAUGH

THE MODERN CARTOON, as a form of political and social commentary, is the invention of eighteenth-century England, where the press was relatively free and the demand for information and comment was vigorous. Political cartoons, unlike newspapers or magazines, were not subject to censorship or libel laws. One did not need to be able to read to understand their message. Car-

A CONFERENCE between the D---L and Doctor D--E.
Togetherwith the Doctor's Epitaph on himself.

toons were sold as separate sheets in print shop windows and by street vendors, and they circulated in coffeehouses. Vicious, often highly personal attacks in pictorial form became an accepted
part of politics. It was a tradition colonial America imitated.

One of the earliest American political cartoons is *A conference between the Devil and Doctor Dove*,
drawn by Henry Dawkins and published in Philadelphia in 1764. Doctor Dove, a writer of scur-
rilous verse for Pennsylvania's Proprietary Party, is shown kneeling before the Devil, his own
pointed tail clearly visible from beneath his coat: "Thou Great Prince of Darkness, assist me in my
Undertakings." The Devil replies, "Well done, thou Good and Faithful Servant."

Presumably Benjamin Franklin was greatly amused by Dawkins' drawing—he owned the particular copy now in the Clements Library. Franklin was living in London when it first appeared.
His devoted but semi-literate wife, Deborah, telling Franklin about the cartoon, wrote, "We have
nothing stiring amongst us but phamlits [pamphlets] and Scurrilitey [sic]."

Purchased from Charles F. Heartman, 1948.

☙ 36 ☙
EARLY BOOK OF JEWISH PRAYERS

DECIDING HISTORICAL PRIORITIES, what was "first," is never quite as easy as it would seem.
There are always qualifications, very reasonable ones, that will complicate the issue.

The Library has a select collection of American Judaica, printed and manuscript, including
correspondence of the great Jewish merchants of the Revolutionary War period, letters of Rebecca

Gratz, an eighteenth-century deed for a syna-
gogue in Philadelphia, and published works of
Mordecai Noah and Isaac Lesser. What is the
first Jewish book published in the present territory of the United States? Well, it depends! In
1926, the American Jewish Historical Society
published a bibliography of American Judaica
to 1850 by the eminent Philadelphia book
dealer A. S. W. Rosenbach. It remains an invaluable guide and is largely all-inclusive for
eighteenth-century titles. Rosenbach starts
with the *Bay Psalm Book* of 1640, the first book
in English printed in America. It was based
upon translations from Hebrew and included
Hebrew type, but since it was written by and
for the Puritans, its attribution as Judaica is
questionable. More convincing might be claims
of primacy for a series of 1722 pamphlets or a
1735 Hebrew grammar published by Judah Monis, which the Library owns. Monis was a Jew

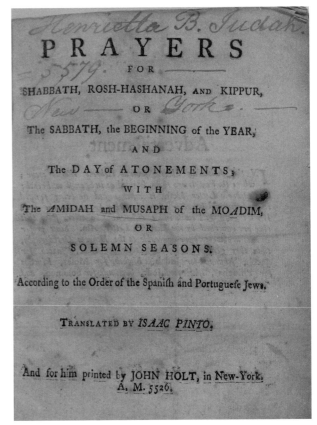

by birth, but by the time he published these works, he had converted to Christianity and was arguing the divinity of Christ on the basis of Hebrew scripture.

The earliest known Jewish immigrants to present-day United States territory were a group of eighteen persons who came to Dutch New Amsterdam from Brazil in 1654. By the middle of the eighteenth century there were also sizable Jewish communities in Newport, Philadelphia, Charleston, and Savannah. The majority were of Spanish and Portuguese ancestry (Sephardic Jews), although Ashkenazic (from central and eastern Europe) immigrants to New York were growing in number. Sephardic forms of worship prevailed in the colonial synagogues.

An eight-page Form of Prayer to celebrate Wolfe's victory over the French (New York, 1760), a fifty-two page book of prayers for Rosh Hashanah and Kippur (New York, 1761), and *Prayers for Shabbath, Rosh-Hashanah, and Kippur* (1766) are what ought to be considered the first authentic Jewish publications in America. The last title, illustrated here, was the first substantial book and the first imprint to carry the Jewish calendar year. Isaac Pinto (1720–1789), the editor of the work, was a merchant, a teacher, and an interpreter. He translated many of the prayers from their original Spanish. Following a timeless pattern for all immigrant groups throughout American history, second and third generations, born in America, did not know the language and the customs of the Old Country. Pinto's work was an attempt to explain Jewish traditions to those unfamiliar with them, and a means of providing prayers in English for those who could not read Hebrew. This prayer book exists in two printing variants, both of which are exceptional rarities.

Acquired by trade with a private collector, and from Clements Estate, 1937.

⤜ 37 ⤛

EPHEMERAL EARLY AMERICAN PRINTING

THE HISTORY OF PRINTING has never been a collecting priority of the Clements Library, in contrast to a number of our highly esteemed peer institutions—the American Antiquarian Society, the Library Company of Philadelphia, and the Library of Congress in particular. The Clements has always emphasized historical content over form. Yet its collections are one of the nation's rich resources for the study of American printing history. In part this is due to the fact that many of the most important sources of our early history are also particularly rare and important imprints. Seventeenth-century New England sermons or pamphlets on the Great Awakening are essential documentary evidence of the thoughts of Americans of the time, but they also are important examples of early American printing.

Many of the unique imprints in the Library were obtained as part of its manuscript collections. Generals Gage and Clinton served as commanders in chief of the British Army in the American colonies from 1763 to 1775 and 1778 to 1782. They and their sub-commanders issued proclamations and accumulated handbills and printed forms that were issued locally. They had agents and spies throughout North America who sent them printed materials that might interest them. Many of these types of imprints—broadsides, handbills, and the like—were issued in small press runs and were meant for the moment only, thrown away after use.

BY FREDERICK HALDIMAND Efqr.,
Brigadier General of His Majety's Forces Commanding the Southern Diftrict of North America, &c. &c.

WHEREAS Jhave been informed that there are a number of English Deferters in the Province of Louifiania who are willing to return into the SERVICE provided they are afsured of obtaining a PARDON. Jhave acquainted His Excellency The Commander in Chief thereof, and have fince Recieved Orders from him to offer a free Pardon to all Deferters from His Britannic Majeftys Troops who shall Surrender themselves at Pensacola On or before the First Dayof March Next.

Jam further Anthorized to affure them, that they will not befent to the Regiments from which they have Deserted, bnt will be put into other Regiments, And that they shall receive Pay from the day of their arrival at Penfacola, where they may come without the leaft difficulty.

And Jdo Promife to Pay to any Mafter of a Vefsel who will bring any of them the fumof 10 Dollars, for the Pafsage & Provisions &c. of cach Deferter upon their Desembarkation at Penfacola, but will not Pay any other charge.

GIVEN under my Hand and feal at Penfacola
the 14th· Day of January 1768.
FREDERICK HALDIMAND.

BY order of the General
FRAN⁵. HUTCHESON.

VU que ladite Ordonnance ne contient rien qui foit contre le Droit Souverain des deux Majeftés, & attendu que Monfieur le Général HALDIMAND nous a écrit à ce fujet ; Nous confentons qu'elle foit publiée dans la Ville Capitalle de la Nouvelle Orléans & autres Poftes dependans de cette Colonie ou Mr. le Lieutenant Boucher deftiné pour cette Commiffion le jugera à propos pour le Service de fon Souverain, & Nous ordonnons à tous les Sujets dépendans de ladite Colonie de ne pas s'y oppofer, & de donner tous les fecours neceffaires pour ladite Publication.

AUBRY

Par Monfeigneur,
SOUBIE.

A. VLLOA.

Por Mandado de fu Sria·
GREGORIO de la SOTILLA.

The proclamation of General Haldimand, shown here, is a typical example. Haldimand, born in Switzerland, joined the British Army as an officer in 1756. He served with distinction in America during the French and Indian War and was made commander of British forces in Florida in 1766. French was his native language, particularly suiting him for service in territories captured by the British in the Seven Years War. From 1778 until 1785 he was governor and military commander in Canada.

The *Proclamation* is a most unusual imprint. As military governor of Florida, Haldimand was stationed at Pensacola. Then, as now, New Orleans, under Spanish control, was a fascinating place, and the British Army had problems with soldiers deserting Florida and crossing into Spanish territory, where the British had no military authority to track them down. This document represents an unusual example of international cooperation. Haldimand's own proclamation is in English. The commander at New Orleans, Antonio de Ulloa, signed the imprint in his native Spanish, and the text of his statement supporting Haldimand's proclamation is in French, the language of the majority of the inhabitants of Louisiana. A unique example of one of the earliest New Orleans imprints, dated 1768, it is the first in which text is printed in English.

Gage Papers, purchased from Clements Estate, 1937.

PICTURING AMERICA FOR A EUROPEAN AUDIENCE

IF IT WERE NOT FOR THE ABILITIES of European artists, engravers, and printers, the modern world would have few visual glimpses of the present United States before the nineteenth century. There were a few locally produced engravings of American towns and scenes which appeared as separate prints or magazine illustrations in the eighteenth century, but most of them were amateurish productions by European standards. Fortunately, among the visitors to the New World there were a number of skilled draftsmen and artists who returned home and shared their artistic efforts with equally skilled engravers. There was an insatiable market in Europe not only for information but for pictures of new lands, strange civilizations, and plants and animals unknown and unimaginable to the Old World.

The wonderful engravings of De Bry, in connection with the American watercolors of John White, have already been described. We are fortunate that a handful of European publishers used authentic American drawings as the basis of engraved book illustrations in the sixteenth and seventeenth centuries. In addition to the De Bry engravings for Hariot's *Virginia*, there are illustrations in the travel accounts published by Champlain and Lahontan of early European settlements, natural wonders, and natives of the northern parts of the United States and Canada. Several Dutch views of New Amsterdam exist in books and atlases. In the eighteenth century a few separate city views and a variety of American pictures were issued in British popular magazines.

A South East View of the City of New York in NORTH AMERICA. Vue du Sud Est de la Ville de New York dans L'AMERIQUE SEPTENTRIONALE.
Drawn on the Spot by Cap.ᵗ Thomas Howdell, of the Royal Artillery. Engraved by P. Canot.

The two greatest collections of North American views published before the American Revolution were (1) those of Frederick Des Barres, engraved as part of his multivolume *American Neptune* (London, 1763–84), which were the official sea charts of North American waters for the Royal Navy, and (2) a series of twenty-eight large engravings published by William Faden in 1768 under the series title of *Scenographia Americana*. The latter was made up of several groupings of views, some of them previously issued, depicting places and actions of the Seven Years War in Canada, Cuba, and the West Indies, views of New York City (one of which is illustrated here), and a series of North American scenes based on drawings by Thomas Pownall. The tradition of Europeans producing the majority and best of existing American views lasted until the middle of the nineteenth century. Increasingly, though, beginning with William Birch's *Views of Philadelphia* (Philadelphia, 1800), artists and engravers on this side of the Atlantic began catching up.

From the earliest stage of his collecting, William Clements made a particular effort to acquire books with visual images of North America. The Library has maintained this traditional emphasis, and its printed, pictorial record of our nation's history, largely in perfect copies, is among the best in the world.

Purchased from Stevens, 1961. Partially a gift of the Clements Library Associates.

⚞ 39 ⚟

OUR FIRST PROFESSIONAL MUSICIAN

AN UNKEMPT MAN with a withered arm, one short leg, one eye, and a predilection for inhaling enormous volumes of snuff, William Billings (1746–1800) certainly had a distinctive profile, but it can also be said that he cast an enormous shadow over American psalmody. Blessed with only a rudimentary education and limited formal training in music, and cursed late in life with troublesome finances, Billings still managed to conduct popular singing schools in Boston from as early as 1769. He wrote over 340 compositions and published six tunebooks. First and most influential among his tunebooks was the *New-England Psalm-Singer* (1770).

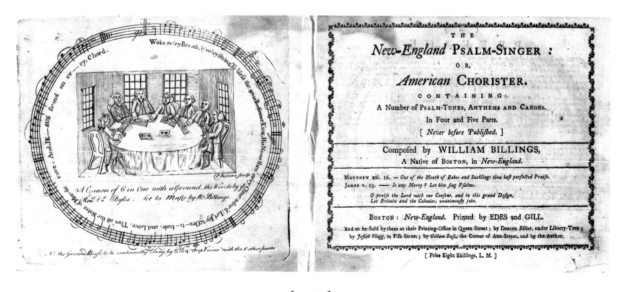

As the title promised, the *New-England Psalm-Singer* was an original work and distinctively American. In his introduction, Billings boasted, "I don't think myself confined to any Rules for Composition laid down by any that went before me," arguing, "it is best for every *Composer* to be his own *Carver*." Until the time of this book's publication, perhaps only a dozen American compositions had ever appeared in print, but Billings' contributions increased the total tenfold. Although drawing on English antecedents, Billings carved a distinctly American niche in psalmody through his unique harmonies and provincial but powerful airs.

Publication of Billings' second volume of tunes was delayed by the Revolution, but his music was eagerly devoured by his countrymen, and his role as a native composer was quickly filled by others, fostering a boom in American-made music. Revolutionary Americans were being encouraged to develop self-reliance — to make their own clothing, grow their own food, and develop their own manufactures — and Billings' advocacy of distinctly American music could not have been more perfectly timed. *The New-England Psalm-Singer* is doubly important as a Revolutionary-era artifact, in that both the music and the frontispiece were engraved by Paul Revere.

Gift of Mrs. Fannie Read Cook, 1937.

☙ 40 ❧

FRANCIS PARKMAN AND THE ROMANCE
OF THE COLONIAL FRONTIER

WHETHER OR NOT IT DETRACTS from the accuracy of written history, a touch of romanticism has played an important role in preserving the memory of the past. If man had no emotional need to remember the past and relay the memories and stories of youth and family to the next generation, there would be no incentive to preserve historical records, old books, or historical sites.

Francis Parkman (1823–1893) was America's greatest romantic narrative historian of the nineteenth century. Although his works no longer hold the eminent place they did fifty years ago on the bookshelf of the average, educated American, they continue to have influence, if only indirectly, as models of the sort of grand historical adventure stories that continue to attract public audiences, whether in the form of true-to-life historical novels, television programs, or films. Parkman was a highly unusual character. Although he was plagued by terrible health through much of his life — near blindness, a nervous disorder that made it difficult to concentrate for long periods of time, and lameness — he was fortunate to come from a wealthy family, allowing him to hire assistants who would read to him and perform secretarial duties. He received a thorough education at preparatory schools and Harvard. He wrote historical narrative in a captivating manner, his imagination and descriptive powers perhaps enhanced by the semi-blindness that forced him to do much of his writing in the dark.

As a boy, he spent a great deal of time in the outdoors, canoeing, hunting, and roaming through the woods. He believed in learning by experience. While on a trip to Europe, he lived for several days in a convent. In 1846, he went to St. Louis and joined a wagon train bound for Oregon in or-

MAJOR ROBERT ROGERS,
Commander in Chief of the INDIANS *in the Back Settlements of* AMERICA.
Published as the Act directs Octᵗ 1776 by Thoˢ Hart.

der to study Indians. He lived with a band of Sioux for several months and got to know fur trappers, half-breeds, and the assorted characters and outcasts who inhabited the frontier regions between white and native civilizations. His book *The Oregon Trail* (1849) remains a classic narrative of the trans-Mississippi frontier, but his real interest was to apply what he had learned to the history of the previous two centuries. He was a great believer in collecting and studying original source materials, and he acquired copies of diaries, letters, and maps from European and American archives and private collectors.

The great theme of his life's work was the conflict between the French and the English for the dominance of North America. In 1851, he published the *History of the Conspiracy of Pontiac*, and between 1865 and 1892 he issued seven more works: *Pioneers of France in the New World* (1865); *The Jesuits in North America* (1867); *The Discovery of the Great West* (1869), which told the story of La Salle and the French expansion into Louisiana; *The Old Regime in Canada* (1874); *Count Frontenac and New France under Louis XIV* (1877); *Montcalm and Wolfe* (1884); and *A Half-Century of Conflict* (1892). His cast of characters, based on meticulous research and then refined by imagination and personal experience, are unforgettable, heroic figures—America's knights, great and terrible, of both European and native origins, clad in buckskins, black robes, warpaint, and military uniforms rather than shining armor.

Inevitably, Parkman became fascinated with Major Robert Rogers, who commanded independent companies of Rangers during the French and Indian War and supplied intelligence to the regular armies. Rogers conducted a series of remarkable raids on enemy territory and became a legendary hero to fellow soldiers. In the 1750s, Robert Rogers and George Washington were the two provincial officers whose names appeared frequently in British newspapers and magazines. In 1760, Rogers was entrusted with command of the troops that took control of the western posts from the French, and after service in South Carolina against the Cherokee in 1761, he helped defend Detroit against Pontiac. In the twentieth century, Kenneth Roberts, in *Northwest Passage* (1939), revived and enhanced Parkman's heroic portrait of Rogers, and today there is a sizable group of Robert Rogers hero-worshipers who have virtually created a cult around this remarkable and very human frontiersman.

There is a question as to whether we know what Rogers looked like or not. Benjamin West included a Provincial Ranger in his famous "Death of Wolfe" painting (the original painting hangs in the Main Room of the Library) which may be Rogers, although recent scholarship suggests otherwise. In 1776, a series of portrait engravings of American military figures was issued in London, including Benedict Arnold, James Sullivan, Israel Putnam, Esek Hopkins, David Wooster, and Robert Rogers. They are very stylized and somewhat similar in facial appearance, leading most critics to doubt the accuracy of the likenesses. This logic makes sense for all the other subjects, none of whom was well-known in London. Rogers, on the other hand, had spent much of ten years in the metropolis and was something of a notable curiosity. It would seem at least possible that this is a relatively faithful likeness.

The Clements' copy of the engraving illustrated here, published in London in 1776 by Thomas Hart, actually belonged to Francis Parkman and is signed by him. Robert Rogers has always held a special fascination for the Clements Library staff, and the Library's manuscript division contains the majority of his surviving correspondence.

Gift of Martayan, Lan, Augustyn, Inc., New York, in honor of Donald A. Watson, Detroit, 1994.

↔ 41 ↔

THE ORDERS PRIMING THE SHOT HEARD ROUND THE WORLD

IN TERMS OF CHANGING THE COURSE of American history, possibly no single written document equals in importance General Thomas Gage's orders, shown here, that sent troops from Boston to march "with the utmost expedition and secrecy to Concord, where you will seize and destroy all the artillery and ammunition, provisions, tents & all other military stores you can find . . . ." This is the original draft, in Gage's hand, written on April 18, 1775, a copy of which was then delivered to Lieutenant Colonel Francis Smith, who commanded the ill-fated expedition that started the American Revolution.

The mission was a dangerous, calculated risk at best, and it was terribly flawed from the beginning. Gage's headquarters was in the city of Boston, then virtually an island. Any sizable movement of troops in the direction of Concord required the use of boats to ferry soldiers, horses, and supplies across the Charles River. Such activity could not escape the innumerable eyes of local citizens hostile to British interests. The Committees of Safety and Correspondence had already created a well-organized intelligence network. Although the force of some seven hundred British troops was very quietly assembled and embarked in the late evening of the eighteenth, Paul Revere and several other American agents were already fully aware of British plans. They were on their way by horseback, giving warning to Concord and surrounding towns, even before the regular troops had formed and begun their march. The small village of Lexington was on the road from Boston to Concord, and Revere reached it at about midnight. There he roused John Hancock and Samuel Adams, American leaders who were particularly obnoxious to the British, as well as the local militia, which began to assemble immediately. Lieutenant Colonel Smith, who did not start his actual march until 2 a.m., was making slow progress, and at Medford he divided his command and sent Major John Pitcairn ahead with slightly over half his forces. He also dispatched a messenger with a Number of small

Four Brass Cannon and two Mortars or Cohorns in the Cellar

or out Houses of Mr Barrett as little on the other side the Bridge
where is also lodged a Quantity of Powder & Leade.

Ten Iron Cannon before the Town=House and two within it
which Town=House is in the Center of the Town, The ammunition
for said Guns within the House

Three Guns of 24 Pounders, lodged in the Prison yard with
a Quantity of Cartridges and Provision

A Quantity of Provision and Ammunition in other Places, the
may the meeting
Principal Deposits are the Houses of Messrs Hubbards, Butler
near Hubbards   the name of
Jones the Sailor, two men of Bond; and particularly at Mr
near
Whitneys who lives on the Right Hand at the Entrance of the
at a
Town, the House plaistered white a small yard in front
and a railed fence a large Quantity of small arms Powder
and Balls is reported to be there deposited in his stores adjoining
the House

A Quantity of Ammunition and Provision together as Numbers
of Cannon and small Arms having been collected at Concord for the avowed
purpose of supporting a Rebellion against his Majesty
Governmnt Sir, you will March with the Corps of Grenadiers and
Light Infantry put under your Command with the utmost Expedition
and Secrey to Concord, where you will seize and destroy
Provisions Tents & all other Military Stores
all the Artillery and Ammunition you can find, you will knock
and destroy the Carriages
off one Trunion at least of each of the Iron Guns, and beat in the
muzzles of the Brass ones so as to render them useless. The
the flints burnt
Powder & flour may be shaken out of the Barrells into the Water, and the
Pockets
men may put the Balls & lead into their Knapsacks throwing them
away by Degrees into the fields Ditches Ponds, &c to whom
have a plan with on which is marked
you shall give you a Return of the Places where the Artillery
&c
& Ammunition is reported to be lodged, and after destroying
the same you will return; and if your men appear much fatigued
you may halt them at Lexington or Cambridge and let them rest in

to Gage, asking for reinforcements, and at 4 a.m., Gage ordered Lord Percy and a thousand additional British soldiers to follow.

Two hours before sunrise on April 19 the stage had been set for the Battle of Lexington, with military engagement virtually inevitable. The Provincial forces had intelligence that there were two, then three sizable units of British regulars marching toward them. To their eyes, this was not simply a raid, but a major, hostile military action. Neither the British nor the Americans had issued clearly defined orders as to "what to do if," and the field commanders at Lexington, on both sides, were subordinate officers who themselves lacked certainty of what was expected of them. We will never know which side actually fired the first shot. Gunfire, church bells, and drums were being used to collect troops and sound the alarm. Orders not to fire, indistinctly heard by nervous men, could easily have been interpreted as "Fire!" Once scattered shots had gone off, the British did fire two distinct and deadly volleys, and a war of seven long years had begun.

By having the papers of General Gage and General Clinton, commanders of the British Army throughout most of the Revolution, as well as other leading generals on both sides of the conflict, the Clements Library owns a significant percentage of the unique documentation of not only Lexington, but many of the military engagements of the war. The manuscripts of a commander are particularly rich sources, in that they contain not only his letters and orders, but spy reports, messages from subordinates, captured letters, and maps. In addition, the Clements' collections include orderly books, papers of junior officers and enlisted men, and nonmilitary manuscripts of the time.

Gage Papers, purchased from Clements Estate, 1937.

ᘖ 42 ᘓ

A STOLEN LETTER FROM RACHEL TO PAUL REVERE

PERSONAL MANUSCRIPTS, private letters written between family members, have a way of maintaining a healthy perspective on even the most exalted of historical personalities. Paul Revere is one of the true heroes of the early days of the American Revolution. A certain amount of scepticism has been voiced over the years as to whether he actually took his famous ride, while the documentary evidence seems to be clearly in his favor. Although a very active and astute businessman with much to lose if singled out by British authorities as a leading rebel, he performed numerous, highly dangerous missions as a messenger in the months before hostilities actually broke out. If it had not been for his ride on the evening of April 18, 1775, John Hancock and Samuel Adams might have been captured at Lexington.

Given the heroic nature of Paul's actions, one might expect a highly patriotic letter from his wife a day or two later. Instead, his wife, Rachel, for whom writing was clearly a difficult and unusual exercise, provided the sort of loving "keep up your spirits" practical support any traveling salesman might receive as he set out from home. She sent money, said that she would send some of the children if the absence became lengthy, warned him to do nothing foolish out of affection for her, such as coming back to Boston, and urged him to put his faith in "a good God." She made it clear that in spite of momentous events taking place, she, with complete faith in the same supe-

my Dear by [crossed out] I send a hundred & twenty five pa...
and beg you will take the best care of your self and not
attempt coming in to this town again and if I have
an opportunity of coming or sending out any thing or
any of the Children I shall do it pray [crossed out] keep up
your spirits and trust your self and us in the hands
of a good god who will take care of us tis all my
Dependance for vain is the help of man adieu my
Love from your
affectionate R Revere

rior being, could take care of herself. As simple as this letter is, it tells us a great deal about Paul Revere and the sort of marriage and family environment he enjoyed.

The history of this particular letter is interesting in itself. Rachel Revere gave it to one of the trusted members of the inner circle of the radical cause, Dr. Benjamin Church, little realizing that he was betraying the "rebels" as General Gage's chief informer. The letter was quickly turned over to the British commander, among whose papers it remains. Paul Revere never saw it.

In our less civilized times, Mrs. Revere and her children might have mysteriously disappeared as a result of this message, or at least their house might have been burned to the ground. Such was not the way any of the commanders of either army chose to fight the American Revolution. The Revere house stands to this day, and there is no indication that retribution was exacted upon the family, other than presumably confiscating the £125 that was in the original letter. Dr. Church, by the way, eventually paid for his sins. He was tried by court martial in October 1775 and found guilty of corresponding with the enemy. Permitted by the Massachusetts Council to leave the state in 1778 for the West Indies, his ship was apparently lost at sea.

Gage Papers, purchased from Clements Estate, 1937.

❧ 43 ❧

BRITISH SOLDIERS AT PLAY: QUEBEC, 1775

ANYONE TRYING TO DOCUMENT the American Revolution with contemporary pictures quickly runs into difficulty. As professional historians, teachers, book publishers, television documentary producers, or historical reenactors will attest, there is a dearth of accurate visual images.

In 1978, the Clements acquired a small collection of John André letters. Included was a naive but charming sketch by André depicting a raucous tavern scene near Quebec in early 1775.

André is best known for his collaboration with the infamous General Benedict Arnold in a plot to turn West Point over to the British in 1780. The tragic consequence of his capture by the Americans as an enemy spy was his own execution. Less is generally known about André's life before he became the victim of Arnold's treason. He appears to have had an excellent reputation among the highest ranking British officers. When the Earl of Shelburne was looking for someone to accompany his young son on his grand tour, General Charles Grey recommended André:"I do not think a better principled young man exists, with much experience of the world, and knowledge for his time. He has been a good deal abroad, understands languages, particularly French and German . . . . He is an uncommon accomplished young man, particularly in this age, with the addition of the most amiable disposition in the world." André declined Shelburne's offer to travel through Europe with young Lord Fitzmaurice, choosing instead to go with the British Army to America.

André was hardly an accomplished artist, but he gave us a rare glimpse of inhabitants of the North American military frontier very much at ease. Fur trappers, traders, half-breeds, Indians, British soldiers, and a bare-breasted woman are having fun, smoking, drinking, and dancing; only the landlady, candle in hand, and a child being ignored by its mother appear to be alarmed. It is an engaging and rare bit of pictorial social history. Such a drawing can serve many audiences. For historians of military uniforms, this is one of the few contemporary illustrations of the dress of British light infantrymen, in this case presumably of members of André's own 7th Regiment of Foot.

None of André's letters mentions the specific entertainment, making it impossible for us to know whether the evening ended peacefully or in a brawl. At about the time the sketch was made, André wrote to his beloved sister in England that he was preparing an illustrated journal of his life

in Canada for her amusement. In one letter, he described sleighing out of Quebec with a lady companion: "We dine, dance rondes, toss pancakes, make a noise and return, sometimes overturn and sometimes are frost bit." Military service was not all tedium and hardship!

Sang Sale purchase at Parke Bernet by Carnegie Book Shop, 1978. Gift of Clements Library Associates.

꿍 44 꿍

THOMAS JEFFERSON, BRITISH AGENT?

MODERN BOOKS ON MILITARY INTELLIGENCE often make the point that the subject is over-glamorized in popular fiction—that rather than the cloak-and-dagger intrigue of movies and novels, most "spy" work involves laborious exercises in research, listening to enemy messages, and tiresome efforts to break codes, accomplished far from enemy lines. This was not the case in the era of the American Revolution. The lack of sophisticated technology, if anything, made the gathering of intelligence all the more important. A basic responsibility of a commander in chief was to develop a large and reliable network of spies and messengers.

Agents were encouraged and recruited at key listening posts, such as river crossings and taverns on frequently traveled roads, to pick up gossip and carefully watch traffic patterns. Others were left or sent behind enemy lines or even encouraged to enlist in enemy service. Identifiable spies for the other side were urged to become double agents, and efforts were constantly made by the British to discern disaffected enemy officers and influential civilians, at the highest level, who could be "brought over." It is an exciting part of American Revolutionary War history which has never received the attention it deserves.

It is no exaggeration to estimate that a fifth of the thousands of letters of the commanders in chief of both armies which survive relate to espionage and intelligence work. The Henry Clinton Papers, the headquarters archives of the British Army from 1778 through 1781, are replete with anonymous spy reports, coded letters, maps, captured correspondence, prisoner interrogations, and eyewitness accounts of enemy movements. Because the ethnic and linguistic backgrounds of combatants on both sides were similar, it was difficult to know who was a friend and who was the enemy. The information contained in a captured letter or the report of a trusted agent was capable of winning battles or saving an army from capture, and if counterintelligence was up to par—feeding false information to the enemy, as was done by the Americans so successfully to forestall reinforcement of Yorktown—it could win a war.

Not all intelligence was good. The anonymous document illustrated here comes from Sir Henry Clinton's papers. It presumably dates from relatively early in the war, sometime between 1775 and 1778. It was an attempt by someone who knew Virginia to point out leaders who might be useful to the British side, who might be bought or convinced to serve British interests by sup-

Colonel Carter Braxton, lives in King William County on Pamunkey, a man of Sense and Influence, but small Property and that hampered with Debt — married to a daughter of Coll. Corbin and might easily be brought over.

Colonel Burrel Basset, lives in New Kent on York River, has no great abilities, but from his Property has considerable Influence, married to a Sister of Mrs Washington, and is I suppose at present a violent Rebel, but I know him to be strongly attached to his own Interests which will always govern his Principles.

Honble Robert Burwell, of the Council, lives at York, a shallow, weak, man, of no great Fortune or Influence.

Doctor Walker, lives near Charlottesville, has large property & great Influence amongst the Planters in his Neighbourhood, a shrewd solid, sensible man, much attached to his own Interests — and a proper Person, if troops over, to contract with for Provisions, Waggons Horses &c ———

Mr Jefferson, a sensible Lawyer, lives also near Charlottesville, and might be of use if he can be brought over.

Richmond, at the Falls of James River, contains about 300 Houses. The Ground hanging over the Town high & commanding, and takes in a very extensive View of the River & Country — The principal Tobacco Ware houses are here.

New Castle, upon the Pamunkey, a Branch of York River, over which there is a Bridge at this Place. The Ground over the Town high, and the great Road from the upper Country passes thro it: The Tobacco Warehouses are here and at Hanover town about four Miles higher up — Contains about the same Number of Houses as Richmond.

Fredericksburgh & Falmouth at the Falls of Rhappahanock, two considerable trading Towns, where the produce of the back Country is deposited for Sale & Exportation — The Ground near them on each Side of the River high — and Vessels of about 100 Tons may come up to the Town — There are here also considerable Tobacco Ware houses.

plying information, raising troops, or cooperating in an invasion of enemy territory. This document is either a report "planted" by an American to entirely mislead the British commander or one of the worst bits of intelligence ever written during the war, because every name mentioned was that of a leading patriot! Even Thomas Jefferson is listed and described as "of use if he can be brought over." True, but of course preposterous. The first page of the report, not shown here, included Richard Kidder Meade, Colonel Burrell (Burwell), Colonel Andrew Lewis, and Colonel Fielding Lewis, who was Washington's brother-in-law.

Most likely, this report was provided by some associate or aide of General Clinton who had known Virginia well in the 1760s or early 1770s but had entirely lost touch. A majority of the intelligence reports in the Clinton Papers are far more accurate and useful than this document, but it does point out one area in which the Americans had an advantage. They knew the country, its geography, and its people in a way that a foreign army never could.

Clinton Papers, purchased from Frances Clinton, 1925, and from Clements Estate, 1937.

AMERICA'S ALL-TIME BEST-SELLER

THOMAS PAINE, a largely self-educated artisan and former excise collector, immigrated to Philadelphia late in 1774. Having met and favorably impressed Benjamin Franklin before leaving England, he came with recommendations that got him a job with Robert Aitkin, printer, and he helped write articles for the *Pennsylvania Magazine*. His previous literary production consisted of a

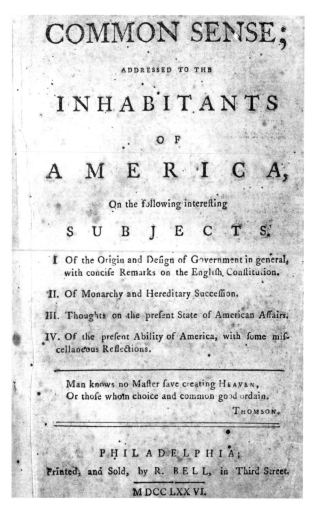

single, privately printed pamphlet, but he had a particular gift for clear, straightforward prose. Philadelphia was not only the largest city in America, it would become the publishing center of the new nation. As the meeting place of the Continental Congress, it was the intellectual hub of the colonies as they moved from protest to war.

Common Sense, issued anonymously in Philadelphia on January 10, 1776, the first edition of which is displayed here, was one of those rare publications timed perfectly, putting into words what many people had been thinking but not quite dared express. By January 1776, the colonies were at war with a formidable British army. The Battles of Lexington and Concord and the Battle of Bunker Hill were months back, colonial troops were besieging Quebec, and Washington was turning short-term soldiers into a trained army with which he could conduct a long-term war. Yet many American colonists and members of Congress could not bring themselves to believe that their King, to whom they had paid homage for so many years, could want to wage a destructive war against his subjects. The whole thing must be a grab for power by the King's corrupt, evil ministers. With each show of British force, in their hearts they knew better.

Common Sense went through a phenomenal twenty-five editions in six months, making an estimated total of 120,000 copies. No best-seller in the history of the United States has ever sold that many copies per capita in that period of time. Paine merely pointed out that the King himself was more hostile to the American rebels than even his ministers and intended to prosecute the war until victory was achieved. He convinced the majority of Americans that the time had come to reject monarchy altogether, declare their independence, and get on with the war.

Purchased from Goodspeed's, 1935.

IN CONGRESS,
JULY 4, 1776,
A DECLARATION
BY THE
REPRESENTATIVES
OF THE
UNITED STATES OF AMERICA,
IN GENERAL CONGRESS ASSEMBLED.

WHEN in the Course of human Events, it becomes necessary for one People to dissolve the political Bands which have connected them with another, and to assume among the Powers of the Earth, the separate and equal Station to which the Laws of Nature and of Nature's God entitle them, a decent Respect to the Opinions of Mankind requires that they should declare the Causes which impel them to the Separation.

We hold these Truths to be self-evident, that all Men are created equal, that they are endowed by their Creator with certain unalienable Rights, that among these are Life, Liberty, and the Pursuit of Happiness:—That to secure these Rights, Governments are instituted among Men, deriving their just Powers from the Consent of the Governed, that whenever any Form of Government becomes destructive of these ends, it is the Right of the People to alter or to abolish it, and to institute new Government, laying its Foundation on such Principles, and organizing its Powers in such Form, as to them shall seem most likely to effect their Safety and Happiness. Prudence, indeed, will dictate that Governments long established should not be changed for light and transient Causes; and accordingly all Experience hath shewn, that Mankind are more disposed to suffer, while Evils are sufferable, than to right themselves by abolishing the Forms to which they are accustomed. But when a long Train of Abuses and Usurpations, pursuing invariably the same Object, evinces a Design to reduce them under absolute Despotism, it is their Right, it is their Duty, to throw off such Government, and to provide new Guards for their future Security. Such has been the patient Sufferance of these Colonies; and such is now the Necessity which constrains them to alter their former Systems of Government. The History of the present King of Great-Britain is a History of repeated Injuries and Usurpations, all having in direct Object the Establishment of an absolute Tyranny over these States. To prove this, let Facts be submitted to a candid World.

He has refused his Assent to Laws, the most wholesome and necessary for the public Good.

He has forbidden his Governors to pass Laws of immediate and pressing Importance, unless suspended in their Operation until his Assent should be obtained; and when so suspended, he has utterly neglected to attend to them.

He has refused to pass other Laws for the Accommodation of large Districts of People, unless those People would relinquish the Right of Representation in the Legislature, a Right inestimable to them, and formidable to Tyrants only.

He has called together Legislative Bodies at Places unusual, uncomfortable, and distant from the Depository of their public Records, for the sole Purpose of fatiguing them into Compliance with his Measures.

He has dissolved Representative Houses repeatedly, for opposing with *manly* Firmness his Invasions on the Rights of the People.

He has refused for a long Time, after such Dissolutions, to cause others to be elected; whereby the Legislative Powers, incapable of Annihilation, have returned to the People at large for their Exercise; the State remaining in the mean Time exposed to all the Dangers of Invasion from without, and Convulsions within.

He has endeavoured to prevent the Population of these States; for that Purpose obstructing the Laws for Naturalization of Foreigners; refusing to pass others to encourage their Migrations hither, and raising the Conditions of new Appropriations of Lands.

He has obstructed the Administration of Justice, by refusing his Assent to Laws for establishing Judiciary Powers.

He has made Judges dependent on his Will alone, for the Tenure of their Offices, and the Amount and Payment of their Salaries.

He has erected a Multitude of new Offices, and sent hither Swarms of Officers to harrass our People, and eat out their Substance.

He has kept among us, in Times of Peace, Standing Armies, without the Consent of our Legislatures.

He has affected to render the Military independent of, and *superior* to the Civil Power.

He has combined with others to subject us to a Jurisdiction foreign to our Constitution, and unacknowledged by our Laws; giving his Assent to their Acts of pretended Legislation:

For quartering large Bodies of armed Troops among us:

For protecting them, by a *mock* Trial, from Punishment for any Murders which they should commit on the Inhabitants of these States:

For cutting off our Trade with all Parts of the World:

For imposing Taxes on us *without* our Consent:

For depriving us, in many Cases, of the Benefits of Trial by Jury:

For transporting us beyond Seas to be tried for pretended Offences:

For abolishing the free System of English Laws in a neighbouring Province, establishing therein an arbitrary Government, and enlarging its Boundaries, so as to render it at once an Example and fit Instrument for introducing the same absolute Rule into these Colonies.

For taking away our Charters, abolishing our most valuable Laws, and altering fundamentally the Forms of our Governments:

For suspending our own Legislatures, and declaring themselves invested with Power to legislate for us in *all* Cases whatsoever.

He has abdicated Government here, by declaring us out of his Protection and waging War against us.

He has plundered our Seas, ravaged our Coasts, burnt our Towns, and destroyed the Lives of our People.

He is, at this Time, transporting large Armies of *foreign* Mercenaries to compleat the Works of Death, Desolation, and Tyranny, already begun with Circumstances of Cruelty and Perfidy scarcely paralleled in the most barbarous Ages, and *totally* unworthy the Head of a civilized Nation.

He has constrained our Fellow Citizens, taken Captive on the high Seas, to bear Arms *against* their Country; to become the Executioners of their Friends and Brethren, or to fall themselves by *their* Hands.

He has excited Domestic Insurrections amongst us, and has endeavoured to bring on the Inhabitants of our Frontiers, the *merciless* Indian Savages, whose known Rule of Warfare, is an undistinguished Destruction of all Ages, Sexes, and Conditions.

In every Stage of these Oppressions we have petitioned for Redress, in the most humble Terms: Our repeated Petitions have been answered only by *repeated* Injury!—A Prince, whose Character is thus marked by *every* Act which may define a Tyrant, is unfit to be the Ruler of a FREE PEOPLE!

Nor have we been wanting in Attention to our British Brethren. We have *warned* them from Time to Time of Attempts by their Legislature to extend an unwarrantable Jurisdiction over us. We have reminded them of the Circumstances of our Emigration and Settlement here. We have appealed to their native Justice and Magnanimity, and we have conjured them by the Ties of our common Kindred to disavow these *Usurpations*, which would inevitably interrupt our Connexions and Correspondence. They too have been *deaf* to the Voice of Justice and of Consanguinity. We must, therefore, acquiesce in the Necessity which denounces our Separation, and hold *them*, as we hold the rest of Mankind, *Enemies* in War; in Peace, Friends.

We, therefore, the Representatives of the UNITED STATES OF AMERICA, in General Congress assembled, appealing to the Supreme Judge of the World for the *Rectitude* of our Intentions, do, in the Name and by the Authority of the good People of these Colonies, *solemnly* Publish and Declare, That these United Colonies are, and of Right ought to be, Free and Independent States; that they are absolved from all Allegiance to the British Crown; and that all political Connexion between them and the State of Great-Britain, is, and ought to be *totally* dissolved; and that as Free and Independent States, they have full Power to levy War, conclude Peace, contract Alliances, establish Commerce, and to do all other Acts and Things which Independent States may of Right do. And for the Support of this Declaration, with a *firm* Reliance on the Protection of Divine Providence, we mutually pledge to each other our LIVES, our Fortunes, and our SACRED HONOR.

Signed by Order *and in* Behalf *of the* Congress,

JOHN HANCOCK, PRESIDENT.
Attest; CHARLES THOMPSON, Secretary.

In COUNCIL, July 17th, 1776.

ORDERED, That the Declaration of Independence be printed; and a Copy sent to the Ministers of each Parish, of every Denomination, within this State; and that they severally be *required* to read the same to their respective Congregations, as soon as divine Service is ended, in the Afternoon, on the first Lord's-Day after they shall have received it:—And after such Publication thereof, to deliver the said Declaration to the Clerks of their several Towns, or Districts; who are hereby required to record the same in their respective Town, or District Books, there to remain as a *perpetual* Memorial thereof.

In the Name, and by Order of the Council,   R. DERBY, Jun. President.

A true Copy Attest,   John Avery, Dep. Sec'y.

SALEM, Massachusetts-Bay: Printed by E. Russell, by Order of Authority.

❦ 46 ❦

DECLARATION OF INDEPENDENCE
IN BROADSIDE FORM

THE FIRST, OFFICIAL PRINTING of the Declaration of Independence was authorized by Congress on July 4, 1776. It was printed that evening by John Dunlap, to be forwarded to the army, to the states, and to state Committees of Correspondence for posting in public places. This is the edition, surviving in two dozen or more copies, that has brought record prices in auction rooms over the last three decades. The Clements Library does not own a copy. Newspapers began publishing the document on July 6, and there were nineteen appearances by July 16. There are sixteen separate "contemporary" broadside *Declarations*. Some of these were officially sanctioned copies, while others were simply the product of enthusiastic newspaper offices wishing to spread the word quickly or provide local constituents with something in the nature of a souvenir. Every one of these later broadside issues of the Declaration is considerably more scarce than the Dunlap edition, but of course they lack the primacy of the first "official" printing. The Salem edition, shown on the previous page, which was the official Massachusetts printing, clearly copied its typographical layout from Dunlap's original. The Library also has eight of the first newspaper printings of the document.

Now, of course, the Declaration of Independence is the most widely known document in our nation's history. Congress had actually voted on independence on July 2. For a few years, the public was uncertain which date to observe, July 2 or July 4, but since July 4 is printed on the document itself, this became the commonly recognized day of celebration by the 1780s. The *Declaration* did not receive a great deal of attention or veneration until the 1820s, when there was an outpouring of patriotic enthusiasm as Lafayette revisited America, as veterans began dying off, as Sanderson's *Lives of the Signers of the Declaration of Independence* (Philadelphia, 1820–24) came out, and as facsimile reprints of the document were produced by several enterprising publishers. These lithographs made ideal wall hangings for the public schools which were just beginning to come into existence throughout the country.

Purchased from Lathrop C. Harper, 1929.

❦ 47 ❦

A REMARKABLE SCHOOLBOY TO
HIS FAMOUS FATHER

ON DECEMBER 6, 1777, ten-year-old William Petty wrote a letter to his father, giving his own interpretation of the latest news from the American War. He was "sorry to hear" that General Washington's army had been "defeated," no doubt a reference to the Battle of the Brandywine, and that General Arnold (still an American hero) had died at the Battle of Saratoga. This latter infor-

> *My dear Papa,*
> *I am very sorry for Washinton's defeat, and Arnolds death, the former is very advan-tageous to General Howe, But it is fully recompensed by the surrender of the eloquent and humane General Burgoyne.*
>
> *Doctor Priestley desires his compliments to you.*
> *I am, my dear Papa, your ever affectionate Son,*
> *William G Petty*
> *Bowood park, Dec 6th*

mation, as with much battlefield news reported in the papers, was incorrect. But bad news was well "recompensed" by good news: "The eloquent and humane" British General Burgoyne had surrendered his army at Saratoga. William, like most young boys, was fascinated by the war. What makes his letter remarkable, with its patriotic American sentiments, is that William was the son of Lord Shelburne, the future British Prime Minister who in 1782 would draft the peace treaty ending the conflict.

For William Granville Petty, the world had always revolved around his "Dear Papa." His mother had died tragically young, a few months after his second birthday. His father was one of the most controversial men in British politics. Shelburne was notorious for his radical support of parliamentary reform, religious toleration, and economic liberalism. He believed strongly that Britain's war against her colonies was bad policy — that it was in his country's best interest to maintain strong political and economic ties with America. So young William's letter was reflecting his father's suspected pro-American sentiments.

But William's letters, preserved in two leather-bound copybooks found among the Shelburne Papers at the Clements Library, reveal much more than current politics. As family history, they offer a glimpse of the British aristocrat's world, where vast landed wealth created great social privilege and political power for an elite few. As intellectual history, they reflect the best in the eighteenth-century Dissenter tradition of education. The great scientist and Dissenting clergyman, Joseph Priestley, was William Petty's tutor, and he designed the course of study that William and his older brother John followed. Priestley believed they should be taught classics, philosophy, history, politics, law, mathematics, modern languages, anatomy, and applied science. The goal of this broad curriculum was to teach man's relation to God. Science demonstrated God's order for the universe, so Priestley had William and his brother watch as he conducted his experiments on "phlogisticated air," later identified as oxygen. Priestley believed that clear, critical thinking was a religious duty, that education was a form of civil liberty. He knew that John and William, by virtue of their father's wealth and prestige, would one day sit in Parliament, so he insisted that his young charges read the newspapers and listen to adults discuss public affairs. William and his brother were expected to write down their own observations and form their own opinions. William's letter to his father, reflecting on Burgoyne's surrender, was an exercise in Priestley's principles of education.

From all evidence, William Petty was a particularly amusing, bright, curious child, but his energy and quick mind belied a fragile constitution. More susceptible than most to childhood illnesses, at ten years, on January 28, 1778, William died from an acute intestinal attack, probably appendicitis, which eighteenth-century medicine could not diagnose, much less treat. His father never entirely recovered from his son's death. The letterbooks not only preserve the memory of an exceptional young man and offer rare insight into private thoughts in his father's household, but provide an important record of enlightened eighteenth-century educational practices in an exceptional British family.

Purchased from Birrell & Garnett, 1929.

⤸ 48 ⤷

AMERICA'S TRAITOR: BENEDICT ARNOLD

BENEDICT ARNOLD (1741–1801) IS ONE OF the most interesting and enigmatic figures in American history. A hero of Ticonderoga, the march to Quebec, the brilliant defensive actions on Lake Champlain, and Saratoga, where he lost a leg, Arnold was vain, mercenary, and resentful of slights, real and imagined. Washington treated Arnold with exceptional kindness and forbearance, but Arnold saw the commander as incompetent, as a personal enemy, and as a rival. Arnold was unquestionably a capable military commander, but he was incapable of true loyalty to anyone or anything but his own self-interest.

When the papers of Sir Henry Clinton were purchased by William L. Clements and first became available for study, the greatest discovery in the collection was the detailed record of Benedict Arnold's treasonable communications with the enemy, beginning in the summer of 1779. Preserved in an extensive series of coded letters, they were far more damning of Arnold than anyone had previously imagined, and they clearly, for the first time, implicated his wife, Peggy Shippen Arnold.

Why did Arnold betray the American cause? Perhaps excusably, he deeply resented criticism he had received from Congress and the State of Pennsylvania over his decisions and financial management of previous campaigns. He also seems to have deeply mistrusted the French and felt that the French Alliance had transformed a previously noble cause into a corrupt conflict in which Europe was again using the American colonies to further selfish ends. The extent to which his wife was Loyalist in sympathy and influential in changing his mind remains open to debate. Money also played a significant role. His personal finances were in turmoil, and in Peggy Shippen, he married a woman who was accustomed to a lifestyle far above his means.

Inclosed in a cover addressed to Mr. Anderson.

Two days since I received a letter without date or signature, informing me that S. Henry — was obliged to me for the intelligence communicated, and that he placed a full confidence in the sincerity of my intentions, &c. &c. — On the 13th Instant I addressed a letter to you expressing my sentiments and expectations, viz. that the following Preliminaries be settled previous to cooperating, — First, that S. Henry secure to me my property, valued at ten thousand pounds Sterling, to be paid to me or my Heirs in case of Loss; and, as soon as that happens shall happen, — hundred pounds per annum to be secured to me for life, in lieu of the pay and emoluments I give up, for my services as they shall deserve — If I point out a plan of cooperation by which S.H. shall possess himself of West Point, the Garrison, &c. &c. &c. twenty thousand pounds Sterling I think will be a cheap purchase for an object of so much importance. At the same time I request a thousand pounds to be paid my Agent — I expect a full and explicit answer — The 20th I set off for West Point. A personal interview with an officer that you can confide in is absolutely necessary to plan matters. In the mean time I shall communicate to our mutual Friend S——y all the intelligence in my power, until I have the pleasure of your answer.

July 15th

Moore

N. the line of my letter of the 13th I did not add seven.

N.B. The postscript only relates to the manner of composing the Cypher in the letter referred to —

Beginning in 1779, to prove his sincerity to the British, Arnold began passing military intelligence to Sir Henry Clinton. In the summer of 1780, he convinced Washington to appoint him as commander of the American garrison at West Point, the key defensive post separating New York City from Canada, doing so with the intention of gaining personal control over a prize (West Point) of sufficient value to the British to consummate a highly lucrative payoff for switching sides. His coded letter of July 15 to John André, Clinton's spymaster, set forth his terms. He requested that the British guarantee him £10,000 Sterling, whether or not his plan was successful, and an additional £20,000 if the British did secure West Point. The prearranged code was based upon a dictionary, providing page and line numbers for omitted words. Once decoded, it is a very calculated, cold-blooded letter, and it is hard to feel much sympathy for Arnold after reading it. Fortunately for the American cause, the plan was discovered shortly before it was to have been put into execution by the chance capture of André, in disguise behind American lines, and the discovery of dispatches in his stockings. Arnold quickly joined the British, and André was executed.

Probably every great war needs to have at least one notable traitor. Arnold paid dearly for his actions in the long run. Sir Henry Clinton, realizing Arnold's military abilities, appointed him a British general and gave him a command in Virginia. But even British officers resented serving with a turncoat. After the war, he attempted various commercial ventures, tried to secure active military assignments, and sought additional compensation from the British government, all without success. The family lived in humble circumstances in London, where Arnold died and is buried.

Clinton Papers, purchased from Clements Estate, 1937.

INVALUABLE DETAILS OF EVERYDAY LIFE, FOUND IN STRANGE PLACES

One of the special pleasures of historical research is finding the unexpected treasure in an unlikely place. Who would think to search the papers of the commander in chief of the British Army during the Revolution to study the food and wine, or furniture and decorative arts in eighteenth-century New York?

In the eighteenth century, civil and military officials paid many expenses that we would consider "public" out of their own pockets. There was a strong incentive, therefore, to keep a meticulously complete record of every expenditure, because final accounts were settled only after leaving office. Payment depended upon the preservation of receipts. Sir Henry Clinton's papers include bills and receipts for every penny which the general expended on himself, his household, and his army, from 1778 to 1782. During much of this time, Clinton was headquartered in New York City, and the documents provide a uniquely rich record of social history and material culture having very little to do with the war itself. We know all the minute details of the commander in chief's lifestyle: his servants, his food, his drinking habits, the names of his tailor and hat maker, and his tastes in music. We know where he lived, where and how he entertained his officers, and the exact number of geese and chickens he kept on his rural farm at the end of Bowery Lane.

Two items are illustrated here to make the point. One is a portion of a nine-page inventory of the furnishings and supplies in William Hick's New York Tavern in April 1780. Hick owned the building and had run the establishment previously, but beginning on May 1, 1780, he was leasing the building, selling the contents, and turning over the management of the business to Charles Roubalet in return for a substantial payment and a two-room apartment for his family. The inventory is a detailed description of the complete furnishings of a very considerable business establishment, including an assembly room, five dining rooms (which could double as bedrooms), two bedrooms, a garret, barroom, kitchen, and cellar. Every piece of furniture, set of dishes and glassware, and piece of cooking equipment are described in minute detail. One could reconstruct this tavern and arrange its complete furnishings, room by room, from this inventory alone. It is the kind of document that can be invaluable to a social historian, archaeologist, historical site interpreter, or even an historical novelist who wants to be precise in small narrative details.

The other item is a printed bill for Roubalet's Tavern, documenting the costs of dinner for Sir Henry and guests on January 19, 1781. It would appear that the party consisted of eight persons who consumed dinner, twelve bottles of wine, a moderate amount of beer and porter, and fruit and coffee for dessert. Five percent seems to have been the normal tip for waiters in this era. Roubalet's Tavern served, occasionally, as an officers' club for the British Army, or at least was considered a safe place to conduct military business. At the particular time this entertainment was held, Clinton was receiving spy reports on the revolt of the Pennsylvania Line, and it undoubtedly provided a lively topic of dinner conversation.

Clinton Papers, purchased from Clements Estate, 1937.

❧ 50 ❧

THE WAR AND WASHINGTON'S TEETH

THERE IS PROBABLY NO FIGURE in history whose teeth have received more attention than George Washington. As a result of smallpox, with which he was infected as a young man while in Barbados, he lost many of his teeth at a fairly early age. This was a constant personal irritation throughout his life, and the various attempts he made to find artificial substitutes have formed the basis of countless jokes and exaggerated stories. Just about every visitor to Mt. Vernon asks to see his wooden teeth. In actuality, his dentures were made of a variety of substances, but wood was not among them.

Given the notoriety of the subject, it was a cause of considerable excitement and amusement when after purchasing the voluminous papers of Sir Henry Clinton, Washington's foe as com-

New Windsor May 29. 1781

Sir,

A day or two ago I requested Col. Harrison to apply to you for a pair of Pincers to fasten the wire of my teeth. — I hope you furnished him with them — I now wish you would send me one of your scrapers, as my teeth stand in need of cleaning, and I have a little prospect of being in Philadel.ª soon. — It will come very safe by the Post — & in return, the money shall be sent so soon as I know the cost of it. —

I am Sir

Yr very Hble Serv.

G Washington

mander in chief of the British Army during the Revolution, that the Clements' librarians discovered an unexpected, handwritten letter from the American commander to his dentist in Philadelphia, ordering wires to hold his dentures in place and a scraper for cleaning his teeth. The letter has been a special showpiece at the Library since it arrived in Ann Arbor in 1937.

As interesting as the letter is by itself, its context is equally fascinating. It is dated May 29, 1781, and was written at New Windsor, New York. Washington had been meeting with Count Rochambeau, commander of the French Army, trying to work out a common plan of action and decide whether to attack New York City. Washington favored such a strategy, and it was probably very fortunate that Cornwallis allowed himself to be cut off at Yorktown, Virginia, from his supplies. It made the New York assault unnecessary. Washington consigned his letter to courier post, and on June 3, the particulars of the capture not being a matter of record, a British agent managed to steal the mail and route it to Sir Henry Clinton in New York City.

For Clinton, the question was whether the letters were authentic, or phony correspondence that had been planted and the capture "arranged" so that he received false intelligence. He pondered the matter for some time and then decided, on the basis of the dental letter specifically, that the capture was "good," and that the intelligence provided by the entire bundle could be relied upon. As he confided to Lord George Germain, "Odd as it may seem, W[ashington']s letter to his tooth

Doctor . . . would not have been found among other communications intended for interception."

This seemingly innocent letter, then, helped reinforce Clinton's belief that Washington intended to attack the city. Although the American commander would soon change his course and begin quickly sending reinforcements to Virginia, he continued to make every effort to convince Clinton that New York City was the ultimate target of offensive operations. Clinton, a man who always played it safe when his own welfare might be at stake, believed it a bit too long, until Washington had much of his army well on its way to Virginia. By then it was too late to save Cornwallis.

There is no reason to think that the letter is not authentic. It is unquestionably in Washington's hand. In other collections, the Library has several bills of Dr. John Baker, suggesting that he was the most capable dentist in the country at that time, with a national clientele.

Clinton Papers, purchased from Clements Estate, 1937.

⊱ 51 ⊰

PEACE AT LAST: THE BROADSIDE THAT ENDED THE WAR

ON OCTOBER 31, 1781, Sir Henry Clinton, commander in chief of the British army, received a fourteen-page letter from General Cornwallis indicating that the latter had surrendered his troops at Yorktown, Virginia, on the nineteenth of the month. The letter is in the Library's collections. In retrospect, Yorktown is celebrated as the last great battle of the war, but that was not at all obvious at the time. New York, Charleston, and Savannah remained under British control, skirmishes were occurring daily, and large British and French fleets continued to maneuver belligerently in the West Indies, with the British beginning to get the upper hand. Neither Clinton, nor Washington, nor George III saw Yorktown as the inevitable conclusion of the conflict.

More telling was the action of the British House of Commons on February 27, 1782, which refused Lord North additional funding to prosecute the war. On March 5, 1782, Parliament authorized the government to make peace with the Americans. Lord North resigned on March 20. It would take three British ministries and seven long months of negotiations in Paris before a preliminary treaty of peace was signed on November 5, 1782. On January 20, 1783, the British signed preliminary articles of peace with France and Spain, and on February 4, 1783, an armistice officially went into effect.

Negotiating a peace treaty is difficult enough, but ratifying it in the age of sail and hand-written, hand-carried letters was an almost endless process. Congress received the text of the provisional treaty on March 13, 1783, and word of the armistice on April 11. The treaty was ratified by Congress on April 15, and finally, on September 3, 1783, the formal Treaty of Peace was signed in Paris. Even this did not complete the process, because under the provisions of the Articles of Confederation, the final treaty now had to be approved in a special session of Congress. Annapolis was

By the UNITED STATES in CONGRESS Aſſembled,

A PROCLAMATION.

WHEREAS definitive articles of peace and friendſhip, between the United States of America and his Britannic majeſty, were concluded and ſigned at Paris, on the 3d day of September, 1783, by the plenipotentiaries of the ſaid United States, and of his ſaid Britannic Majeſty, duly and reſpectively authorized for that purpoſe; which definitive articles are in the words following.

In the Name of the Moſt Holy and Undivided
TRINITY.

IT having pleaſed the Divine Providence to diſpoſe the hearts of the moſt ſerene and moſt potent Prince George the Third, by the Grace of God, King of Great-Britain, France and Ireland, Defender of the Faith, Duke of Brunſwick and Lunenburg, Arch-Treaſurer and Prince Elector of the Holy Roman Empire, &c. and of the United States of America, to forget all paſt miſunderſtandings and differences, that have unhappily interrupted the good correſpondence and friendſhip which they mutually wiſh to reſtore; and to eſtabliſh ſuch a beneficial and ſatisfactory intercourſe between the two countries, upon the ground of reciprocal advantages and mutual convenience, as may promote and ſecure to both perpetual peace and harmony: And having for this deſirable end, already laid the foundation of peace and reconciliation, by the proviſional articles, ſigned at Paris, on the 30th of November, 1782, by the commiſſioners empowered on each part, which articles were agreed to be inſerted in, and to conſtitute the treaty of peace propoſed to be concluded between the crown of Great-Britain and the ſaid United States, but which treaty was not to be concluded until terms of peace ſhould be agreed upon between Great-Britain and France, and his Britannic majeſty ſhould be ready to conclude ſuch treaty accordingly; and the treaty between Great-Britain and France, having ſince been concluded, his Britannic majeſty and the United States of America, in order to carry into full effect the proviſional articles abovementioned, according to the tenor thereof, have conſtituted and appointed, that is to ſay, His Britannic majeſty on his part, David Hartley, eſquire, member of the parliament of Great-Britain, and the ſaid United States on their part, John Adams, eſquire, late a commiſſioner of the United States of America at the court of Verſailles, late delegate in congreſs from the ſtate of Maſſachuſetts, and chief juſtice of the ſaid ſtate, and miniſter plenipotentiary of the ſaid United States, to their high mightineſſes the States General of the United Netherlands; Benjamin Franklin, eſquire, late delegate in congreſs from the ſtate of Pennſylvania, preſident of the convention of the ſaid ſtate, and miniſter plenipotentiary from the United States of America at the court of Verſailles; John Jay, eſquire, late preſident of congreſs, and chief juſtice of the ſtate of New-York, and miniſter plenipotentiary from the ſaid United States at the Court of Madrid, to be the plenipotentiaries for the concluding and ſigning the preſent definitive treaty; who after having reciprocally communicated their reſpective full powers, have agreed upon and confirmed the following articles.

ARTICLE 1ſt. His Britannic Majeſty acknowledges the ſaid United States, viz. New-Hampſhire, Maſſachuſetts-Bay, Rhode-Iſland and Providence Plantations, Connecticut, New-York, New-Jerſey, Pennſylvania, Delaware, Maryland, Virginia, North-Carolina, South-Carolina and Georgia, to be free, ſovereign and independent ſtates: that he treats with them as ſuch, and for himſelf, his heirs and ſucceſſors, relinquiſhes all claims to the government, propriety and territorial rights of the ſame, and every part thereof:

ARTICLE. 2d. And that all diſputes which might ariſe in future on the ſubject of the boundaries of the ſaid United States may be prevented, it is hereby agreed and declared, that the following are and ſhall be their boundaries, viz.

From the north weſt angle of Nova-Scotia, viz. that angle which is formed by a line drawn due north from the ſource of Saint-Croix river to the Highlands; along the ſaid Highlands which divide thoſe rivers that empty themſelves into the river Saint Lawrence from thoſe which fall into the Atlantic Ocean, to the north-weſternmoſt head of Connecticut river, thence down along the middle of that river to the forty-fifth degree of north latitude; from thence by a line due weſt on ſaid latitude, until it ſtrikes the river Iroquois or Cataraquy; thence along the middle of ſaid river into lake Ontario, through the middle of ſaid lake until it ſtrikes the communication by water between that lake and lake Erie; thence along the middle of ſaid communication into lake Erie, through the middle of ſaid lake until it arrives at the water communication between that lake and lake Huron; thence along the middle of ſaid water communication into the lake Huron; thence through the middle of ſaid lake to the water communication between that lake and lake Superior; thence through lake Superior northward of the iſles, Royal and Philipeaux to the long lake; thence through the middle of ſaid long lake and the water communication between it and the lake of the Woods, to the ſaid lake of the Woods; thence through the ſaid lake to the moſt north-weſtern point thereof, and from thence on a due weſt courſe to the river Miſſiſippi; thence by a line to be drawn along the middle of the ſaid river Miſſiſippi, until it ſhall interſect the northernmoſt part of the thirty-firſt degree of north latitude. South by a line to be drawn due eaſt from the determination of the line laſt mentioned, in the latitude of thirty-one degrees north of the equator, to the middle of the river Apalachicola or Catahouche; thence along the middle thereof to its junction with the Flint river; thence ſtraight to the head of Saint Mary's river; and thence down along the middle of Saint Mary's river to the Atlantic Ocean. Eaſt by a line to be drawn along the middle of the river Saint-Croix, from its mouth in the bay of Fundy to its ſource, and from its ſource directly north to the aforeſaid Highlands which divide the rivers that fall into the Atlantic Ocean from thoſe which fall into the river Saint Lawrence: comprehending all iſlands within twenty leagues of any part of the ſhores of the United States, and lying between lines to be drawn due eaſt from the points where the aforeſaid boundaries between Nova-Scotia on the one part, and Eaſt Florida on the other, ſhall reſpectively touch the bay of Fundy, and the Atlantic Ocean; excepting ſuch iſlands as now are or heretofore have been within the limits of the ſaid province of Nova Scotia.

ARTICLE. 3d. It is agreed that the people of the United States ſhall continue to enjoy unmoleſted the right to take fiſh of every kind on the Grand Bank, and on all the other banks of Newfoundland; alſo in the gulph of Saint Lawrence, and at all other places in the ſea, where the inhabitants of both countries uſed at any time heretofore to fiſh; and alſo that the inhabitants of the United States ſhall have liberty to take fiſh of every kind on ſuch part of the coaſt of Newfoundland as Britiſh fiſhermen ſhall uſe, (but not to dry or cure the ſame on that Iſland) and alſo on the coaſts, bays and creeks of all other of his Britannic Majeſty's dominions in America; and that the American fiſhermen ſhall have liberty to dry and cure fiſh in any of the unſettled bays, harbours and creeks of Nova-Scotia, Magdalen iſlands, and Labradore, ſo long as the ſame ſhall remain unſettled, but ſo ſoon as the ſame or either of them ſhall be ſettled, it ſhall not be lawful for the ſaid fiſhermen to dry or cure fiſh at ſuch ſettlement, without a previous agreement for that purpoſe with the inhabitants, proprietors or poſſeſſors of the ground.

ARTICLE 4th. It is agreed that creditors on either ſide, ſhall meet with no lawful impediment to the recovery of the full value in ſterling money, of all bona fide debts heretofore contracted.

ARTICLE 5th. It is agreed that the Congreſs ſhall earneſtly recommend it to the legiſlatures of the reſpective ſtates, to provide for the reſtitution of all eſtates, rights and properties, which have been confiſcated, belonging to real Britiſh ſubjects, and alſo of the eſtates, rights and properties of perſons reſident in diſtricts in the poſſeſſion of his majeſty's arms, and who have not borne arms againſt the ſaid United States. And that perſons of any other deſcription ſhall have free liberty to go to any part or parts of any of the Thirteen United States, and therein to remain twelve months unmoleſted in their endeavours to obtain the reſtitution of ſuch of their eſtates, rights and properties, as may have been confiſcated; and that Congreſs ſhall alſo earneſtly recommend to the ſeveral ſtates a reconſideration and reviſion of all acts or laws regarding the premiſes, ſo as to render the ſaid laws or acts perfectly conſiſtent, not only with juſtice and equity, but with that ſpirit of conciliation, which on the return of the bleſſings of peace ſhould univerſally prevail. And that Congreſs ſhall alſo earneſtly recommend to the ſeveral ſtates, that the eſtates, rights and properties of ſuch laſt mentioned perſons ſhall be reſtored to them; they refunding to any perſons who may be now in poſſeſſion the bona fide price (where any has been given) which ſuch perſons may have paid on purchaſing any of the ſaid lands, rights or properties ſince the confiſcation. And it is agreed that all perſons who have any intereſt in confiſcated lands, either by debts, marriage ſettlements, or otherwiſe, ſhall meet with no lawful impediment in the proſecution of their juſt rights.

ARTICLE 6th. That there ſhall be no future confiſcations made, nor any proſecutions commenced againſt any perſon or perſons for or by reaſon of the part which he or they may have taken in the preſent war; and that no perſon ſhall on that account, ſuffer any future loſs or damage, either in his perſon liberty or property, and that thoſe who may be in confinement on ſuch charges, at the time of the ratification of the treaty in America, ſhall be immediately ſet at liberty, and the proſecutions ſo commenced be diſcontinued.

ARTICLE 7th. There ſhall be a firm and perpetual peace between his Britannic Majeſty and the ſaid States, and between the ſubjects of the one, and the citizens of the other, wherefore all hoſtilities both by ſea and land ſhall from henceforth ceaſe: all priſoners on both ſides ſhall be ſet at liberty, and his Britannic Majeſty ſhall with all convenient ſpeed, and without cauſing any deſtruction, or carrying away any negroes or other property of the American inhabitants, withdraw all his armies, garriſons and fleets from the ſaid United States and from every poſt place and harbour within the ſame; leaving in all fortifications the American artillery that may be therein, and ſhall alſo order and cauſe all archives, records deeds and papers, belonging to any of the ſaid ſtates, or their citizens, which in the courſe of the war may have fallen into the hands of his officers, to be forthwith reſtored and delivered to the proper ſtates and perſons to whom they belong.

ARTICLE 8th. The navigation of the river Miſſiſippi, from its ſource to the Ocean, ſhall forever remain free and open to the ſubjects of Great-Britain and the citizens of the United States.

ARTICLE 9th. In caſe it ſhould ſo happen that any place or territory belonging to Great-Britain or to the United States, ſhould have been conquered by the arms of either from the other, before the arrival of the ſaid proviſional articles in America, it is agreed, that the ſame ſhall be reſtored without difficulty, and without requiring any compenſation.

ARTICLE 10th. The ſolemn ratifications of the preſent treaty, expedited in good and due form, ſhall be exchanged between the contracting parties, in the ſpace of ſix months, or ſooner if poſſible, to be computed from the day of the ſignature of the preſent treaty. In witneſs whereof, we the underſigned, their miniſters plenipotentiary, have in their name and in virtue of our full powers, ſigned with our hands the preſent definitive treaty, and cauſed the ſeals of our arms to be affixed thereto.

DONE at Paris, this third day of September, in the year of our Lord one thouſand ſeven hundred and eighty-three.

(L. S.) D. HARTLEY, (L. S.) JOHN ADAMS,
(L. S.) B. FRANKLIN,
(L. S.) JOHN JAY.

AND we the United States in Congreſs aſſembled, having ſeen and duly conſidered the definitive articles aforeſaid, did by a certain act under the ſeal of the United States, bearing date this 14th day of January 1784, approve, ratify and confirm the ſame and every part and clauſe thereof, engaging and promiſing that we would ſincerely and faithfully perform and obſerve the ſame, and never ſuffer them to be violated by any one, or tranſgreſſed in any manner as far as ſhould be in our power: and being ſincerely diſpoſed to carry the ſaid articles into execution truly, honeſtly and with good faith, according to the intent and meaning thereof, we have thought proper by theſe preſents, to notify the premiſes to all the good citizens of theſe United States, hereby requiring and enjoining all bodies of magiſtracy, legiſlative, executive and judiciary, all perſons bearing office, civil or military, of whatever rank, degree or powers, and all others the good citizens of theſe States of every vocation and condition, that reverencing thoſe ſtipulations entered into on their behalf, under the authority of that fœderal bond by which their exiſtence as an independent people is bound up together, and is known and acknowledged by the nations of the world, and with that good faith which is every man's ſureſt guide within their ſeveral offices juriſdictions and vocations, they carry into effect the ſaid definitive articles, and every clauſe and ſentence thereof, ſincerely, ſtrictly and completely.

GIVEN under the Seal of the United States, Witneſs his Excellency THOMAS MIFFLIN, our Preſident, at Annapolis, this fourteenth day of January, in the year of our Lord one thouſand ſeven hundred and eighty-four, and of the ſovereignty and independence of the United States of America the eighth.

Cha Thomson secy

ANNAPOLIS: Printed by JOHN DUNLAP, Printer for the United States in Congreſs aſſembled.

then the nation's capital. Delegates were slow to assemble, but on January 14, 1784, the necessary votes were cast and peace was declared. The rare broadside shown here, signed by Charles Thompson, officially announced the end of the Revolutionary War.

The Library has outstanding manuscript holdings on the lengthy diplomatic process that resulted in the 1783 peace treaty, including the papers of Lord Shelburne, David Hartley, Lord Sydney, Lord Strachey, and the Duke of Manchester. The Library's Josiah Harmar Papers have a fascinating postscript to the entire business. One of the conditions placed on the United States at the time of the treaty's signing on September 3 was that the document, with proof of Congressional ratification, be back in Paris by March 3, 1784, to be official. Harmar was chosen as courier, and he had only six weeks to meet the deadline. In spite of every possible effort, the weather did not cooperate, and Harmar did not reach Paris until March 29. Fortunately, the wisest of the American diplomatic commissioners, Benjamin Franklin, had foreseen the possibility and negotiated extra time! When Harmar arrived and presented the signed, ratified document, the process was complete.

Exchange with Library of Congress, 1964.

❧ 52 ❧

IMPROBABLE DIARIST

JACOB NAGLE'S HANDWRITTEN AUTOBIOGRAPHY is one of the most improbable and most important manuscripts in the Clements Library's collections. The odds of such a record existing and surviving are a bookmaker's dream.

Although raised in a fairly prominent frontier family, Jacob became essentially a lifetime orphan of the American Revolution. He joined the Continental Army in 1777 at the age of fifteen and served about a year. He then signed up for the Navy but never got to sea. He joined the privateering service, was captured at sea by the British in 1781, and served for twenty years in the Royal Navy, largely as a common seaman. He was a member of the First Fleet which settled Australia and Norfolk Island, served with Lord Nelson in the Mediterranean, deserted the Navy to ship with the East India Company to India, later sailed with the same company to China, and was a merchant seaman for two decades. He ended up a restless nomad who, well into his seventies, thought nothing of walking from Ohio to Washington, D.C. or Washington to Philadelphia without a dollar in his pocket.

Highly unusual circumstances account for the existence of this manuscript. Jacob Nagle did receive a good primary school education, and he inherited an iron constitution, remarkable strength of character, and great natural intelligence. He forgot all the niceties of spelling and grammar over the years, but he had excellent handwriting, a bountiful vocabulary, a remarkable memory, and an irrepressible desire to preserve a record of his adventures. He kept diaries all his life, losing them, reconstructing them, and recopying until he penned a final, most complete version, which is the one preserved at the Library. The result is that Jacob Nagle created one of the few

In 1776 the Brittish leaving Boston Landing at Long Island & took New York
In 1777 Lord How Landed at the head of Elk, which Washington purceives
he ment for Philadelphia, therefore he came to meet him, at this time my Father
Sent for me, at this time there was a number of Officers in Reading upon
Liberty, but was demanded to join the army, amongst the rest was Jack Bittle
Commesary general, which my Mother gave him Charge of me, to be delivered
to my Father, we went on to join the army, but on the road he pretended
he had Lost some dispatches which was for Washington, the Officers all
returned with him for Seven or eight miles; when he gave up the Search
and we returned, & joined the army, the next day, Marching through
Wilmington Mr Bittle took me to my Father who was then Leutenant Cornel
of the Ninth Pensylvania Rigment, & Shortly after Full Cornel of the Tenth Pensylvania
Rigment, I was then not quite Sixteen, when the army Encamped my Father
took me to Cor Prockter who Commanded the grand park of Artillery, I Laid
in his Marklee that night, and the next day I messed with ajudent Stofnor
who had the Charge of me, being a young Soldier, we then marched and
the army Encamped on the Brandewine on the Right of Shade Jord on the high
ground, our Artilery was Ranged in front of an Orchard, the Night before the
Brittish arived the Infantry hove up a brest work, so that the muzzels of the
guns would Run over it, a Cross the Road on the left was a Buckwheat field
oppsit to a wood, & the Brandewine, between them, the provision wagging
being Sent a way we ware three day without Provisions, Excepting what the
Farmers brought in to Sell, in their waggons, & what the Soldiers Could

book-length diaries which exists by a member of the working class, uncensored and unedited. It is probably the finest existing record of a common sailor of the eighteenth century.

The section illustrated is from the very beginning of the diary, when Nagle joined Washington's army in Wilmington, Delaware, just before the Battle of the Brandywine. In a passage typical of the entire narrative, he remembered certain details and had certain insights which are recorded nowhere else. *The Nagle Journal*, edited by John C. Dann, was published in its entirety in 1988.

Purchased at Hamilton Auction by Carnegie Book Shop, 1982.
Gift of John and Emily Wheeler, Bay City, Michigan.

SOUTH SEA PATTERNS: A UNIQUE SAMPLER
OF CAPTAIN COOK

WHEN CAPTAIN COOK'S *Discovery* returned from the third voyage of 1780 — Cook having been killed two years earlier by natives at Kealakekua Bay, Hawaii, and buried in a sea coffin — the ship carried with it plants, specimens, and artifacts of great fascination. Among them were many rolls of tapa cloth which the Polynesian women made from the bark of the paper mulberry tree. Alexander Shaw, a London merchant, was able to obtain specimens of the textured cloth with its striking patterns and designs and put together *A Catalogue of the Different Specimens of Cloth Collected in the Three Voyages of Captain Cook, to the Southern Hemisphere; with a Particular Account of the Manner of Manufacturing the Same in the Various Islands of the South Seas.* He printed his list as a pamphlet in 1787, bound it with a selection of 45 to 60 swatches of the cloth, two or four to a page, and distributed copies to friends. The book is a great rarity, and the Clements Library copy is uniquely special.

Thomas Pennant (1726–1798) was one of the most admired naturalists of the eighteenth century, and when he saw a copy of the book, he called on Shaw and obtained every existing sample, both from Shaw and apparently other sources, cut them to full page size, and bound them with

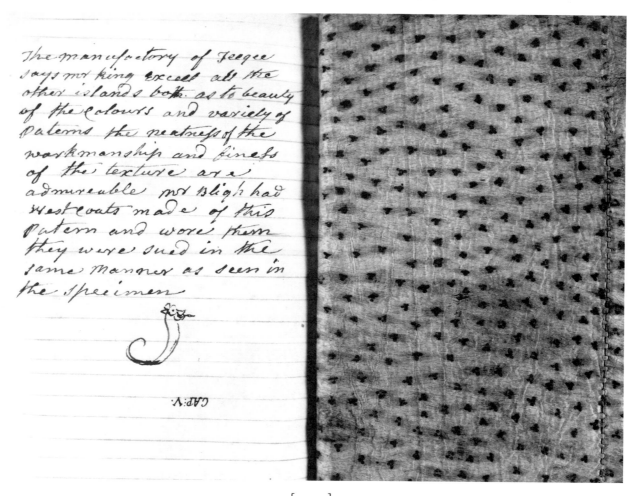

Shaw's essay. To supplement the printed identifications, he sought out and interviewed several of Cook's sailors, writing on blank interleaves where, when, and by whom each sample was acquired, and how the different types of cloth were used by the natives. The result was a fat book containing 92 samples and a unique body of ethnological information. The sample illustrated here was from the Fiji Islands and was particularly admired by Cook's able lieutenant, William Bligh, later of HMS *Bounty* fame. Bligh had the cloth made into stylish waistcoats.

Pennant's book is the jewel of an extensive collection of eighteenth-century Pacific documentary material at the Clements Library. The cloth samples, after two hundred years, are strikingly vivid. Some, as Pennant noted, are waterproof. This copy of Shaw's book was later owned by Sir Leicester Harmsworth, brother of Viscount Northcliffe, who founded the *Daily Mail* in 1896 and is considered the father of modern British journalism.

Purchased from Maggs, 1958.

⋙ 54 ⋘

COMMISSIONING A REGULAR ARMY

THE SUCCESSFUL CONCLUSION of the American Revolution left the United States with an embarrassing vestige of the struggle for independence—a standing military force in the form of the Continental Army. It was soon reduced to a mere skeleton of its former self, but just as "downsizing" was accomplished, a new military threat arose west of the Allegheny Mountains, where the native peoples of the Ohio valley continued their long resistance to the waves of settlers flooding their land.

As early as the spring of 1783, Congress had begun to study the feasibility of a peacetime army. The need to maintain troops to garrison western forts and to confront the Indians vied with a republican distaste for full-time soldiers and a fear that the rights of individual states and citizens might be infringed. British refusal to relinquish military posts on American territory along the Great Lakes exacerbated the frontier crisis. Congress finally and reluctantly took action. On June 3, 1784, it resolved to form a "First American Regiment" of 700 men for one-year's service. The last remnants of the old Continental Army had been officially disbanded just the day before.

The route to a federal army was indirect. In an attempt to keep expenses low, Congress decided that the states most concerned about unrest on the northwestern frontier—Pennsylvania, New York, New Jersey, and Connecticut—should provide the troops and officers. Congress "recommended" that these states raise the needed soldiers. Since Pennsylvania was responsible for the largest share of manpower, that state was given the privilege of appointing a "Lieutenant Colonel Commandant" of the new regiment, who would also become commander of the army. The state's Supreme Executive Council chose Josiah Harmar, a veteran of the wartime Pennsylvania Line who had served since the autumn of 1775 and had received a brevet colonelcy late in 1783. Harmar's commission, "in pursuance of the Resolution of Congress," was issued on August 12, 1784. The document came not from the Continental Congress but rather "In the Name and by the Authority of

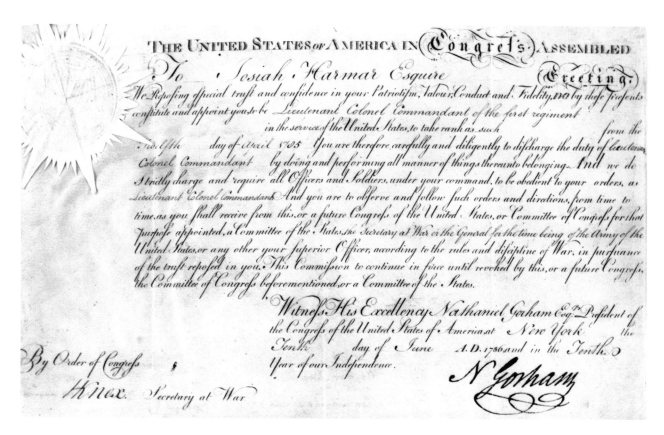

the Freemen of the Commonwealth of Pennsylvania." Harmar's troops were enlisted for one year, and his appointment was to "continue in force untill revoked by this or any succeeding Supreme executive Council."

Lieutenant Colonel Commandant Josiah Harmar's tiny army was organized on the lines of its Continental predecessor. Its year passed quickly, and in April 1785 Congress authorized new enlistments for a three-year period. Harmar's new commission, the first issued by Congress rather than Pennsylvania, was effective April 12, 1785, although not presented to him or signed until the following year. Presumably there was a delay in getting the document printed, and presentation had to await Harmar's return from western field duty. This commission, from a documentary standpoint, marks the birth of the modern United States Army.

Purchased from Josiah Harmar, 1936.

ᥫ 55 ᥫ

A NATION OF SQUARES

NOTHING IS MORE STRIKING to an air traveler in the United States, flying from the East coast westward, than the contrasting land patterns of the East and the Middle West. East of the Ohio River one is over areas of colonial settlement, where land grants represented the topography, the whims of the provincial surveyor, or the prerogatives of the proprietors. West of the Ohio, where fences, hedgerows, and roads create a checkerboard pattern, the observer has arrived over the areas largely granted and settled after the American Revolution.

The Continental Congress has earned a poor historical reputation over the years for being better at talking than doing anything to solve a problem. It did have a difficult time raising money and acting decisively, but in several ways, particularly centralizing authority over foreign affairs and taking charge of western lands, it made significant progress in moving the United States from thirteen separate governments to one. The colonial charters of Virginia, Massachusetts, Connecticut, New York, North and South Carolina, and Georgia all included claims, conflicting with each other, to land beyond the Allegheny Mountains. This had led to heated debate in Congress between the states claiming western territory and those which did not, and it was only the relinquishment of these claims by New York, Connecticut, and Virginia that made possible ratification of the Articles of Confederation in 1781. Massachusetts and North Carolina ceded their lands to Congress in 1784. South Carolina did not do so until 1787, and Georgia did not act until 1802.

The impetus for doing anything about western lands was initially financial. Sale of these vast tracts of wilderness was one of the few sources of income available to the central government, and the Revolution had left many bills to pay, among them promises of land grants to both state and Continental veterans, all of which Congress agreed to satisfy in taking control of this territory. The question was, should Congress sell land quickly to investors for income, or should it do so gradually, in small parcels, to persons who might actually become settlers? Should the land be surveyed before or after it had been sold?

The Land Ordinance of 1784, which never actually went into effect, was largely the work of Thomas Jefferson. Its lasting contribution was the establishment of the principles of prior surveys and rectangular tracts of land, with boundary lines running north and south, east and west. This plan was modified by Congressional committee, and on May 25, 1785, the Land Ordinance of 1785 was approved by Congress, establishing what became the basic system for surveying the West. The primary unit was the township, six miles square, containing 36 numbered "sections" of 640 acres each. Six lots in each township were reserved, one for education, one for religious purposes, and four to Congress for future disposal. The law attempted to provide a balance between investors and settlers, requiring that some sections in every township be sold as a whole, while others could be purchased in fractional divisions. The tracts were to be sold at auction at a minimum of one dollar per acre, payable either in specie or Revolutionary War debt certificates. Lands were surveyed only after Indian titles had been extinguished by federal treaty. The base survey line was essentially an extension of the Mason and Dixon survey separating Maryland and Pennsylvania, westward from the Ohio River, and the north and south line was to start at the same point, running from the Ohio River to Lake Erie.

From the very beginning, the land system became entangled in politics and was complicated by features of the natural terrain, slightly inaccurate surveys, and compass variations. But the essential surveying system remained intact throughout the nineteenth century, and it worked, providing a predictable but flexible framework for the country's expansion, and making farm ownership an attainable dream for average Americans and immigrants well into the present century. Beyond the Allegheny Mountains, from the air, most of the United States is a land of squares, and most midwestern Americans, spring and fall, have to drive to and from work with the sun directly in

SCALE *of forty chains to an inch*

Nº 36 640 Acres John Burnham	Nº 30 640 Acres John Burnham	Nº 24 640 Acres Nathᴸ Whitmore	Nº 18 640 Acres Nathᴸ Whitmore	Nº 12 640 Acres Benj.ⁿ Wadsworth	Nº 6 640 Acres Benjⁿ Wadsworth
Nº 35 640 Acres John Burnham of Lynnfield	Nº 29 640 Acres Ministry	Nº 23 640 Acres Jnᵒ Treadwell	Nº 17 640 Acres John Treadwell	Nº 11 640 Acres Congress	Nº 5 640 Acres Nathᴸ Browne
Nº 34 640 Acres Benjⁿ Wadsworth	Nº 35 262 Acres / Nº 34 262 Acres / Nº 29 262 Acres	Nº 23 262 Acres / Nº 17 262 Acres / Nº 18 262 Acres	Nº 16 640 Acres School	Nº 5 262 Acres / Nº 4 262 Acres / Nº 12 262 Acres	Nº 4 640 Acres Mathew Park Elijah Shoap
Nº 33 640 Acres Peter Oliver	Nº 33 262 Acres / Nº 28 262 Acres	Nº 20 262 Acres	Nº 36 262 Acres / Nº 6 262 Acres	Nº 3 262 Acres / Nº 2 262 Acres	Nº 3 640 Acres Willᵐ Pierce
Nº 32 640 Acres Joseph Willard	Nº 26 640 Acres Congress	Nº 25 262 Acres / Nº 19 262 Acres	Nº 31 262 Acres / Nº 1 262 Acres / Nº 7 262 Acres / Nº 13 262 Acres	Nº 8 640 Acres Congress	Nº 2 640 Acres Willᵐ Pierce
Nº 31 640 Acres John Safford	Nº 25 640 Acres Obadiah Parsons	Nº 19 640 Acres Wᵐ Cleveland	Nº 13 640 Acres John Burnham	Nº 7 640 Acres Massᵈ Cutler	Nº 1 640 Acres Massᵈ Cutler

N.B. The fractions or lots of 262 acres
bear the same numbers as the mile
squares or sections to which they
are annexed.
Each lot lies for the quantity of acres
marked, but in many instances does not
hold out measure.
In Ohio company's purchase. A copy.

+ First quality of upland & standing alone supposed land level.
‡ Middle or second quality of upland when alone supposed land level.
⟿ Streams of water & the figures in red ink their width in links.
↑ Ridge or long hill of gradual ascent.
• Bottom or interval land.
⟂ Hills short & steep.
Ɩ Hilly ridge broken poor land.

+ Stones & ledges of rocks.
⟿ Springs of water.
P Red paint.

Rufus Putnam

their eyes, unless they can use a road based on one of the old Indian trails pre-dating federal surveys.

The map shown here, delineating a township of present-day Meigs County, Ohio, was drawn in the 1780s by Rufus Putnam. The Library is rich in materials on the development of the nation's early land systems, including rare, official copies of the Land Ordinances of the 1780s and 1790s and correspondence of Thomas Hutchins and Rufus Putnam, the first surveyors who established the lines on which all land grants of the old Northwest Territory are based.

Purchased from Mary Benjamin, 1972.

⤜ 56 ⤛

FORTIFYING THE FRONTIER

JOSIAH HARMAR'S TINY ARMY of the 1780s pushed its way into the Ohio wilderness with an effective strategy in mind: establish fortified points of deposit and defense where supplies could be amassed and troops lodged in safety. Although the United States Army experienced several setbacks in its long struggle with the Indians of the Old Northwest, this strategy remained consistent until the 1830s, when the danger of Indian warfare was essentially eliminated by forced native migration to the West. Soldiers of this era spent much of their time erecting forts.

The northwestern forts varied greatly in form according to the site, the needs of their garrisons, and the capabilities of the officers who constructed them. All were situated at locations calculated to control important routes of travel and communication or to overawe the native residents. All made use of timber and earth, the building materials available to an army in a forested and undeveloped environment: stockades, horizontal log walls, and wooden blockhouses were the most common features of this military architecture. Particularly well documented in the Clements Library collections is Fort Franklin, established at Venango, Pennsylvania, in 1787. The post was intended to project the power of the United States among the Indians of the upper Allegheny, but it also put American authority one step closer to the Great Lakes, an area still contested with Britain. Fort Franklin reoccupied a familiar site near the mouth of French Creek where French and British posts of earlier conflicts had guarded the way from Pittsburgh to the lakes.

Chosen to establish this new post was Captain Jonathan Heart, one of the more experienced officers of Harmar's command. Like Harmar, Heart had fought through the entire Revolution. He was retained among the Connecticut contingent when the army was reconstituted in 1784. Captain Heart was also a talented draftsman, cartographer, and topographical artist. These were desirable skills developed by many eighteenth-century military men and represented by numerous drawings and plans in the Clements Library collections. Six of Heart's drawings and maps are among the Library's Harmar Papers, and further examples of his finely executed and highly de-

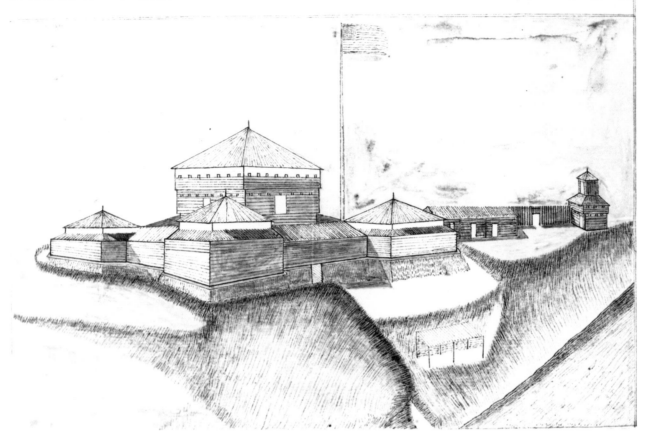

tailed work may be found in other institutions. Unfortunately, Heart would meet his death at St. Clair's defeat on November 4, 1791.

"An East View of Fort [Franklin] on French Creek" provides an excellent example of how officers in the field apprised their superiors of their progress in following orders. Heart received his instructions to establish the French Creek post early in April 1787. He arrived to select a site at Venango on May 11, and by June 1 he could report a defensible blockhouse and wall. Three weeks later, on June 25, Captain Heart sent Colonel Harmar the delicately colored sketch illustrated here. The works were not yet finished, and Heart felt it necessary to add that he "had taken the Liberty to represent them not according to their present appearance, but as I presume they will appear when compleated." Construction was far enough advanced for the captain to add that "Should its appearance recommend it Sufficiently to deserve a Name, I could wish the Colo[nel] will please inform me what it is to be calld." This request was emphasized by a conspicuous blank space in the title block. Harmar responded with approval in December and added: "You wish a name for your fortress—as it is in the State of Pennsylvania, let it be named <u>Fort Franklin</u>."

Purchased from Josiah Harmar, 1936.

"GOVERNMENT . . . MUST EITHER FALL
INTO ANARCHY OR BE SUPPORTED WITH VIGOR"

THEODORICK BLAND (1742–1790) was the classic Virginia aristocrat. On the basis of family and education, he might have been expected to have sided with the British in the Revolution, but in fact he became an ardent patriot. Descended from wealthy seventeenth-century London merchants, early residents of Jamestown, and even a descendant of Pocahontas through the Randolph line, Bland was sent to school in England. He graduated in medicine from the University of Edinburgh in 1763. Returning to Virginia after more than ten years' absence, he practiced medicine until 1771, then became a planter. He was one of a daring group of colonists who removed the armaments from the Governor's Palace in Williamsburg in June 1775. Appointed captain of the First Virginia Cavalry and colonel of the 1st Continental Dragoons, he served at Brandywine, Germantown, and Valley Forge and, in 1778, was put in charge of Convention prisoners (British and Hessian troops captured at Saratoga) who were marched to Charlottesville.

Bland retired from military service in 1779 and was elected by the Virginia legislature to serve in the Continental Congress from 1780 to 1783. He was a member of the Virginia House of Delegates from 1786 through 1788 and was a leading member of the Virginia Ratification Convention of 1788, joining Patrick Henry in opposing the new Federal Constitution. In spite of this opposition, he was elected to the House of Representatives in the first Congress and served until his death on June 1, 1790.

The letter illustrated here was written to Patrick Henry on March 9, 1790, as Congress was considering and putting into effect Alexander Hamilton's bold financial program. On the very day the letter was written, a Committee of the Whole Congress had "come to a resolution to assume the state debts which are also to be funded, the states to have Credit for such part of their debt as they have paid in interest or Extinguished by their own Exertions." It is a long and thoughtful letter and must have been difficult to write, because Bland was throwing his whole support behind the Federalist program. What would his dear friend and ally in opposing centralized government in the ratification convention think of his seemingly contradictory actions? Bland's thinking, which he explains in detail, is fascinating:

"The transactions of Congress from the first days of its commencing its operations to this hour has confirmed me in the opinion which I entertained on the day of its adoption by our state, viz. that the power in whom was vested the sword and the Purse and a paramount Authority could have no competitor—from that moment I have bounded my loyns to the single object of securing (in timorem) the great and essential rights of freemen from the incroachments of Power . . . . This is the Polar Star of my Politics. The sacrifice of state rights has in my opinion been offered up and has already Bled its vital drops—let those who led it to the altar bring thither their repentence as an atonement . . . . Having sworn to support the Constitution I feel myself committed on all occasions to try how far its Energy may be made usefull for the preservation of peace and Harmony—to this point are all my secondary views directed. Clashing powers and interfearing Juris-

Dr Sr   New York March 9th 1790.

The friendly wish with which your obliging
favor of the 8th Ultimo was concluded, for my health was
but Just realized after a severe fit of the Gout when
your friendly and agreeable letter reached me — Scarce
had I begun my career of Politics in the great Sa-
-lædin when that fell Monster Siesed my hands and
feet, Knees and Elbows — where he wreaked his vengeance
for near a fortnight — but I thank God has spared my
head, and left it in a Better state than it has been
for ten months Past, being now free of Vertigo — And I
once more enjoy the pleasing hope of a good state of health
with only Semi annual returns of that painfull Crisis
of other disorders —

The transactions of Congress from the first
days of its commencing its operations to this hour
has confirmed me in the opinion which I entertained
on the day of its adoption by our State — viz that the
power in whom was vested the Sword and the Purse
and a paramount Authority could have no competi-
-tor — from that moment I have bounded my hopes
to the single object of securing (in terrorem) the great
and essential rights of freemen — from the encroachments
of Power — so far as to Authorise resistance when they ch'd
be either openly attacked or insidiously undermined —

This is the Polar Star of my Politics. The Sacrifice
of State rights has in my opinion been offered up and
has already Bled its vital drops — let those who led it to
the Altar bring thither their repentance as an atonement —

I find they are beginning to be astonished at their
own works and every step which the federal Govern-
-ment takes shakes that resolution which they so fully
possessed at the adoption and they like the Stormy ocean
when it returns to a Calm, wonder at the ruin they
have made — Having sworn to support the Constitu-

dictions appear to me the weaker side of our present incongruous machine—well am I aware that from strong Collisions sparks are generated which will inevitably light up a flame unquenchable—but (perhaps) with Blood. You will not then be surprised to find me on every occasion (except where the great rights of man are concerned) on the Side of Energy—and *Consolidation*—for I never was a Milk and water Politician, and government with all its *Essential* powers once assumed for so extended a dominion I am firmly convinced must either fall into Anarchy or be supported with Vigor. The first is an unbridled monster, and the second may peradventure be restrained—of the two evils then let us choose the last. Thus have I explained to you my dear Sr. the Principles by which my Political Conduct is activated. Happy shall I be if they meet your approbation—for next to that of my own Conscience the approbation of the good man and the Virtuous patriot is the first wish of my heart."

Bland need not have worried about Henry's reactions. Essentially following the same logic, once the Bill of Rights had been added as the first ten amendments to the Constitution, Patrick Henry also became a proponent of a strong central government. This letter in many ways demonstrates, better than the document itself, the causes and the results which made the Constitution such a brilliant vehicle for governing a nation of immense territory and highly diverse constituents. The generation of our Founding Fathers, not merely those who framed the Constitution but even those who opposed it, had the wisdom and ability to put the country's interests above selfish and petty politics. They knew that the Constitution was flawed from the first and did not expect too much of it. Bland had been quite passionate in the ratification convention of 1788, but a mere two years later, he came to appreciate what wise American politicians have come to understand ever since—that the U.S. Constitution itself was the product of the very same sort of political compromise that alone would make the system operate.

Purchased from MacManus, 1991. Gift of Clements Library Associates in honor of
Duane Norman Diedrich, Chairman.

☙ 58 ☙

YELLOW FEVER AND BLACK JUSTICE

IT BEGAN NEAR THE WHARVES in June, and by August it had spread throughout the city, sowing discord and reaping bodies. In 1793, yellow fever made its first appearance in Philadelphia in a generation, striking a population with little immunity and setting off a chain reaction of accusations over responsibility for its origin, its treatment, and the behavior of the citizens during the crisis. Ten to fifteen percent of the city's 45,000 residents died.

Surprisingly, the French colony of Saint Domingue (present-day Haiti) was at the heart of the swirling controversies. With Toussaint L'Ouverture's revolution in full swing, Philadelphia was inundated with refugees fleeing the violence. Philadelphia Federalists knew three things: Santo Domingo was host to the most radical ideas of the French Revolution; the island was regularly visited by yellow fever; the fever appeared in Philadelphia not long after the refugees. Clearly the plague was a foreign import, and to some Federalists it seemed almost to have political implications. Democratic Republicans, on the other hand, tended to be more favorable to the French and Haitian Revolutions, and they were more inclined to believe the fever originated locally, a product of poor sanitation and the "miasmas," or evening mists which arose from undrained marshes along the Delaware and Schuylkill Rivers.

In part because the Haitian revolution was led by "African" slaves, and in part because of the uneasy race relations in the United States, Philadelphia's Black community was caught in the middle. As the yellow fever epidemic became widespread in the summer of 1793, many citizens abandoned the city, creating a severe labor shortage and leaving behind very few people who were willing to aid the sick or inter the dead. Most of the poor, which included the preponderance of Black citizens, lacked the means to escape. At least some African Americans also had the advantage of an inherited or built-up immunity to yellow fever, and therefore Black men and women were in great demand to nurse the sick, bury the dead, and perform all sorts of jobs normally accomplished by white laborers.

Two men in particular, Richard Allen and Absalom Jones, figured largely in this story. Both were born into slavery, had taught themselves to read and write, purchased their freedom, and had risen to the highest levels of Black society in Philadelphia. Allen would become the founder of the African Methodist Episcopal Church and Jones, the African Protestant Episcopal Church. The two men helped to start the African Society in 1787, a benevolent organization that lent assistance to impoverished members of Philadelphia's large African-American community—numbering about 2,500 at the time of the epidemic.

Within a month of the onset of the fever, Allen and Jones mobilized the African Society to aid the afflicted of all races, visiting the sick, supplying nurses when possible, gathering and burying the dead, and caring for the survivors. In the face of the desertion of the city by much of its white leadership, the African Society became the most active and most effective relief organization during the epidemic. In September, Mayor Matthew Clarkson even announced that those wishing to help in the crisis should apply to Allen and Jones. With such an extraordinary record, one might assume that Philadelphia's African Americans would receive thanks and appreciation. But among others, Mathew Carey, the brilliant but irrascible Irish-born printer, vociferously accused the

African Society of profiteering from the epidemic by charging exorbitant prices for their work. In fact, most members of the Society accepted only what was offered by families, and the African Society was driven deeply into debt during the crisis, registering a deficit at the end of the year of over £177.

Allen and Jones responded boldly and in print to Carey's charges. In *Narrative of the Proceedings of the Black People . . . .* (Philadelphia, 1793) they meticulously documented their experiences during the epidemic and the actions of whites they had seen "in a manner that would make humanity shudder." They recorded incidents of theft from the dying and dead and shameful profiteering. Allen and Jones were equally careful to document the numerous incidents in which African Americans had acted with "more humanity, more sensibility" than whites and when they had worked for little or no compensation.

The *Narrative* remains not only one of the most important first-hand accounts of the great epidemic of 1793, describing both heroism and deep venality, but also provides a rare glimpse of the eighteenth-century African-American urban community.

Purchased from Charles F. Heartman, 1957.

☙ 59 ☙

THE GREAT SCIENTIST IN PASTEL

TODAY, VISITORS TO INDEPENDENCE HALL in Philadelphia can see an unusual group of small, life portraits of Washington, Jefferson, Hamilton, Burr, Monroe, and many other Founding Fathers and their contemporaries. One is immediately struck by the rich colors and simple truthfulness of these likenesses. Unlike so many oil paintings, which because of their size, composition, and formality, distract from the subject, these provide the viewer a sense of seeing the true appearance of the persons being portrayed. It is this quality of accuracy that gives the pastel portraits created by James and Ellen Sharples so valuable a place in the history of American portraiture.

As a medium, pastel is relatively fast and flexible, allowing the artist to express an intimacy not possible in oil, or the engravings made from paintings which provide the majority of eighteenth-century portraits. Ellen and James Sharples performed a great service to our country by capturing not only the faces and personalities of the new republic's great leaders, but also those of many lesser-known men and women, people who lacked the money for, or had no interest themselves in commissioning a formal portrait. James Sharples was a well-established professional artist living in Bath, England, when he and his wife, a talented amateur painter, undertook their sojourn in the United States. The public on both sides of the Atlantic was hungry for pictures of leading Americans.

In 1793, the family sailed from Portsmouth with their three young children. They made Philadelphia their base for most of the seven years they spent in the United States, but from the outset they were also traveling artists. James, an amateur inventor and relentless creator of useless contraptions, constructed a carriage large enough to accommodate his wife, three children, and his drawing materials. Among his equipment, Sharples carried a "physionotrace," a mechanical instrument used to take head measurements for all his profile portraits. James Sharples did not lack for sitters, but the artist's fortunes were rather precarious until his wife Ellen, an extraordinarily resourceful woman, took matters into her own hands. As she wrote in her diary, the family's delicate financial situation and her husband's tendency to forgo the profits of portrait-making for the "uncertainties of his mechanical pursuits" convinced her "to make my drawing which had been learnt and practiced as an ornamental art for amusement, available to a useful purpose." To supplement their income, she began making copies of her husband's work. "These I undertook and was so far successful as to have as many commissions as I could execute; they were thought equal to the originals, price the same; we lived in good style associating in the first society."

The Library has only one Sharples portrait, that of Joseph Priestley, but it is a fine example of a particularly notable individual. Priestley is best remembered as the man who "discovered" oxygen and identified the chemical nature of combustion, but he was a man of many talents and, in his day, considerable notoriety. Lord Shelburne, many of whose papers are in the Clements Library, was Priestley's patron and employer at the time he made his most notable contributions to science. He was an ardent Unitarian and a firm supporter of constitutional government. He was vocally sympathetic to the French Revolution in its early stages, and his home in Birmingham was attacked and his laboratory burned during anti-French riots in that city in 1791. Threatened with government prosecution as the war with the French Republic took on serious proportions, Priestley fled to Philadelphia in 1794, where he was "captured" in pastel by the Sharpleses as a man of middle age. Priestley was welcomed in America as a noted scientist and intellectual, but distrusted because of his religious views. He spent the last years of his life in relatively happy seclusion at his country home in Northumberland, Pennsylvania, and is honored today as one of America's notable early scientists.

Purchased from Clive Farahar, 1995. Gift of Clements Library Associates in memory of William C. Finkenstaedt, Board member and grandson of W. L. Clements.

☙ 60 ❧

THE FIRST AMERICAN COOKBOOK

GREAT BOOKS, particularly great early American books, are often unassuming in appearance. Amelia Simmons' *American Cookery* (Hartford, 1796) is a very modest, typical pamphlet of its day, but its importance can hardly be overemphasized. It is, in fact, the first American cookbook.

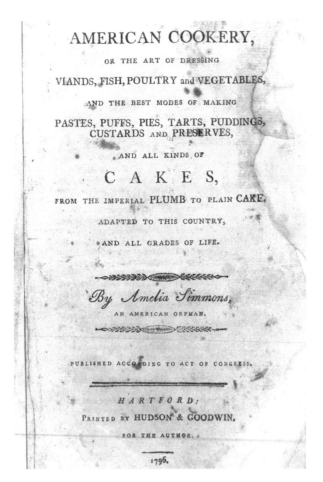

AMERICAN COOKERY,

OR THE ART OF DRESSING

VIANDS, FISH, POULTRY and VEGETABLES,

AND THE BEST MODES OF MAKING

PASTES, PUFFS, PIES, TARTS, PUDDINGS,
CUSTARDS AND PRESERVES,

AND ALL KINDS OF

C A K E S,

FROM THE IMPERIAL PLUMB TO PLAIN CAKE,

ADAPTED TO THIS COUNTRY,

AND ALL GRADES OF LIFE.

By Amelia Simmons,

AN AMERICAN ORPHAN.

PUBLISHED ACCORDING TO ACT OF CONGRESS.

H A R T F O R D:

PRINTED BY HUDSON & GOODWIN,

FOR THE AUTHOR.

1796.

Jan Longone of Ann Arbor is an authority on the history of American cookery and cookbooks (her husband Dan Longone shares the same honors with regard to American wine), and in *American Cookbooks and Wine Books, 1797–1950* (Ann Arbor, 1984), the historical catalogue accompanying a Clements Library exhibit, she explained that "the originality of her [Simmons'] work lies in its recognition and use of truly American products. There are five recipes using corn meal (corn is indigenous to America): three for Indian Pudding, one for Johnny or Hoe Cake and one for Indian Slapjacks. This is the first known appearance for any of these recipes in any printed cookbook. Other American innovations were the use of corncobs in the smoking of bacon, the suggestion of cranberry sauce as an accompaniment to roast turkey (both cranberries and turkey are also indigenous to the New World), and the use of watermelon rind to make American citron. Perhaps the most far-reaching innovation was the introduction of Pearlash, a well-known staple in the colonial American household, as a chemical leavening in doughs. This practice resulted in the compounding of modern baking powders."

Purchased from Scribner Book Store, 1956.

ᑌᑊ 61 ᑊᑌ

THE DEATH OF WASHINGTON

TOBIAS LEAR WAS DEVOTED to George Washington. Lear had been Washington's constant companion since 1785, his private secretary during the Presidency, and an intimate member of the Mount Vernon household during the remaining years of Washington's life. Just before his inauguration, when Washington was looking for a suitable young gentleman to serve as his private secretary, General Benjamin Lincoln had recommended Lear. The New Hampshire native had graduated from Harvard with distinction, continued his studies in Europe, and traveled extensively. His father, a prosperous Portsmouth shipmaster, was well known to Washington for his service during the Revolutionary War.

Tobias Lear was a most fortunate choice. Intelligent, sensitive, and discreet, he was a natural diplomat. He had a wide range of social connections with Federalists and Republicans alike, and Washington soon came to depend on his political instincts. As private secretary, it was Lear's task his eyes streaking gratitude; but unable to utter a word without great distress. — About ten o'clock he made several attempts to speak to me before he could effect it — at length, he said, "I am just going, Have me "decently buried, and do not let my body be put into the Vault "~~till~~ in less than two days after I am dead". — I bowed assent. — He looked at me again, and said "Do you understand me" — I replied Yes Sir, "Tis well" said he. — About ten minutes before he expired his breathing became much easier — he lay quietly — he withdrew his hand from mine & felt his own pulse — I spoke to Dr Craik who sat by the fire — he came to the bed side. — The General's hand fell from his wrist — I took it in mine and laid it upon my breast — Dr Craik put his hands over his eyes and he expired without a struggle or a sigh! ——— While we were fixed in silent grief — Mrs Washington asked, with a firm & collected Voice, "Is he gone', — I could not speak, but held up my hand as a signal that he was. — "Tis well" said She, "Tis all now over. — I have no more trials to pass through. I shall soon follow him! ———

to keep the "Books of the President of the United States," in which every item of expense was entered. Eventually Washington entrusted to him the management of his private estates as well. Above all, Lear was totally loyal, and Washington gradually came to regard him as a surrogate son. Lear held a similar regard for the President. Of Washington, Lear noted that "I have never found a single thing that could lessen my respect for him. A complete knowledge of his honesty, uprightness and candor in all his private transactions, has sometimes led me to think him more than a man."

Lear left Washington's employment to go into private business in 1793, following the death of his young wife, but in 1798 a threat of imminent war with France developed as a result of high-handed treatment of American ships and diplomatic insults. President Adams appointed Washington commander of a provisional army to deal with the crisis, and Washington asked Lear to return to Mt. Vernon as a lieutenant colonel and his military secretary.

As was their daily habit while at Mt. Vernon, on December 12, 1799, Lear and Washington had ridden out together to inspect work on the farms. A heavy snowstorm started shortly after they left, but upon their return Washington claimed his greatcoat had protected him from the weather. That evening he appeared well. The next day Washington noted, in what would be his last journal entry, that the snow had continued. What is known about the events that followed comes from a letter by Tobias Lear in the Clements Library which he headed "A Circumstantial account of the last illness and death of General Washington noted by T. Lear, on Sunday following his death, which happened on Saturday Evening, December 14, 1799 between the hours of ten and eleven."

During the early evening of December 13, as Washington sat with his wife and Lear after dinner, reading aloud from newspapers, he admitted to having a sore throat. Lear's suggestion that he take some medicine was met with the retort, "You know I never take anything for a cold. Let it go as it came." By three o'clock in the morning Washington awoke, feeling "extremely unwell." He could scarcely speak or breathe. Dr. Craik was summoned, but before he arrived Washington asked that an overseer who treated sick slaves be brought in to begin bleeding him. Both Lear and Martha tried to intervene, but Washington insisted. Half a pint was taken. Dr. Craik, his lifelong friend, arrived, and the doctor took more blood from Washington's arm. Two more physicians were called. In the meantime Washington was bled a third time.

The doctors then consulted. Doctors Craik and Brown thought he had quinsey (tonsillitis), but Dr. Dick, the youngest of the three, insisted that Washington was suffering from "a violent inflammation of the membranes of the throat, which it had almost closed, and which, if not immediately arrested, would result in death." He urged an operation that would open the trachea below the infection and allow Washington to breathe. Craik and Brown disagreed. At least, Dick urged, do not bleed him again: "He needs all his strength, bleeding will diminish it." Dr. Dick was overruled, and Washington was bled a fourth time.

In late afternoon, when Washington was able to swallow a little, he was given various purges. Medical historians are certain that Washington died from a combination of hemorrhage and dehydration. Through repeated bleeding, the general lost about three liters of blood, a lethal amount that resulted in hypovolemic shock. Simply put, he did not have enough blood circulating in his body to sustain life, and the purges had depleted his body fluids. In hindsight, the treatment as much as the disease killed the patient, but given the state of eighteenth-century medicine, Dr. Craik was justified in saying "we were governed by the best light we had; we thought we were right."

As the hours wore on, Lear sitting by the bedside holding his hand, Washington said, "I find I am going. My breath cannot continue long. I believed from the first attack it would be fatal." Lear described the final moments: "About ten o'clock, he made several attempts to speak to me before he could effect it. At length he said, 'I am just going. Have me decently buried, and do not let my body be put into the vault in less than two days after I am dead.' I bowed assent. He looked at me again, and said, 'Do you understand me[?],' I replied Yes Sir. 'Tis Well,' said he. About ten minutes before he expired his breathing became much easier. He lay quietly. He withdrew his hand from mine and felt his own pulse. I spoke to Dr. Craik who sat by the fire. He came to the bedside. The General's hand fell from his wrist. I took it in mine and laid it upon my breast. Dr. Craik put his hand over his eyes and he expired without a struggle or a Sigh!"

Purchased from William F. Havemeyer by Joseph Sabin, 1921. Gift of W. L. Clements, 1923.

NELSON AND EMMA: THE SECRET LETTERS

THE CLEMENTS LIBRARY has several dozen letters written by Horatio Nelson, England's greatest naval hero. There are early documents of his career in American waters, one collection covering the Battle of Copenhagen, and another extensive group of letters from H.M.S. *Victory*. There are also two secret letters, written to Lady Hamilton as "Mrs. Thompson," before and after the birth of their daughter, Horatia.

When the Hamiltons arrived in London from Naples in November 1800 they were soon settled into a house at 23 Piccadilly. On January 1, 1801, Nelson was appointed second in command of the channel fleet with the rank of vice admiral. He was necessarily separated from Emma. Apprehensive about sending letters to the house where she lived with her husband, Sir William Hamilton, he devised a simple fiction. He would write to her about one of his sailors named Thompson, whose lover was being befriended by Lady Hamilton. This clandestine route of correspondence was supposedly necessary since marriage to Thompson was being opposed by an uncle. Nelson, who at moments dreamed of bliss with Emma in a Norfolk cottage, had many good reasons for wanting to correspond freely with her, one of which was jealousy. He had learned that the lustful Prince of Wales had met Emma at a London dinner party and that she had "hit his fancy."

One of the Thompson letters in the Clements Library is signed by Nelson, but the one printed here is not. The letter is undated also, but the year is 1801. It is addressed "to the Care of Lady Hamilton," and says:

My Dear Mrs. T. Poor Thompson seems to have forgot all his ill health and all his mortifications and sorrows in the thoughts that he will soon bury them all in your dear dear bosom. He seems almost beside himself. I hope you have always mind'd what Lady H[amilto]n

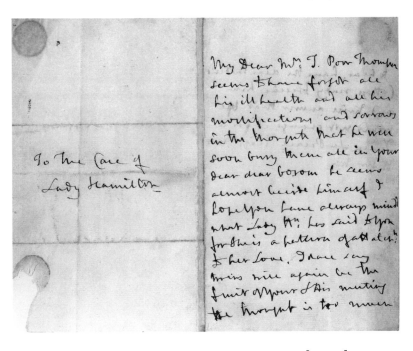
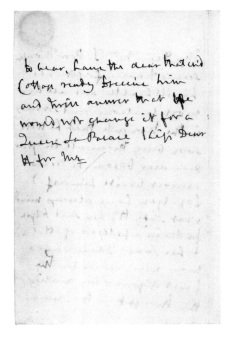

has said to you for she is a pattern of attatch[men]t to her Love. I dare say twins will again be the fruit of Your & His meeting. The thought is too much to bear, have the dear thatch'd Cottage ready to receive him and I will answer that He would not change it for a Queen & a Palace. Kiss Dear H. for Me.

Horatia was born on January 28 or 29, 1801, and was boarded with a nurse, Mrs. Gibson, in Little Titchfield Street, London. Nelson was given three days leave soon after her birth, and Emma took him there to see their daughter. The girl would be christened Horatia Nelson Thompson on May 13, 1803, a month after the death of Sir William Hamilton and but two years and five months before Nelson's heroic demise at the Battle of Trafalgar.

Gift of Hubert H. Smith family, Bay City, Michigan, 1953.

⤫ 63 ⤪

DRAWING THE GREAT LAKES FRONTIER

MANY OF OUR BEST GLIMPSES of early frontier topography, architecture, and everyday life come from the pens and brushes of army officers who served in the forts dotting the margins of the Great Lakes and the hinterlands of Canada and the United States. While military engineers were more likely to concern themselves with straightforward renderings of fortifications and topography, other officers, many of whom also had received some formal training in drawing as part of their military education, undertook sketches as a gentlemanly pursuit or for the elucidation of friends at home. Some, like Surgeon Edward Walsh, intended to publish their drawings and observations.

Edward Walsh (1756–1832) was an Irishman who did not begin his military career until he was more than forty years of age. He obtained a medical education at Edinburgh, where he published a few sketches before graduating in 1791. Walsh began his professional practice aboard a West India packet, but in May 1797 he obtained an appointment as assistant surgeon of the 29th Regiment of Foot. Walsh had extensive service in Ireland during the '98 Rebellion and saw further action after he became surgeon of the 49th Regiment in August 1800. The doctor was wounded in the hand while his regiment served as marines aboard British vessels at the Battle of Copenhagen. Fortunately, the injury was not such as to permanently impair his artistic or medical abilities.

The Clements Library's ten watercolor views and six nature studies by Walsh were produced after the 49th arrived in Canada in 1802. The regiment's garrison duties centered at Fort George (Niagara-on-the-Lake, Ontario), where it was stationed from 1803. The commander of the post, Lieutenant Colonel Isaac Brock, would later gain fame and meet an early death in 1812 at nearby Queenston Heights. Walsh left Canada in 1806 when he transferred to the 62nd Regiment of Foot. He later served with the 6th Dragoon Guards in the Peninsular campaigns and as a Medical Department physician at Waterloo before retiring on half-pay in 1816 or 1817 at the age of sixty.

The Fort of Old Niagara, taken from Navy Hall, with the Embouchure of the Strait into Lake Ontario

Although Edward Walsh's watercolors bear dates from 1803 to 1806, his most productive year was 1804. That spring he began working on his nature studies, followed by views of Fort Niagara and Fort George, and Mohawk Chief Joseph Brant's home on Lake Ontario. Walsh then embarked on a journey up the lakes to Sault Ste. Marie, which he reached by August 20. On the way he depicted Fort Chippewa, Fort Erie, and Fort St. Joseph as well as the rapids at Sault Ste. Marie and Detroit from across the river. Inevitably, Walsh painted Niagara Falls, but he is not known to have done sketches of British Fort Malden at Amherstburg or American-held Fort Mackinac. Four of Walsh's drawings were later engraved in London, suggesting that he may have intended to publish a more extensive series of American views.

"The Fort of Old Niagara," dated April 26, 1804, and illustrated here, is one of Walsh's most attractive compositions. It allows us to gaze across the broad sweep of the lower Niagara River to Lake Ontario and the post — Fort Niagara — given up to the United States in 1796 when Walsh's own Fort George was built. A strong northwest breeze spreads huge garrison colors over the American fort. In the foreground, local Indians and British sailors lounge near the Navy Hall wharf where a schooner of the Provincial Marine is moored, held against the powerful current by hawsers tied to bollards made of condemned cannon. The artist reveals a little of himself as well. As in several of his drawings, he included himself in the composition, and can be seen on the wharf, leaning comfortably on his walking stick.

Purchased from John Wise, 1939. Gift of Detroit Friends of the Clements Library.

FINE FURNITURE AT FIXED PRICES

Not all books are published to provide information for the general public. In fact, there are certain types of publications that are intended specifically to keep secrets among a select constituency. The Masons and other secret societies published guides to rituals that were to be hidden from nonmembers. Inventors, apothecaries, and even cooks occasionally issued broadsides, receipts, pamphlets, and books of extremely high price, attempting to restrict circulation to those willing to pay. Nineteenth-century financial institutions occasionally published "subscription only" mug books of suspected criminals or credit-rating books to help banks and investors avoid doing business with deadbeats and charlatans.

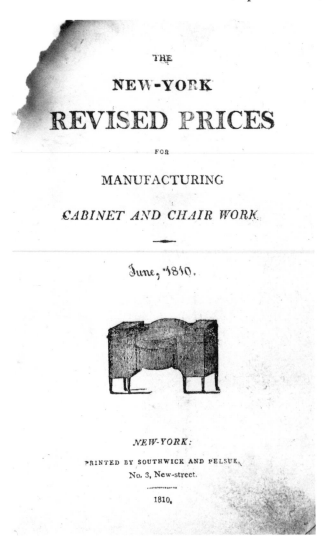

The New-York Revised Prices for Manufacturing Cabinet and Chair Work (New York, 1810) was issued by the New-York Society of Cabinet Makers and intended for the eyes of members only. This may be the only copy of this particular guide to survive, although similar price books, all of them scarce, were issued in Philadelphia, New York, and Baltimore in the late eighteenth and early nineteenth centuries. The purpose for restricting circulation of this book was to limit the number of individuals having the skills necessary to produce the finest cabinetwork, control the quality and dignity of the trade, and maintain prices. In joining the society and subscribing to this publication, members were agreeing not to undercut each other's prices. What text there is in this volume is of a highly technical nature, presumably informative to the skilled craftsman but unintelligible to the layman.

Neither the art of printing nor the American tradition of free circulation of information have been particularly kind to any organization that has attempted to keep secrets. The skilled craftsmen who belonged to the New-York Society of Cabinet Makers would be largely displaced by machinery as the century wore on, but their book provides rare insights into not only the techniques of furniture making, but also early efforts to organize skilled labor and "fix" prices.

Gift of Seymour K. Padnos, Holland, Michigan, in honor of Stuart Padnos, 1992.

QUESTING QUAKER AND THE BOUNTY MUTINEERS

IN THE FALL OF 1813, Captain Mayhew Folger, his wife, Mary, and a growing family of children packed their belongings and left beloved Nantucket for Philadelphia and then Ohio. It was a dramatic break from a lifestyle intimately tied to the sea, which Folgers had pursued for generations, but it could not be helped. The War of 1812 and an accompanying blockade of American ports by the British Navy had put an end to the lucrative whaling, sealing, and trading voyages that were the primary source of income on the island. Captain Folger was more fortunate than many. Although his last voyage had involved exceptional hardship, it proved in the end to be profitable and provided enough capital for him to make a new start elsewhere. Relatives had moved to the Philadelphia area a few years earlier and made it easy for them to settle there temporarily, until the war with Britain ended and frontier settlement was again possible.

We have no record of how Mayhew Folger and Samuel Coates got to know each other during the Folgers' brief stay in Philadelphia, but there are a variety of possibilities. Coates, a substantial merchant whose investments over several decades had involved coastal and international trading ventures, may have known Folger as a ship's captain. They were both Quakers and may have attended the same meetings. Folger, like Coates, was a man of intellectual interests, and the former undoubtedly wandered into the Library Company of Philadelphia, of which Coates was an officer, to examine its cabinet of curiosities or look at the latest books on Pacific travels.

However it happened, Folger was invited to Samuel Coates' comfortable home at Second and Chesnut Streets and told a story of personal adventure in 1808 that only he could tell. Captain Mayhew Folger, while on a sealing voyage in the Pacific, had found Pitcairn Island and solved the nineteen-year mystery of the whereabouts of the last of the mutineers of H.M.S. *Bounty*. Coates dutifully recorded his every word, and the six-page letter, which he later mailed to his sister-in-law, is the longest and most detailed record of a remarkable American discovery. Captain Folger carefully described the events of February 7, 1808, when a canoe set off from shore and hailed Folger's ship, the *Topaz*. Folger spent several hours on shore, visiting with Alec Smith, alias John Adams, the last living mutineer, and his colony of Polynesians and half-English, half-Polynesian children and grandchildren. They exchanged small gifts and established the first contacts with the outside world that the settlement had had since its founding in 1790. A native of Nantucket, a mariner, and a Quaker, Folger could relate to and empathize with the Pitcairn colony as could have few other men. Folger can now be seen, in a very real sense, as the prime creator of the *Bounty* myth — the transformation of an armed insurrection into something of an idyll — since it was his sensitivity and concern for the only surviving mutineer and his "family" on Pitcairn Island that set the tone of universal reaction to his discovery, nineteen years after the mutiny itself.

Walter Hayes, of the Clements Library's Board, used the Folger letter and other previously undiscovered documents in British and American archives to write *The Captain from Nantucket and the Mutiny on the Bounty*, published by the Clements Library in 1996.

Gift of Marian S. Carson, Philadelphia, 1988.

⋙ 66 ⋘

THE DISASTROUS INVASION OF CANADA

BRIGADIER GENERAL WILLIAM HULL's *Proclamation* of July 12, 1812, opened the first military campaign of the War of 1812. Tensions had been extremely high on the frontiers of Ohio and Indiana for more than a year, since the governor of Indiana Territory, William Henry Harrison, had defeated the Indians at the Battle of Tippecanoe. Proof of British support of a native uprising by Tecumseh and his brother, the Prophet, had supposedly been found on the Tippecanoe battlefield, and there had been a series of isolated raids on settlers' cabins and incidents of killings and scalpings. An army had been raised in Ohio to defend Detroit. William Hull, first Governor of Michigan Territory and a noted veteran of the American Revolution, was placed in command. The "War Hawks" in Congress, younger members from western constituencies, were calling for a declaration of war and an invasion of British Canada as the only sure method of bringing permanent peace to the American frontier.

Hull's army arrived in Detroit on July 5, 1812, and crossed into Canada on the 12th. Had he attacked the weak British garrison at Fort Malden quickly, he could have won a decisive victory. Instead, he decided to wait for Canadians to join his army, giving the British an opportunity to steal the initiative. The British garrison at St. Joseph Island had simultaneously sent a small party to attack Fort Mackinac, and the post was taken easily on July 17, resulting in a terrifying rumor that several thousand Indians were now marching on Detroit. Colonel Henry Proctor and regular British reinforcements rushed from Niagara and established full control of river communications. A force of British troops and Indians were sent across the river below Detroit, and after several minor engagements, they captured Hull's letters to the War Department and cut the fragile overland line of communication and supply from Ohio.

Without even making an attempt to fight, fearing an Indian attack on the civilian population, Hull ordered his troops back to Detroit and surrendered to General Isaac Brock, who had just ar-

By WILLIAM HULL, *Brigadier General and Commander of the North Western Army of the United States.*

A PROCLAMATION.

INHABITANTS OF CANADA! After thirty years of PEACE & prosperity, the UNITED STATES have been driven to Arms. The injuries & aggreffions, the infults & indignities of Great Britain have *once more* left them no alternative but manly refiftance, or unconditional fubmiffion. The ARMY under my command, has invaded your country, & the Standard of the UNION now waves over the Territory of CANADA. To the peaceable unoffending inhabitant, it brings neither danger nor difficulty. I come to *find* enemies, not to *make* them. I come to *protect*, not to *injure* you.

Separated by an immenfe Ocean, & an extenfive Wildernefs from Great Britain, you have no participation in her Counfels, no intereft in her conduct. You have felt her Tyrany, you have feen her injuftice, but I do not afk *you* to avenge the one or to redrefs the other. The UNITED STATES are fufficiently powerful to afford you every fecurity, confiftent with their rights, & your expectations. I tender you the invaluable bleffings of Civil Political & Religious Liberty, & their neceffary refult individual and general profperity; That Liberty which gave decifion to our counfels and energy to our conduct, in our ftruggle for INDEPENDENCE, and which conducted us fafely and triumphantly, thro' the ftormy period of the Revolution. That Liberty which has raifed us to an elevated rank among the Nations of the world, and which has afforded us a greater meafure of PEACE and Security, of wealth and improvement, than ever fell to the lot of any people.

In the name of my *Country* and by the authority of my *Government,* I promife you protection to your *persons, property* and *rights.* Remain at your homes. Purfue your peaceful and cuftomary avocations. Raife not your hands againft your brethren. Many of your fathers fought for the freedom & INDEPENDENCE we now enjoy. Being children therefore of the fame family with us, and heirs to the fame heritage, the arrival of an Army of friends, muft be hailed by you with a cordial welcome. You will be emancipated from Tyrany and oppreffion, and reftored to the dignified ftation of freemen Had I any doubt of eventual fuccefs, I might afk your affiftance, but I do not. I come prepared for every contingency. I have a force which will look down all oppofition, & that force is but the vanguard of a much greater If contrary to your own intereft, and the juft expectation of my Country, you fhould take part in the approaching conteft, you will be confidered & treated as enemies, & the horrors & calamities of war will ftalk before you.

If the barbarous & favage policy of Great Britain be purfued, and the favages are let loofe to murder our Citizens, & butcher our women and children, this war, will be a war of extermination.

The firft ftroke of the Tomahawk, the firft attempt with the fcalping knife, will be the fignal for one indifcriminate fcene of defolation. *No white man found fighting by the fide of an Indian, will be taken prifoner.* Inftant deftruction will be his lot. If the dictates of reafon, duty, juftice and humanity cannot prevent the employment of a force which refpects no rights, & knows no wrong, it will be prevented by a fevere and relentlefs fyftem of retaliation.

I doubt not your courage and firmnefs : I will not doubt your attachment to Liberty. If you tender your fervices voluntarily, they will be accepted readily.

The UNITED STATES offer you *Peace, Liberty* and *Security.* Your choice lies between thefe & WAR flavery, and *deftruction.* Choofe then, but choofe wifely ; and may he who knows the juftice of our caufe, and who holds in his hand the fate of Nations, guide you to a refult the moft compatible with your rights and intereft, your Peace and profperity.

BY THE GENERAL

Capt: 13th. *U. S. Regt: of Infantry and Aid de camp.*

rived on the field, on August 16. It was a shameful and embarrassing start to the war, particularly one which had been announced by Hull in such confident and self-righteous terms! Two more years of fighting did little to change the status quo, and when peace was made, territorial boundaries were left exactly as they had been before the conflict.

In actual fact, though, the War of 1812 was a decisive event. After a series of defeats in the Northwest, the Americans rallied in 1813, successfully defending Fort Meigs, near present-day Toledo, and defeating British naval forces on Lake Erie, invading Canada, and mortally wounding Tecumseh at the Battle of the Thames. The war sealed the fate of the Indians in the Midwest and opened the territories of Michigan, Indiana, Wisconsin, and Illinois for settlement thereafter. The British would quickly forget that there ever had been a War of 1812 in America. Citizens of the United States would take pride in their naval achievements on Lake Erie, Lake Champlain, and the high seas, brag about Jackson's victory at the Battle of New Orleans, and develop amnesia in relation to their disastrous Canadian invasions or the humiliating British burning of the Capitol and the White House.

The Canadians, however, never will forget the war. The Hull proclamation was a perfect example of American arrogance and miscalculation. Hull was certain that anyone would prefer living under the American flag to British "despotism," and confident that an army of "free" Americans could defeat any force on earth. The British and Canadian army quickly outmaneuvered and beat him, and they also held their ground against American invasion forces on the Niagara frontier and the St. Lawrence. In the process, a formerly heterogeneous group of old French settlers, Loyalist refugees from the American Revolution, and British and American immigrants, with little sense of community previously, found a common bond on which to create a distinct nation. Opposition to the encroachments of the United States, even today, remains one of the few things all Canadians agree on, and a primary element of Canadian nationalism.

The Hull proclamation, illustrated here, was printed on a second-hand printing press, brought to Detroit by Father Gabriel Richard, which accomplished all press work in Michigan Territory between 1809 and 1816. The Library has a fine collection of early Detroit imprints and rich, unique source materials on the War of 1812.

Purchased from Lathrop C. Harper, 1919. Gift of W. L. Clements, 1923.

☙ 67 ❧

FREE ENTERPRISE SYSTEM AT FULL STEAM

THE UNITED STATES was, perhaps, particularly fortunate in having Britain as an influence and model in the establishment of its economy and way of doing business. Something in the mixture was conducive to free enterprise and technological innovation, and beginning even in the colonial period, with Franklin's stove and Oliver Evans' automatic flour mills, skilled artisans began inventing new, more efficient machinery, and men of wealth figured out ways to make money on other people's efforts. Long familiarity with the joint stock company and increasingly easy incorporation laws after the Revolution meant that good ideas could attract the capital necessary to turn them into reality.

The steam engine was a British invention, but an American, John Fitch, built the first steamboat in 1787. Robert Fulton launched the *Clermont* in 1807, the first truly practical vessel, and within less than a decade, dozens of privately financed steamboat companies were competing for investment funds and profitable routes of travel. The *Eagle*, Captain Moses Rogers commanding, began regular service between Philadelphia and Bordentown, New Jersey, in late July 1813 under the auspices of the New York and Philadelphia New Steam Boat Line. Its construction and fitting out were apparently financed in Philadelphia by the sale of stock certificates such as the one shown here. It competed on the same route with the *Phoenix*, but there seems to have been plenty of

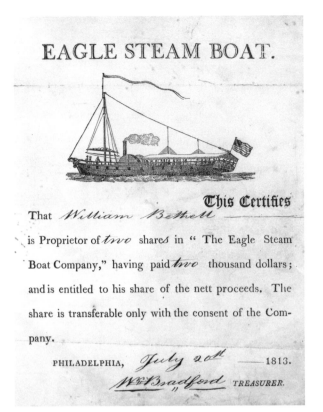

EAGLE STEAM BOAT.

This Certifies

That *William Bethell* ____

is Proprietor of *two* shares in " The Eagle Steam Boat Company," having paid *two* thousand dollars; and is entitled to his share of the nett proceeds. The share is transferable only with the consent of the Company.

PHILADELPHIA, *July 20th* ____ 1813.

Wm Bradford TREASURER.

business for both. The *Eagle* left the wharf in Philadelphia at 7 a.m. each Monday, Wednesday, and Friday, and it returned on the following days. At Bordentown it met a stagecoach and a steamboat for New Brunswick. In the summer season it also met a stage for Long Branch, the most fashionable seaside resort of its day. An existing diary of a voyage on August 11, 1813, described the accommodations on the vessel as elegant and dinner as equal to that served in the best hotels. There were 130 passengers on board.

Few of the early steamboats lasted more than a year or two. Advertisements for the *Eagle* appear regularly in the newspaper from July 31 to October 20, 1813, and then the vessel suddenly drops from view. The 1814 Philadelphia directory, which was probably printed in the fall of the previous year, lists the *Eagle*, but newspapers give no indication that it was again in service. Whether or not William Bethell ever recouped his $2,000 investment, recorded on the stock certificate, is uncertain.

Gift of Clarence Wolf, Philadelphia, 1980.

❧ 68 ❧

WARTIME PROPAGANDA IN GRAPHIC FORM

THE COUNTRY WAS BADLY DIVIDED when it declared war against Britain in 1812, and early reversals at Mackinac, Detroit, and Chicago created a military crisis on the frontier. The Americans not only needed victories, they also needed something to arouse public outrage, to inspire the lukewarm patriot, and to embarrass the opponent of the war into silence. Following Hull's surrender at Detroit in August 1812, William Henry Harrison was put in command of an army of Kentucky and Ohio troops and charged with recapturing the lost territory. This was eventually accomplished, but first the Americans would sustain another defeat which was probably worth more than any possible victory.

General James Winchester was sent with an advance party of Harrison's army to present-day Monroe, Michigan, where he was surrounded and forced to surrender on January 22, 1813. After the surrender, the very responsible British commander, General Procter, lost control of the Indians, and for a day afterwards the native warriors looted and burned homes and murdered and scalped prisoners and civilians. The event became notorious as "The River Raisin Massacre." The

MASSACRE of the AMERICAN PRISONERS, at FRENCH-TOWN, on the River Raisin, by the SAVAGES Under the Command of the British Gen! PROCTOR : January 23? 1813.

Library owns the only surviving copy of this contemporary, hand-colored engraving. It is a strikingly effective picture, but entirely inaccurate in detail. Monroe had been settled for thirty years when the massacre occurred, and the houses were more substantial than rude, frontier log cabins. The appearance and orientation of the river is entirely wrong, and the area has no hills.

But accuracy has little to do with this sort of print. Its purpose is to appeal to the emotions. It is propaganda, every bit as inflammatory as a World War I poster showing German soldiers killing innocent women and children. Newspapers and magazines throughout the country screamed in bold headlines about Indian tortures encouraged by British rum. In ensuing engagements, soldiers were sent into action with the battle cry "Remember the Raisin."

There are many contemporary prints of military and naval action during the War of 1812 that attempted to be accurate, or at least realistic, and others that are editorial cartoons and exercises of patriotic imagination. Each type has a place in the history of the event, and the Library has a fine collection of all varieties.

Purchased from Kennedy & Co., 1951.

DRINKING SONG TO NATIONAL ANTHEM

AFTER THE HUMILIATING ATTACK on our national capital in August 1814, the British fleet, then in complete control of Chesapeake Bay, set its sights on Baltimore. There was one primary obstacle, Fort McHenry, which commanded the mouth of the harbor. The British arrived and began shelling the fortification on September 13. In the company of the enemy's warships was an American sloop under a flag of truce, the *Minden*, which had been engaged in an exchange of prisoners. Admiral Cochrane, the British commander, had treated the vessel respectfully, but he insisted that it remain under guard until the attack on Baltimore had been completed. Aboard the *Minden*, in company with John S. Skinner, U.S. commissioner for the exchange of prisoners, was Francis Scott Key, attorney general for the District of Columbia.

The guns of Fort McHenry were manned by a motley group of army and navy personnel, but they performed their duty with exceptional skill. Shot after broadside shot hit the mark, but when the sun went down, the fort resolutely held firm and continued to keep the fleet at bay. Shots were fired throughout the night, and at "the dawn's early light" Key was thrilled to discover that the American flag continued to wave above Fort McHenry. On the spot he penned the words to what has become the national anthem of the United States. The British were forced to give up their attempted attack, the *Minden* was released, and the fleet sailed down the Bay.

Within a few days of the event, Key consulted Thomas Carr, a sheet music publisher, who sug-

gested setting the piece to a noted eighteenth-century drinking song entitled "To Anacreon in Heaven." A handbill of the text was issued in September or October as "Defense of Ft. McHenry," and at some point in early November, Carr issued this piece of sheet music — the very first printing of words and music under the present title, for piano and voice. This first printing is identifiable by a typographical printing error in the subtitle ("pariotic" instead of "patriotic"). It is the sort of thing that provides a bit of satisfaction to those who have ever edited something for publication, certain they had eliminated every error, only to find a glaring typo on the first look at the finished product!

Francis Scott Key was neither the first nor the last American to use this English tune. It had been set to "Adams and Liberty" by the Massachusetts Charitable Fire Society of Boston and for a song commemorating Washington's death entitled "When Death's Gloom Angel Was Bending His Bow." It was Admiral Dewey, during the Spanish-American War, who unofficially ordered that "The Star Spangled Banner" be considered the national anthem. It was not until 1931 that Congress officially recognized it as such.

Purchased from Caravan Book Shop, 1967. Gift of Clements Library Friends of Flint, Michigan.

❧ 70 ❧

THE PEACE OF CHRISTMAS EVE

IT TENDS TO BE MUCH EASIER to get into a war than out of it. The United States unilaterally started the War of 1812. In his Declaration of War, delivered to Congress on June 18, 1812, President Madison listed four major grievances: the impressment of American seamen on the high seas; violations of the neutral rights of the United States; the blockade of American ports; the refusal of the British to revoke the Orders in Council, which prohibited the United States from trading with France or French allies. There was a certain irony in the message, in that all of the stated causes, as humiliating as they may have been to national pride, primarily affected the pocketbooks of northern and eastern merchants and shippers, most of whom were entirely opposed to going to war.

Militarily, the war proved to be decisive for neither side. The Americans were rather quickly shown that conquest of Canada was unlikely. The British and Indians registered immediate success in the West, taking Detroit, Fort Dearborn (Chicago), and Fort Mackinac, but a little over a year later Perry's victory on Lake Erie and the Battle of the Thames reversed the situation. The Niagara and St. Lawrence frontiers witnessed indecisive campaigns on both sides. The Americans burned York (Toronto), the British burned Washington, D.C., but neither extended these actions into territorial gains. The British, with overwhelming naval strength, controlled coastal waters, although a small but effective American navy gained begrudging respect, and American privateers inflicted considerable damage to British merchant shipping throughout the world. The United States was fortunate that America was never more than a secondary front for Britain, which was primarily concerned with defeating Napoleon.

Serious peace negotiations began in the summer of 1814 in Ghent, Belgium. The Americans sat down at the table, requesting that the maritime rights referred to in Madison's Declaration of this day, or sooner if practicable.

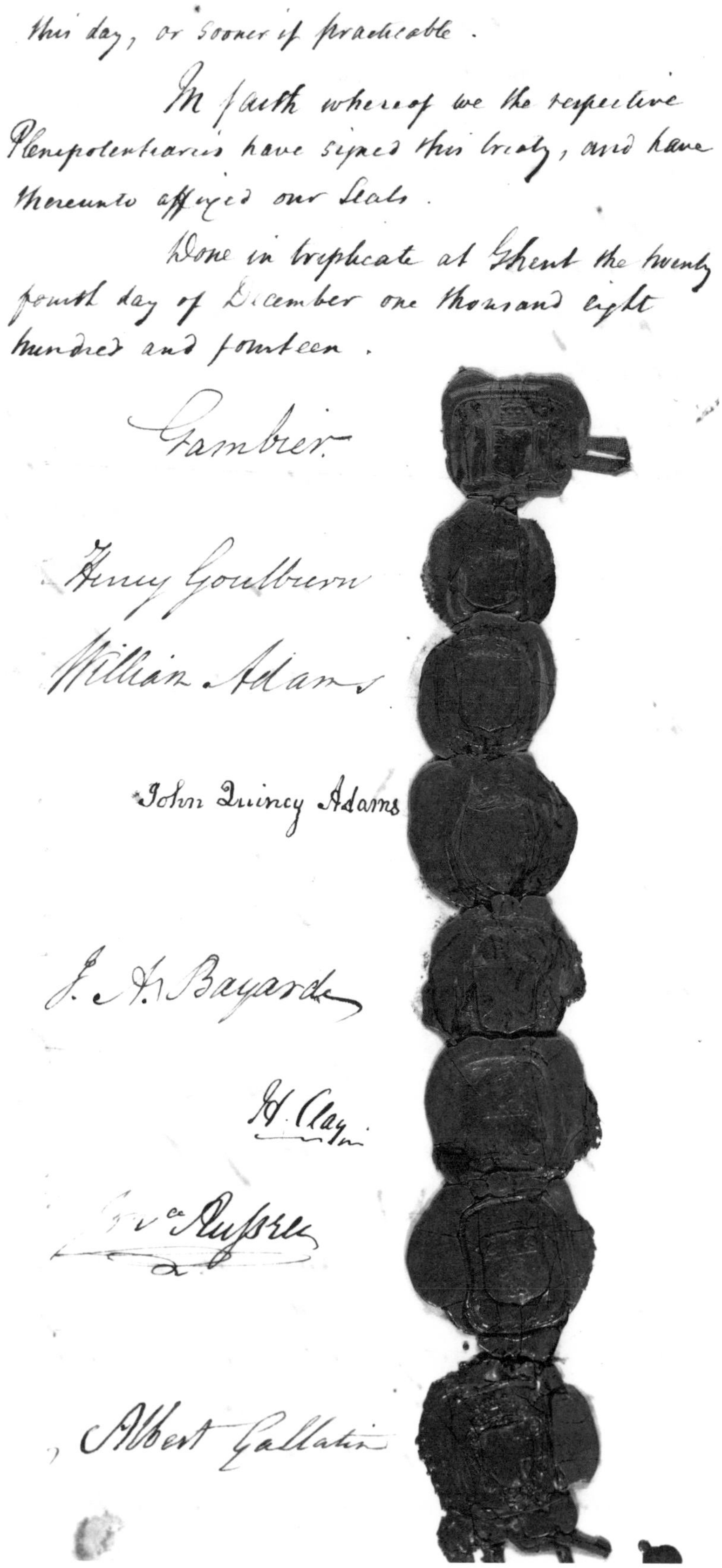

In faith whereof we the respective Plenipotentiaries have signed this treaty, and have thereunto affixed our Seals.

Done in triplicate at Ghent the twenty fourth day of December one thousand eight hundred and fourteen.

Gambier

Henry Goulburn

William Adams

John Quincy Adams

J. A. Bayard

H. Clay

Jon. Russell

Albert Gallatin

Signature page of the Treaty of Ghent, December 24, 1814

Albert Gallatin

John Quincy Adams

Henry Clay

James A. Bayard

War be recognized. The British insisted on significant boundary concessions west of the Great Lakes, the creation of an Indian buffer state between the United States and Canada, and retention of territory presently held. In the end, neither side achieved any of their stated goals. Britain's hero of the day, the Duke of Wellington, not only refused to take command of the British army in America but stated that British territorial goals were unrealistic, given Perry's victory on Lake Erie. The British ministry began to appreciate the magnitude of the national debt created by the Napoleonic wars, and by late November 1814 both sides were primarily interested in ending the war.

The American commissioners at the peace table were Jonathan Russell, Albert Gallatin, John Quincy Adams, Henry Clay, and James A. Bayard. It was a particularly distinguished group, Russell and Adams being career diplomats, Gallatin the brilliant former secretary of the treasury under Jefferson and Madison, Clay the leading spokesman for western interests in Congress, and Bayard, a former U.S. senator. Adams later became President, and Clay, although never elected to the presidency, wielded great power in Congress for half a century.

Negotiations were amicable and went fairly rapidly in December, as each side gave up previous demands and agreed to deal with most existing problems by study and negotiation after the peace had been made. Both sides had hoped to finish their work before Christmas, but finishing touches seemed to stretch on endlessly on December 24. To expedite matters, Henry Clay sat down and wrote out this particular draft. It was an "official" signed copy, serving the immediate purpose of allowing the weary diplomats to get some sleep and celebrate Christmas properly, but it was presumably replaced by a more formal copy a day or two later. One of the British commissioners, Henry Goulburn, then kept the Henry Clay copy as a souvenir. The Clements Library acquired the manuscript with Goulburn's letters and papers documenting the peace negotiations.

The Library also owns the papers of Christopher Hughes, a career United States diplomat in the first decades of the nineteenth century. He served as secretary to the American delegation in Ghent, and as a souvenir of his own, he had a Dutch artist, P. van Huffel, draw pencil sketches of four of the American negotiators.

Goulburn Papers purchased from Meyers & Co., 1941. Gift of Lawrence Reynolds, Detroit. Pencil sketches from Christopher Hughes Papers. Gift of Jesse S. Reeves, Ann Arbor, 1943.

❧ 71 ☙

PIRATING THE WORD OF GOD

ANY LIST OF THE MOST INFLUENTIAL American books would have to include *The Book of Mormon*, written by Joseph Smith, supposedly on the basis of divine inspiration, and first issued by a small-town newspaper publisher in Palmyra, New York, in 1830. In combination with a group of sermons and further divine revelations collected under the title *Doctrine and Covenants* (Kirtland, Ohio, 1835), it formed the distinctive scriptural basis of the Church of Jesus Christ of Latter-Day Saints. The Mormon Church has since developed into one of the most successful religious denominations in the modern world.

Joseph Smith and his early followers, as well as *The Book of Mormon*, were highly controversial from the very beginning. Abner Cole, editor of *The Reflector*, an irregularly issued local newspaper, was one of the skeptics, although his paper is an important source for factual information on early Mormon beginnings. The manuscript of *The Book of Mormon* itself was delivered to the printer in August 1829, and the complete book was first available in March 1830. It happened that Egbert B. Grandin, printer and binder of the volume, also was the printer of *The Reflector*. By some surreptitious method, Abner Cole, *The Reflector's* editor, managed to get hold of sheets of *The Book of Mormon* while it was being printed. He issued a pirated edition of three chapters in January 1830, before Joseph Smith was able to stop him.

Although illegally printed, the item illustrated here represents the first appearance of the text of one of the notable religious books of modern times. The Library has exceptionally fine collections on the earliest beginnings of the Mormons, the Shakers, the Seventh-Day Adventists, and the Christian Scientists—all indigenous American religious denominations based upon distinctive divine revelations, which have had considerable influence in the world at large.

Purchased from Peter Crawley, 1973.

❧ 72 ❧

THE SECRETS OF INDIAN MEDICINE

FROM THE TIME of their earliest contacts with Native American peoples, the European settlers of North America developed respect for the Indians' ability to treat and cure disease using natural products of the fields and forests. Much of the scientific literature of the colonial period involved the collecting and identifying of native plants. As European training and traditions came to dominate formal medical practice in the late eighteenth century, botanical medicine fell out of favor in urban areas. The uneducated, the poor, and the residents of frontier areas, however, never lost faith in herbal medicines, which were available at little cost from the local medicine women or "root doctors."

John Tennent, author of the first medical self-help guide, published in Philadelphia and Williamsburg in 1734, relied heavily on "Indian physick" and other preparations used by the natives. The first American farrier, or horse-doctoring book, published in Wilmington, Delaware, in 1764, included an appendix of native plants and herbs and listed "Discreet Indians" among its authors. From the early nineteenth century until well into the patent medicine era, nontraditional physicians frequently claimed to have learned about natural cures from "Indian doctors," thereby ensuring a level of trust from the general public.

The 1832 pamphlet displayed here is particularly interesting in that it appears to be an authentic, if brief, Indian doctoring book, presumably published for sale to whites. The Cherokee Nation had established a press at New Echota, Georgia, in 1828, which printed in both the English and native alphabets. The Library has an extensive run of the bilingual *Cherokee Phoenix*, the newspaper issued by the tribe, and the press produced a number of printed laws and school books before being forced to close in 1835.

Whether or not this medical item was produced on the Cherokee press, it would seem to be an authentic work of native authorship. Containing none of the extravagant claims to cure every ailment found in most botanical medical guides, the sixteen-page pamphlet includes clear descriptions of how to mix various roots, herbs, and barks to cure common diseases, aches, and pains. Ingredients include rattlesnake grease, live frogs, turpentine, red lead, and hog's fat! Its publication may have been motivated by a desire simply to preserve accumulated botanical wisdom, or perhaps to serve as a basis for a native industry, supplying natural medicines in the way that Shaker communities were beginning to do in nearby Kentucky and Ohio. This seems to be the only known copy of the pamphlet.

Purchased from Stephen Resnick, 1984. Gift of John and Emily Wheeler, Bay City, Michigan.

❧ 73 ❧

ANDREW JACKSON AS THE GREAT FATHER

ANDREW JACKSON WON THE PRESIDENCY in 1828, decisively defeating the incumbent, John Quincy Adams, in perhaps the most vicious campaign in American history. A westerner and celebrated military hero, an ordinary citizen of humble birth and plain tastes, a passionate democrat, President Jackson would give new meaning to the concept of "government by the people." For better or worse, his election marked the beginning of modern American politics. Few anticipated the

dynamic leadership Jackson would bring to his office, nor the sweeping reforms he would promote—great economic, political, and cultural changes designed to democratize America.

In his first message to Congress in December 1829, Jackson made the stunning proposal to move all Indians to unoccupied lands west of the Mississippi. The presence of tribes within several states had led to mounting tension, even bloodshed. Jackson's prejudice, fostered by his experience in wars against Tennessee Creeks and Florida Seminoles over a decade earlier, was well known. Like Jefferson, Jackson believed removal was the best solution to an intractable problem. After heated debate in both houses, Congress narrowly passed the Indian Removal Bill on May 28, 1830. Lands held by tribes within states were exchanged for land designated Indian Territory in what would become Oklahoma. Tragically, thousands died in the course of removal, a national disgrace remembered as "The Trail of Tears."

American political culture was transformed during Jackson's administration. Technology had revolutionized the popular market for political cartoons in the 1820s. Commercial lithography, a relatively inexpensive, flexible process by which impressions are taken from designs inked on stone, replaced the difficult process of engraving on metal. Cartoons could be mass produced on cheap, single sheets. Jackson, more than any of his predecessors in office, had captured America's imagination. Colorful and controversial, striking in appearance, he was an easy target for graphic satire. The result was a flood of cartoons during the course of his presidency, from 1828 to 1837.

Among the Clements Library's extensive collection of American satirical prints is this unique cartoon, brilliantly mocking Jackson's betrayal of the native people that he, in particular, was supposed to protect.

Purchased at Phillips Sale by Carnegie Book Shop, 1980.

SEX: A TIMELESS SUBJECT OF PUBLIC CONSTERNATION

In the era when factories and shops coexisted with residential dwellings in downtown centers, when emigration from abroad was constantly enlarging the population and helping to keep wage rates down, and when ports were served by countless ships whose crews dispersed on shore while cargoes were being loaded and unloaded, cities were full of a disproportionate number of young, single men. While they could afford quarters in rooming houses and modest entertainment, few of them had sufficient funds to support wives and families. Widespread prostitution was an inevitable result, even in somewhat puritanical America.

City officials in Boston, New York, and Philadelphia officially frowned upon prostitution and the crime, disease, and drunkenness with which it is generally associated. In practice, about the best they could do was to try to force it off the streets and unofficially restrict houses of ill fame to certain neighborhoods, away from the residences of the middle and upper classes. In New York City, the Five Points area and then the Tenderloin District, uptown on the west side, became particularly notorious. *The Directory or Pocket Companion, Containing a List of All the Gay Houses and Ladies of Pleasure in the City of New-York* (New York, 1840) is one of the exceptionally rare printed guides to New York's bordellos.

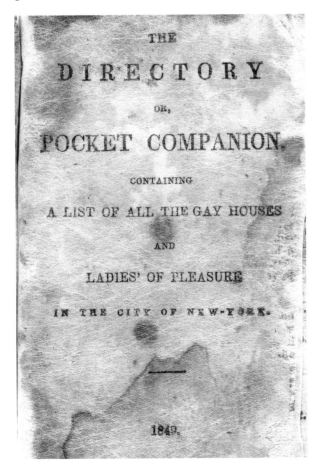

FIRST ANNUAL REPORT

OF THE

EXECUTIVE COMMITTEE

OF THE

NEW YORK

MAGDALEN SOCIETY.

INSTITUTED JANUARY 1, 1830.

From the 2d New-York Edition, with corroborative notes and a Plate,

Philadelphia:

For sale, Wholesale and Retail, by J. Scarlett, No. 8 Market-street; 174, South Second-Street; 324, South Fourth-Street; and 249, South Front-Street.

1831.

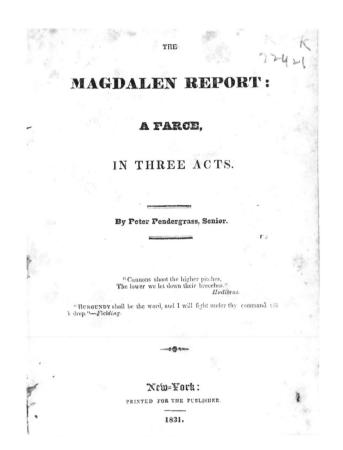

THE

MAGDALEN REPORT:

A FARCE,

IN THREE ACTS.

By Peter Pendergrass, Senior.

"Cannons shoot the higher pitches,
The lower we let down their breeches."
Hudibras.

"BURGUNDY shall be the word, and I will fight under thy command till
I drop."—*Fielding.*

New-York:
PRINTED FOR THE PUBLISHER.
1831.

FRUITS

OF PHILOSOPHY:

OR

THE PRIVATE COMPANION

OF

YOUNG MARRIED PEOPLE.

BY CHARLES KNOWLTON, M. D.,
Author of "Modern Materialism."

"Knowledge is Wealth."
Old Saying.

SECOND EDITION, WITH ADDITIONS.

BOSTON:
1833.

With the rise of an evangelical urban missionary movement in the early decades of the nineteenth century, the religious element made attempts to eliminate prostitution by saving the girls and setting them on the path of virtue. The Magdalen Society of New York, formed in 1830, sent agents into the streets to locate houses of ill fame and convince prostitutes to quit the business, take up residence in proper boarding houses, and develop the skills needed to earn a respectable living. The society published its first annual report in 1831. It was, for its day, a fairly shocking bit of investigative reporting, and it received widespread attention. The issue shown here is a contemporary Philadelphia reprint.

One anonymous author who read the report found it a source of amusement. He wrote a short three act play entitled *The Magdalen Report: A Farce in Three Acts* (New York, 1831). The gist of the drama was that young men of New York, entirely unaware previously that such activity existed, owed the society a vote of thanks for warning them to be highly suspicious of even the most respectable appearing women! The farce is as scarce as the guidebook—unknown bibliographically except for this copy.

Charles Knowlton was a Massachusetts-born and Dartmouth-educated physician and a decided freethinker who did not shy away from controversy. *Fruits of Philosophy; or, The Private Companion of Young Married People*, first published anonymously in New York in 1832, appeared under the author's name in the expanded second edition illustrated here. The anonymous publisher supplied a preface which briefly summarized the basic philosophy of the treatise: "It is a notorious fact that the families of the married often increase beyond what a regard for the young beings coming into existence, or the happiness of those who give them birth, would dictate; and philanthropists, of first rate moral character, in different parts of the world, have for years been endeavouring to obtain and disseminate a knowledge of means whereby men and women may refrain at will from be-coming parents, without even a partial sacrifice of the pleasure with which attends the gratification of their productive instinct."

Knowlton was prosecuted, fined, and jailed in Massachusetts for the book, but it continued to be issued by freethought publishers in the United States and Britain. Annie Besant reprinted it in England in the 1870s, was prosecuted, and acquitted in a highly publicized trial in 1877. Thereafter it sold in many editions throughout the world. The theories expressed in this book, and prostitution, remain as controversial in today's world as they were in the 1840s.

"Directory" purchased at Christie's by MacManus, 1995; "First Annual Report" purchased from Richard Wormser, 1962; "Magdalen Report . . . Farce" purchased from Howard Mott, 1991; Knowlton purchased from The Americanist, 1995.

❧ 75 ❧

PROFESSIONAL WOMAN WITH A PEN

WHILE IT IS PROBABLY NOT TRUE that the fainting couch was the favorite piece of furniture for women in the 1830s, we might easily think so if the only evidence we had was the fiction of the day. Meek, submissive, and dependent upon men for subsistence, the heroines of antebellum sentimental novels exerted their influence only indirectly, through prayer and living example, suffering and moral suasion, or if all else failed, through falling into a dead but timely faint. Lydia Huntley Sigourney (1791–1865) was among the most popular antebellum authors of sentimental fiction, a best-selling writer who helped define the genre. But Sigourney's life belies many of the stereotypes she helped to perpetuate.

A native of Hartford, Lydia Huntley was educated in the common schools before embarking on a highly successful career as an educator. By 1814, still in her early twenties, she had opened a school of her own, and in the following year she published a well-received tract, *Moral Pieces, in Prose and Verse.* She married, in 1819, Charles Sigourney, a widower with three children. Although well intentioned, Charles proved to be a terrible financial manager, and as a result, Lydia turned to writing to supplement the family income, composing poetry and prose for a periodical magazine industry that was exploding in popularity. Although today her writing seems overly didactic and steeped in a prim religious moralism, it was so enormously popular in the 1830s that editors paid simply to have Sigourney's name on the masthead.

As her popularity grew, Sigourney became a hard-edged professional businesswoman. Although she struggled at times with feelings of inadequacy, she knew her worth on the market and knew how to get it. Through her friend and literary agent, George Griffin, she developed into a tough contract negotiator, driving her asking price from 12.5 percent of the profits in 1834 to 20% and more in 1837. She also dictated marketing strategies and coordinated reviews, determined the timing of publication to coincide with the season at which they would be most profitable, and, when necessary, shopped publisher against publisher, looking for the best reputation as much as for the best deal. "It wonderfully sharpens a woman's wits to support herself," she wrote.

from her, in New-Haven. — Your opinion of any favourable influence upon our "Sketches", from my presence in your metropolis, must arise from your kind partiality. — Literary men, and poets, will only go certain lengths, for their fraternity. There are secrets in their trade, as well as in all others. — Their efforts to uphold the body corporate, are subject to certain checks. — I have little dependence on Bryant or Halleck for aid:— something, they will say from necessity,— but nothing more. — Excuse me, if I have written too plainly.— Could I see you,— it would be easy to substantiate these remarks. — We, like the painters, must seek for a character from trans-atlantick criticism. — While I express these opinions,— I feel painfully,— how little I have done, deserving of notice. — But I have been inspired with desires to do more worthily,— since you have encouraged & stimulated my labours. — You have illustrated for me, the spirit of the promise which Henry the Great of France, addressed to the princes of Bourbon, during the heat of the battle of "Coutras, — "please God, — I will shew you, I am your elder brother." — You will not, I trust infer, from ought I

Lydia H. Sigourney to George Griffin, April 6, 1834

Sigourney's hard-nosed attitude was born of experience. "As a body of men," she informed Griffin, "I have feared the publishers, ever since I have had anything to do with them. They seem to me wily, & not liberal, neither disposed to be the natural allies of authors, but rather to forage upon them." Nor was she any more kindly disposed toward her male peers: "Literary men, and poets, will only go to certain lengths, for their fraternity. There are secrets in their trade, as well as in all others. Their efforts to uphold the body corporate, are subject to certain checks. I have little dependence on Bryant or Halleck for aid . . . ." Sigourney outlived them all, an iron fist beneath the sentimental velvet glove.

The Clements Library has a very strong collection of early American literature — our earliest novels, plays, poetry, and literary periodicals — much of it barely readable today! The Library does not generally collect post-Civil War literature. The Clements Library is also particularly rich in the sources of women's intellectual history. In addition to the professional correspondence of Lydia Sigourney, illustrated here, noted women authors represented in the manuscript collections include Lydia Maria Child, the Grimké sisters, Harriet Beecher Stowe, Catherine Beecher, Delia Bacon, and the family of Catherine Maria Sedgwick.

Purchased from Schmitt Investors, 1995.

MOUNTAIN MEN AND INCREDIBLY LARGE TREES

ZENAS LEONARD WAS TYPICAL of countless young men before and since, tired of living at home and bored with the routines of farm labor. Reaching the age of twenty-one, his restlessness first took him to the big city, Pittsburgh, where he briefly worked in a store. He then decided that he wanted to become a fur trapper. St. Louis, with its river connections into the far West, had become the center of the trade by the 1820s. Yearly caravans of pack horses and wagons were sent by the mercantile firms to meet the "mountain men" and Indians at "summer rendezvous" points in the eastern foothills of the Rockies. The trappers and Indians had been collecting pelts throughout the winter, which they sold and traded for supplies to get them through the next winter, and the pack trains returned to St. Louis loaded with furs for the European and East Coast markets.

Leonard arrived in St. Louis in April 1831, was hired by a leading fur merchant, and set out as clerk with a party for Idaho. In 1833, at Green River rendezvous, he met up with Captain Bonneville and signed up as a member of the Walker Party, a portion of Bonneville's group which was sent to explore the region of the Great Salt Lake. Documentation is too limited to know whether Walker was following orders or elaborating on them, but after a harrowing crossing of the deserts of Utah and Nevada, this party headed west and was the first group of Americans to climb the Rockies and Sierras and actually make it to the Pacific coast, seemingly the first to enter Yosemite Valley and see the giant sequoias. They rejoined Bonneville at the summer rendezvous of 1834. Leonard stayed in the Rockies one more year as a trapper and then returned home to Pennsylvania, where he wrote a narrative of his travels. A portion of it was published in installments in the local *Clearfield Republican,* and in 1839, pestered for additional copies, the newspaper office issued the entire narrative in book form. Leonard himself, by this time, had returned west, settling as an Indian trader on the Santa Fe Trail at Sibley, Missouri. He died there at age 48 in 1857.

Published so obscurely, Leonard's *Narrative* was little more than a rumor to collectors for many years and remains an almost

NARRATIVE

OF THE

ADVENTURES OF

ZENAS LEONARD,

A NATIVE OF CLEARFIELD COUNTY, PA. WHO SPENT FIVE
YEARS IN TRAPPING FOR FURS, TRADING WITH
THE INDIANS, &c., &c., OF THE
ROCKY MOUNTAINS:

WRITTEN BY HIMSELF.

———

PRINTED AND PUBLISHED
BY D. W. MOORE,
CLEARFIELD, PA.
1839.

unobtainable rarity today. In terms of content, it is an essential text, being the only first-hand narrative of the Walker expedition to survive. What makes it a particularly wonderful book is its improbability. Leonard was nothing more than a typical kid who didn't know what he wanted to do in life. He craved adventure, and by good fortune he signed on with a group of men who would make history but fail to record it themselves. The Walker Expedition was an incredibly difficult undertaking, but at Leonard's age, physical hardship was nothing. For him, the entire experience was one of exciting adventure, and he captured that wide-eyed quality in the book, which he never intended to publish.

In the process of building their holdings, libraries and collectors are deeply indebted to bibliographers for identifying the "musts" of a comprehensive collection in any particular subject. For narratives of western exploration, Henry R. Wagner and Charles L. Camp's *The Plains & Rockies*, 4th edition, edited by Robert H. Becker (San Francisco, 1982) is the bible. The Library has added missing Wagner-Camp titles whenever possible for decades, and it possesses most of the significant narratives, even the greatest rarities. The importance of these "overland narratives" can hardly be overemphasized, because they provide the first descriptions we have of the topography, the flora and fauna, and the native populations of North America.

Gift of Everett D. Graff, Chicago, 1945.

ෙ 77 ෙ

THE POLITICS OF LOG CABINS AND HARD CIDER

How could you resist an invitation like the one extended by the accompanying poster? It offers a chance to escape the heat at home on a summer evening and go to a political rally. Undoubtedly there would be free food, with an ample supply of hard cider. Rousing speeches, political songs, and probably a torch parade through the streets would finish it off.

National politics had come a long way in 1840 from what the Founding Fathers had envisioned when they wrote the first generation of state constitutions and the U. S. Consitution of 1788. The Revolutionary generation, although in agreement that the country did not need a hereditary monarch, was equally distrustful of the common man. Popular voting was generally restricted to choosing members of the lower legislative chamber, and voting was largely restricted to white male property owners. No one envisioned the rise of political parties. Upper houses in the legislatures, as well as the federal Electoral College, were expected to be made up of men of education, property, and wisdom, who to some extent would counteract the dangerous tendencies of democracy. The President, appointed by the Electoral College, was expected to be nothing less than the wisest natural leader in the country, chosen by men who were themselves wise and disinterested enough to make their choice, heedless of the momentary enthusiasms of the mob.

The entire system began to break down immediately. Before Washington's term of office had

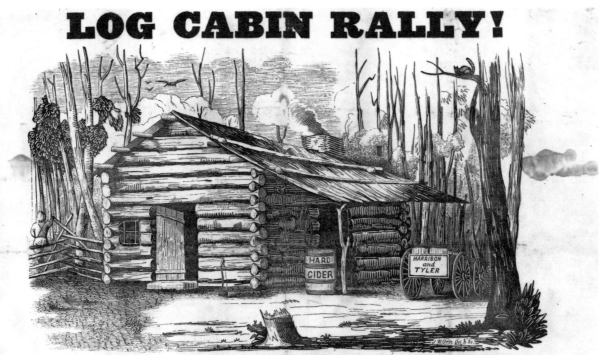

LOG CABIN RALLY!

THIS EVEN'G.

The Whigs of Detroit are requested to meet at the Log Cabin THIS EVENING, at half past seven o'clock.

The freemen of Indiana, Kentucky and North Carolina are calling upon the Whigs of Michigan to follow their glorious example. To do so, fellow citizens, we must be active. The meeting to-night is not only to congratulate each other at the victories achieved in the past, but to prepare for an equally glorious victory in the future.

Turn out, then, Freemen of Detroit! Let EVERY MAN be at his post.

DETROIT, Friday August 28, 1840.   By Order of the Committee.

ended, political groups had developed in Congress and spread to the states, dividing legislatures and voters between two distinct political parties. Thomas Jefferson became the figurehead of the opposition, and his election to the Presidency in 1800 gave a kind of legitimacy to two-party politics. The War of 1812 discredited the Federalist Party, and for a brief period from 1816 to 1821, the "Era of Good Feelings," party politics seemed to be on the wane, only to be revived with a vengeance between 1821 and 1824, when five men began campaigning ardently to become James Monroe's successor. John Quincy Adams won the struggle by enlisting the support of his rival Henry Clay, but this "nefarious bargain" only spurred the supporters of General Andrew Jackson to heightened efforts. From 1824, when the Jacksonian Democrats began seriously organizing themselves for victory in 1828, to the election of Lincoln in 1860, politics vied with religion as the most popular form of entertainment in America.

The Jacksonian Democrats portrayed themselves as the party of the common man, the independent farmer, and the westerner versus the forces of aristocracy, wealth, corruption, and East Coast snobbery. They organized state and county committees, held rallies and conventions, and worked in the legislatures and state constitutional conventions to abolish property restrictions for voting and any sort of officeholding not elected by the popular majority or appointed by the winner. Jackson won the 1828 and 1832 elections with unprecedented voter turnout, and the opposition National Democrat or Whig Party adopted Jacksonian political techniques, adding a few of their own.

The Whig Party nominated William Henry Harrison in 1839. In spite of the fact that he was actually born to a wealthy Virginia family, lived in elegance, and was a merciless and high-handed politician and military officer, he was portrayed as a simple product of a frontier log cabin, a gentle patriot, and someone who would enjoy nothing more than sitting around, sipping hard cider, and swapping stories with some of the boys about their exploits as hunters or Indian fighters.

Modern critics of today's politics decry the opportunism and hypocrisy of our system, as if this was something new. They lament the fact that the real issues and problems of the nation are ignored. Sophisticated, seemingly amoral political advisers shape the candidates' images into whatever form seems to work. Voters are analyzed with cold-blooded cynicism, and special approaches are devised to appeal to their particular beliefs, their fears, and their pocketbooks. Winning is everything. The whole process may be an embarrassment when contrasted to the ideals of the Founding Fathers, but it is, and has been, the American way for more than 150 years.

Purchased from the family of a private collector, 1985.

⮾ 78 ⮾

THE FORGOTTEN BUT WELL-DOCUMENTED WAR

THE MEXICAN WAR, 1846 to 1848, is an event largely forgotten by Americans unless they live in the southwestern part of the country, yet it significantly affected the United States in innumerable ways. At the time, it was a decidedly political and sectional war, largely supported by southerners and Democrats, generally opposed by northern Whigs. The fact that the country has forgotten the details is to some extent the result of a guilty national conscience. While there were some very real diplomatic and military justifications for going to war, the peace treaty could hardly be defended on the grounds of international fairness. We literally deprived Mexico of half its territory — taking from them their frontier, which might have been so useful in accommodating an expanding population.

The Mexican War was, overall, a resounding triumph for the professional military services of the United States. Zachary Taylor and Winfield Scott, with better trained and better equipped men, defeated far larger armies, and a West Point-trained corps of officers performed brilliantly. Among their numbers were most of the men who would become successful commanders during the Civil War.

The conflict is also notable for its historical and visual documentation. It was the first armed conflict in the world in which photographs as well as chromolithographs and woodcut maps and pictures recorded the action, even while the war was in progress. Several dozen daguerreotypes exist of troops in the field and outdoor scenes associated with the war in Mexico and Texas as well as portraits of men in uniform. Newspapers and magazines contained occasional maps, portraits of the leading officers, and pictures of battlefields and Mexican scenery.

During and immediately after the war, there also was a considerable market in colored litho-

graphs showing American victories, the breathtaking desert and mountain scenery, and elegant Spanish-style city views, so different from anything most Americans had seen previously. Duval, Sarony & Major, Endicott, and particularly Nathaniel Currier produced numerous views based upon the latest news reports, perfecting the techniques of cheap popular prints for which Currier & Ives would become so famous in the era of the Civil War. In addition to the inexpensive views, several fine and expensive prints, issued individually and as sets, were produced, the most notable being a series of twelve used by George W. Kendall as illustrations for *The War between the United States and Mexico Illustrated* (New York, 1851). The view of General Scott and his army entering Mexico City is shown here. Until the Civil War, the very finest lithography was being done in Europe. Kendall hired Carl Nebel, a German artist who had previously visited Mexico, to execute the artwork and the Parisian firm of Rose-Joseph Lemercier to produce the lithographs.

Because the Mexican War was followed so closely by the Civil War, its history and significance are easily lost. Zachary Taylor's heroics on the battlefield gained him the Presidency, but he died before accomplishing anything. Winfield Scott attempted to win the office but failed. A few dozen participants wrote personal narratives, but there was little popular interest in them, and they are almost all rare books today.

What the Mexican War did do, in the long term, was to eliminate a buffer of vast, sparsely settled territory between two distinctly different cultures — the largely English and northern European Protestant world of the United States and the Spanish and Indian Catholic civilization of Mexico.

Gift of W. L. Clements, 1923.

GO WEST YOUNG MAN: THE EMIGRANT'S GUIDE

THE INSPIRATION THAT TOOK the Pilgrim Fathers to America was enriched by more material considerations by the middle of the nineteenth century. It was a period of extraordinary economic growth and prosperity in the United States, and the incentive to leave the Old World behind seemed increasingly compelling. By 1840 the United States had nearly 3,000 miles of railroad. Within a few years Samuel Morse would transmit the first message on a telegraph line, Elias Howe would patent the sewing machine, and John Deere would be selling steel plows. Evidence of America's growing concern for its own culture was to be observed in the founding of the Philharmonic Society of New York and the American Association for the Advancement of Science. In 1848 came the California gold rush. The land of opportunity was ever more attractive, and European governments, which had previously welcomed emigration of excess population, began to worry about the loss of able-bodied workers.

Not even the great Charles Dickens, the most famous and articulate critic of American society, could dampen his countrymen's enthusiasm for the United States. By the mid-forties the London *Athenaeum* mentioned the growth of guide books for prospective emigrants. "Among the multitude of Hints and Directions with which the press just literally teems," it noted, "we have been amused by the illustrative version of the emigration lesson delivered by Mr. Percy Cruikshank." This little book of cartoons, *Hints to Emigrants or Incidents, in the Emigration of John Smith of Smith-*

Upon inspecting the land which you have purchased, you will at once
see your work before you. Proceed vigorously to remove the timber

Town, consisted of nine "dreadful warnings." Drawn and etched by Percy Cruikshank, the nephew of George Cruikshank, Charles Dickens' own illustrator, it is a worthy addition to the work of four generations of Cruikshank family artists.

Percy Cruikshank had learned the art of cartooning by engraving his father's humorous book illustrations. Since the arrival of *Punch* in 1841, the English public had an insatiable appetite for satirical prints. Cruikshank's little work, published in 1849, was a great success. The etching illustrated here is typical of Cruikshank's style. As the *Morning Post* said, "The inspection of the land with the enormous pine-trees which have to be vigorously removed is a rich engraving, the bare inspection of which would be sufficient to deter the most energetic and sanguine from even thinking of a location in North America." *Hints to Emigrants* is only one item in the Library's extensive store of immigration literature, but one of the most entertaining.

Purchased from Stevens, 1982.

❧ 80 ❧

ROBERT E. LEE'S FAMILY CHRISTMAS AT ARLINGTON, 1851

IN 1851, ROBERT E. LEE was a colonel in the army's Corps of Engineers, assigned to superintend harbor fortifications in Baltimore. Taking holiday leave, he and his family took a train from Baltimore to Washington to spend Christmas with Mrs. Lee's father, George Washington Parke Custis. The father-in-law was the somewhat eccentric grandson of Martha Washington by her first husband, and he lived at Arlington, the mansion that now is the center of Arlington National Cemetery. Six of the Lee children accompanied their parents on the journey. Mildred was the much-adored youngest child, and it should be noted that Angelina, referred to in the letter as having been left behind in Baltimore, was a doll.

The oldest child of the family, George W. Parke Custis Lee, was unable to join the family, being a cadet at West Point, and his father wrote this affectionate description of the family Christmas celebration so that he would not feel he had been forgotten. Lee was a man of rigid dignity in public. A letter such as this provides a marvelous and rare glimpse of his private personality.

"Arlington 28 Decr. 1851

I have grieved my dearest Son that you are not here with us. But because you are not present you are not the less thought of by every member of the family. You are Constantly wished for. Constantly missed. I hope you are well & happy, & that we shall all be united next June. We came on last Wednesday mor[nin]g. It was a bitter Cold day, & we were kept waiting an hour at the Depot in Baltimore for the cars, which were detained by the Snow & frost on the rails. We found your G[ran]d Father at the Washington Depot & Daniel & old Carriage & horses & young Daniel on the Colt <u>Mildred</u>. Your Mother, G[ran]d Father, Mary, Eliza, the little people & the baggage, I thought load enough for the Carriage, so Roony & I took our feet in our hands & walked over. We looked for the Anne Chase in which to get a lift to Roachs hill, but Congratulated ourselves afterwards that we missed her for She only overtook us after we had passed Jackson City, & was scarcely out of Sight when we turned up the Washington Turnpike. The Snow impeded the Carriage as well as us, & we reached here shortly after it. The Children were delighted at getting back & passed the ev[enin]g in devising pleasures for the morrow. They were in upon us before day xmas mor[nin]g to overhaul their stockings. Mildred thinks she drew the prize, in the shape of a beautiful new Doll. Angelina's infirmities were so great that she was left in B[altimore] & this new treasure was entirely unexpected. The cakes, candies, books etc. were overlooked in the Caresses she bestowed upon her, & she was scarcely out of her arms all day. Roony got among his a nice p[ai]r of boots, which he particularly wanted, & the girls I hope were equally pleased with their presents, books & trinkets. Your Mother, Mary, Roony & I went in to Church. Roony & the twins skated back in the Canal (Roony having taken in the skates for the purpose) & we filled his place in the Carriage with Miss Sarah Stuart, one of M's Comrades. Minny Lloyd was detained at home to assist her mother at dinner, but your Aunt Maria brought her & Miss Lucretia Fitzhugh out the next day, & Wallace Stiles & his brother arriving at the same time, we had quite a table full. The young people have been quite assiduous in their attentions to each other, as their amusements have necessarily been indoors, but the beaux have successfully maintained their reserve so far, notwithstanding the Captivating advances of the Belles. The first day they tried skating but the ice was soft & rough & it was abandoned in despair. They have not moved out of the house since. To day the twins were obliged to leave us & when the Carriage came to the door, Minny Lloyd & Sarah Stuart reluctantly Confessed that their Mamas ordered them to return in the *first* Carriage. We have only therefore Wallace & Edw[ar]d Stiles & Miss Lucretia Fitzhugh in addition to our family Circle. I need not describe to you our amusements. You have witnessed them so often, nor the Turkey, old ham, plumb pudding, mince pies etc. at dinner. I hope you will often enjoy them again or Some equally as good.

"The weather has been bitter Cold. I do not recollect such Cold weather. I Can only judge by my feelings, since the winter of 1835. I have not been to Washington yet, but will endeavor to get over tomorrow, & am writing this to mail there, that you may not entirely miss your accustomed letter. The family have retired but I know I should be charged with much love from every individual were they aware of my writing. So I will give it without bidding. May you have many happy years. All bringing you an increase of virtue & wisdom. All witnessing your prosperity in this life. All bringing you nearer everlasting happiness hereafter. May God in his great mercy grant me this my Constant prayer…With kind remembrances to Jerome, T___ W. Lawrence etc. I remain as ever your devoted father.

R. E. Lee"

Purchased from Goodspeed's, 1979. Gift of Clements Library Associates in memory of Helen Schoff.

ᥫ᭰ 81 ᥫ᭰

FOLLOWING THE NORTH STAR

THE UNDERGROUND RAILROAD traversed the North, linking "stations" in countless small towns and farms along the route to Canada and liberty. One of the towering figures of abolitionism, Frederick Douglass (1817?–1895) knew firsthand about the Railroad as both passenger and conductor.

Born a slave on Maryland's Eastern Shore, Douglass was only twenty-one when he escaped from the docks of Baltimore, where he had been hired out as a ship's caulker. With the assistance of the New York Vigilance Committee, an organization founded by African Americans to assist fugitive slaves, Douglass settled in New Bedford, Massachusetts, and although racism prevented him from plying his trade, he soon found his calling as a publicist for the abolition of slavery. Displaying an extraordinary talent as an orator and armed with the moral authority of his experiences, Douglass earned the attention of William Lloyd Garrison and Wendell Phillips. He toured the North with them to deliver countless lectures on the evils of slavery and the necessity of immediate emancipation. But there was a problem. Douglass spoke too well. "People doubted if I had ever been a slave," he wrote, "They said I did not talk like a slave, look like a slave, nor act like a slave."

Thus, in 1845 Douglass wrote his autobiography, *Narrative of the Life of Frederick Douglass*, as testimony to the authenticity of his experiences and as a tool to advance the cause. It was an instant success, giving names, dates, places, and other details that provided unequivocal verification of his claims. It established Douglass as a figure of national importance. After returning from a lecture tour of Britain in 1847, he broke with Garrison and established his own newspaper in Rochester, New York, the *North Star*, later known as *Frederick Douglass' Paper*. Although never very profitable, the paper managed to stay solvent with the liberal assistance of groups such as the Rochester Ladies Anti-Slavery Society, whose records are housed at the Clements Library. It became one of the most important antislavery voices in the nation.

As he always did, Douglass put his preaching into practice. The offices of the newspaper became an important stop on the Underground Railroad, where fugitives could find a safe resting place, food, and drink. In many cases, Douglass arranged for small sums of money to assist the fugitives on the last leg of their journey to Canada. Once again, the Rochester Ladies coordinated

My Dear Miss Porter,

You will oblige me by sending me three Dollars to assist to assist John Williams, a man on his way from slavery to freedom. He comes from the neighborhood from which I escaped and I believe him to be genuine.

Yours with respect and gratitude,
Frederick Douglass

April 29th

much of the funding. The handwritten note illustrated here was penned by Douglass and slipped into the hand of fugitive John Williams, to provide him safe passage and financial support at the next Underground Railroad station in the Rochester area.

When Williams was brought to Douglass' office, we can only imagine what ran through the great abolitionist's mind. The fugitive was a man "from the neighborhood from which I escaped," replaying Douglass' own past, taking a different geographic route, but aspiring to the same ultimate goal of self liberation. Douglass' comment, "I believe him to be genuine," seems perplexing. Why doubt Williams? The answer, perhaps, lies in the context of the great public debate in the 1850s over the authenticity and veracity of "slave narratives." Allegations that white antislavery worker Lydia Maria Child had ghost written Harriet Jacobs' *Incidents in the Life of a Slave Girl*, and that some narratives had been fabricated, were used to discredit abolitionism. As author of two of the most widely read narratives, Douglass was keenly aware of the politics of authenticity and was undoubtedly sensitive to the issue.

The antislavery movement is among the great, long-time interests of the Clements Library, and its collections reflect all of its aspects. From conservative colonizationists like David Lee Child, Joshua Danforth, Morris Barton, and James Duncan, to moderate political activists like James Gillespie Birney and Owen Lovejoy, to the comprehensive radicalism of the Grimké sisters, Theodore Dwight Weld, the Rochester Ladies, and Harriet deGarmo Fuller, the Clements' manuscripts offer a remarkable perspective on the motives and tactics of organized abolitionism. In addition, the Library has an exceptionally strong collection of antislavery pamphlets, periodicals, and newspapers, as well as numerous publications defending the institution.

Rochester Ladies Anti-Slavery Society Papers purchased at local auction by Stephen Resnick, 1983.

PRESERVING THE MEMORY OF THE DEAD

A THEORY CURRENT IN THE MID-NINETEENTH CENTURY held that an image of the last moment of life was permanently inscribed in the eye of the deceased. For many Americans, photography became the eye of the living, preserving an image of a deceased loved one for eternity. Within a few years of its introduction in 1839, photography had become an integral part of a burgeoning culture of death, an indispensible ritual in the mourning process of many Americans.

In the 1850s, the passing of a family member was often marked with the summoning of a photographer, even before the body was laid out for viewing. Partly because of the primitive state of embalming, postmortem photographs were taken as soon after death as possible. Especially in the case of the death of an infant, parents were expected to pose with the corpse, often cradling it in their arms, life-like except for closed eyes. In this way, the bonds of familial love were made tangible for all to see and, permanent in the photographic silver, were proof of the conquest of love over death.

One of America's best known daguerreotypists, Marcus Aurelius Root (1808–1888), clearly understood the impulse. "By heliography," he wrote (using a synonym for photography), "our loved ones, dead or distant, our friends and acquaintances, however far removed, are retained within

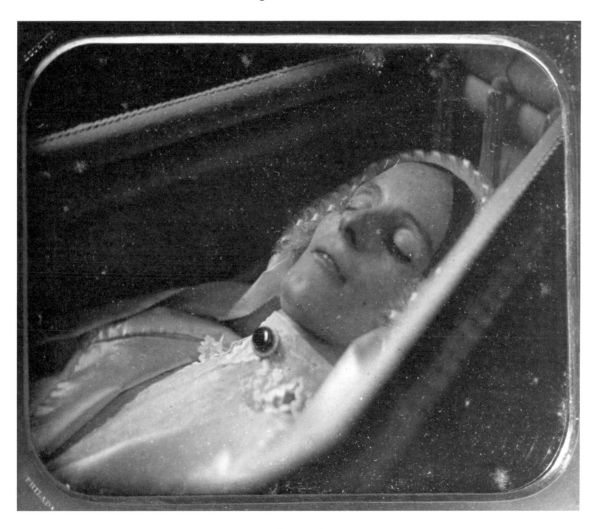

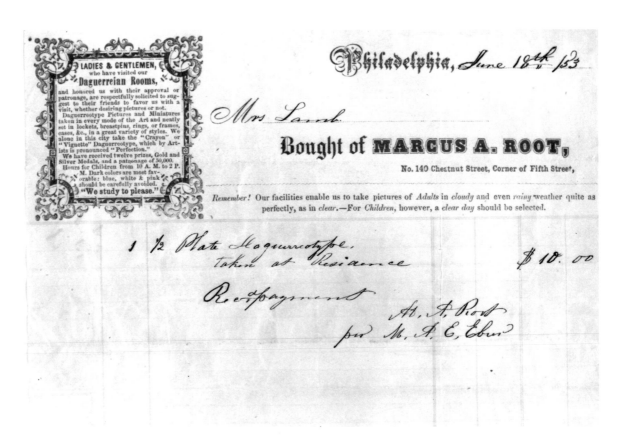

daily and hourly vision. To what extent domestic and social affections and sentiments are conserved and perpetuated by these 'shadows' of the loved and valued originals, every one may judge. In this competitive and selfish world of ours, whatever tends to vivify and strengthen the social feelings should be hailed as a benediction."

When wealthy Philadelphian Harriet Lamb died in June 1853, Marcus Root carted his camera to her family's home for the tidy sum of ten dollars. The family spared no expense, and the funeral director supplied trappings of the most exquisite sort: oak coffin with silk lining and bunting, gloves, and pillows. The refinements of the funeral arrangements are reflected in the daguerreotype as well—its cost reflected in the care lavished on the plush velvet pad and brass mat and the elegant wood and leather case housing the delicate silvered plate. When the case is opened, the photograph is intended as a private mourning experience, for the viewer's eyes alone. Not only has this cultural artifact survived for nearly one hundred and fifty years, but the bills of the funeral and the photographer have as well. It is one of the few daguerreotypes accompanied by such information.

Although modern medicine and sanitation were beginning to improve mortality statistics by the time this photograph was taken, it was not until the end of the century, when the germ theory and the causes of infection were beginning to be understood, that striking progress was made. Until then, death was a frequent visitor to every home, constantly depriving rich and poor of infants and children and young men and women, such as Harriet Lamb, just as they were entering adulthood. This portrait is morbid to the modern American eye, but it documents a common occurrence in past generations. The omnipresence of death inevitably affected the outlook of nineteenth-century Americans.

Purchased from Tamerlane Books, 1996.

RUNAWAY SLAVE POSTER: AN INSTITUTION
CONDEMNS ITSELF

THE LIBRARY'S COLLECTIONS contain many source materials which document the almost unimaginable brutality of slavery as it was practiced, from the log books of slave ships and correspondence of slave dealers to newspaper advertisements. There is something particularly shocking in a poster such as the one displayed here, advertising to find a human being, as if he were a lost horse, and putting a value on him in dollar figures. Although six feet tall and twenty-seven years old, he is referred to as a "boy" and is not provided the dignity of a last name. "Copper color" would suggest that Henry was of mixed blood, very possibly a brother or even child of this or a previous master. Most shocking is the physical description, including "his right eye burnt out, causing a scar down to the corner of his mouth." This is not a self-inflicted wound, and it was either the result of inhumane working conditions or torturous punishment.

Two decades before this advertisement was issued, Theodore Dwight Weld, one of the early antislavery leaders, came up with a brilliant idea. He, his wife, Angelina Grimké Weld, and sister-in-law Sarah Grimké, all of whose papers are at the Library, solicited copies of southern newspapers and collected descriptions from persons who had lived and visited in the South and observed slavery firsthand. From these, they published, under the auspices of the American Anti-Slavery

$100,00
REWARD.

Ranaway from the subscriber living about 8 miles north of Liberty, Mo., on the 26th August, a negro man named HENRY, aged 27 years, about 6 feet high, copper color, his right eye burnt out, causing a scar down to the corner of his mouth, and weighs about 170 lbs.
☞I will give $100 for the apprehension and delivery to me of said boy if taken out of the State; $40 out of Clay county, and $20 in the county. WM. T. ONAN.
Sept. 23, 1857.

Society, *American Slavery As It Is: Testimony of a Thousand Witnesses* (New York, 1839). The publication provided brilliant and irrefutable documentation of the harshness and cruelty of the system, largely in the words of slave holders themselves. The broadside illustrated here serves the same purpose. Historical libraries have as great a responsibility to preserve documentation of the flaws as they do the triumphs of the nation's past.

Purchased from Randall House Books, 1981.

❦ 84 ❦

PHANTOM CITY, PRESERVED IN PRINT

DONIPHAN COUNTY, bounded on the east by the Missouri River, was one of the earliest areas of settlement in Kansas. Sometime in the spring of 1857, a homesteaders' association was formed to establish a ferry and river town a few miles south of Doniphan, and they named it Geary City in honor of one of the territorial governors. As of April 1857 the "town" contained a single squatter's cabin, a stream, and a forest of virgin timber on a site which gradually rose in ascending levels from the river. One month later, it had a newspaper, and by September the *Geary City Era* reported that the timber had been cleared, streets had been graded, and a ferry established. There were several stores, a post office receiving daily mail deliveries, a lime kiln, brick kiln, two saw mills, and a sizable hotel, with a second one almost completed. Coal had recently been discovered within the village limits, several steam boats made regularly scheduled stops daily, roads were being constructed to the back country, and more than two hundred persons were gainfully employed, providing most of the services expected in any civilized community. Kansas was an exciting place, politically, at that period of time, a battleground between proslavery and antislavery forces to determine whether it would eventually enter the Union as a free or slave state.

The *Geary City Era* was four pages in length, issued every Saturday evening. This particular paper had a most unusual arrangement, in that it had two and sometimes three editors simultaneously, adhering to different political parties—one a Whig, one a Democrat (but a Free Soil Democrat), and the third an American Party enthusiast. They took turns writing editorials. Otherwise, it was typical of the papers issued in more than a thousand small towns and villages throughout the country: literary pieces on the first page, national and local news on the inner pages, and advertisements on the final page. In spite of being issued on the edge of civilization in a sparsely populated region, the *Geary City Era* was but one of six such weeklies in Doniphan County alone and twenty-eight newspapers in Kansas Territory. Newspaper presses in this era did job printing of advertising matter, and the newspaper page shown here, printed entirely in bold type, was obviously issued simultaneously as a poster.

Based upon the local news and advertisements in the *Era*, Geary City seemed to be well on its way to growth and prosperity in 1858. But something happened, and in the latter part of 1858 progress came to an abrupt halt. In the issue of October 9, 1858, the *Era* announced that the Republican editor had quit and the Democratic editor was moving the paper to Troy, the county seat,

BEWARE OF IMPOSITION!!

We earnestly hope and confidently believe that

Every Free State Voter

will carefully examine his ticket, and compare it with the one under the editorial head of the Geary City Era. It is the only one authorized by the

GRASSHOPPER FALLS CONVENTION, IN AUGUST LAST,

and endorsed by the Convention of Delegates which met at

PALERMO, ON THE FIFTH DAY OF SEPTEMBER LAST.

The enemy have and are attempting, as we have conclusive evidence, by

Spurious Tickets and Fraud!

to divide our vote, and thus to weaken us and elect their candidates.

☞ UNITE TOGETHER!--Stand shoulder to shoulder in unbroken columns, and, with united effort, we can succeed in ROUTING THE FOE, AND OBTAINING A COMPLETE VICTORY!

COME TO THE POLLS!!

Let no man stay away, whatever be his political opinions, and then let us endeavor, quietly and harmoniously, to accomplish the great work of FREEING KANSAS FROM FOREIGN RULE!! Vote early!

PAY NO TAX!!

The GOVERNOR, the PRESIDENT, and the CABINET, unite in the opinion that there can no Tax be exacted, and in the law there is no mention of any Tax. ☞ READ THE GOVERNOR'S PROCLAMATION!

TAKE NO TEST OATH!!

Which is wholly annulled and blotted out of the Statutes of Kansas. Act only on the DEFENSIVE. SUFFER NO IMPOSITION!!

BE READY FOR ANY EMERGENCY.

where he would issue the first number of the *Troy Democrat* at the beginning of November. Probably the leading cause was the short but severe economic depression of 1858–59. Perhaps the site was not all it had seemed to be at first. By 1870 a bill was introduced in the legislature to vacate the town's streets and alleys. Geary City disappeared from the map. We think of it as an exclusive phenomenon of the American west, but "boom town" to "ghost town" was a commonplace and accepted part of the American settlement process, beginning with Jamestown itself. Geary City's entire existence, to a considerable degree, depends upon the chance survival of a single file of a newspaper!

Gift of Dr. and Mrs. Joseph Cerny, Ann Arbor, 1976.

⤬ 85 ⤬

JOHN BROWN'S PROVISIONAL CONSTITUTION

THE SAVAGE ARM OF A WRATHFUL GOD, John Brown (1800–1859) was an American demon or demigod, depending on the politics of the observer. Born of old New England stock, before he

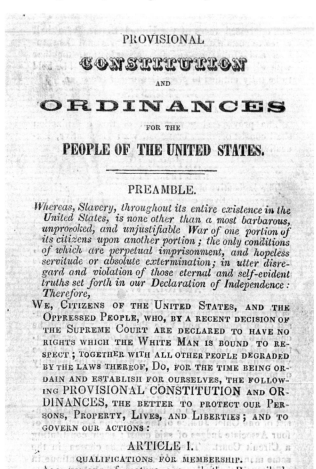

turned fifty Brown had proven himself an abysmal failure at nearly everything in life except procreation. He had twenty children by two wives. As a drover, tanner, shepherd, and merchant, he could not make ends meet, and with each personal crisis, like a Biblical patriarch, he led his brood to a different home in Pennsylvania, New York, Connecticut, or Ohio.

Brown had long had a fascination with abolitionism, and in the 1850s his interest turned into a fixation. Galvanized by the question of whether slavery ought to be allowed in the territories, Brown turned the full force of his will to the active destruction of the slaveholding system. "Bleeding Kansas" had descended into chaos as proslavery and antislavery forces sought to resolve the question in the territory by force. Following his sons to Kansas in 1856, Brown led a band of antislavery guerrillas who inflamed the countryside, liberating slaves and assaulting slaveholders.

With the respect and financial support of some highly educated, highly placed men,

Brown conceived a plan to spark a larger war to liberate enslaved Americans. By leading a tightly knit band of armed men into the heart of the South, he reasoned that slaves and white abolitionists would flock to his side and precipitate the end of slavery by force of arms. At the time, Brown was depicted as a fanatic, a monomaniac, but his schemes were characterised by tremendous intelligence and calculation. What Brown felt he needed to complete his plan was a constitution, founded on the principles of equality, "those eternal and self-evident truths" set out in the Declaration of Independence, to lend legitimacy to his authority and order to his enterprise.

Brown labored over the constitution, drafting ideas while staying at Frederick Douglass' house in Rochester in January 1858. On May 8, his Harper's Ferry raid already in the planning stage, he called a secret meeting of his supporters in Chatham, Ontario, which was the center of an extensive African-American community made up largely of runaway slaves. Forty-six men, including the great African-American intellectual, Martin Delany, debated the various articles, which carefully laid out not only a justification for the annihilation of slavery, but the framework for a provisional government. Brown was elected commander in chief. One article carefully indicated that the intention of the new government was not to dissolve the Union or overthrow the government, but simply "Amendment and Repeal." Through Brown's strongarm tactics and charismatic energy, the Provisional Constitution was easily ratified.

As Brown was preparing to return to the United States, the constitution was whisked away to St. Catharines, Ontario, where it was published by William H. Day, an African-American graduate of Oberlin College. Two versions of the constitution are known, one printed on white paper, the other (this copy) on blue. Both are extremely rare. No more than a few hundred were issued, but the rarity may be equally a result of a peculiar subsequent history. The finished pamphlets were sent to Brown, who took them to the Freeman Farm where he and his soldiers stayed before their raid on Harper's Ferry. He apparently intended to distribute them as the crusade to liberate slaves advanced. After the defeat of Brown's forces, a number of copies remained strewn about the Harper's Ferry Armory. These were used for cartridge paper by the militia as they took target practice, an ignominious end to a document that had such high intentions.

Purchased from Abraham Lincoln Bookshop, 1948.

❧ 86 ❧

BUFFALO HUNTING ON CANADA'S WESTERN PLAINS, 1862

IN AUGUST 1862, young Charles Adolphus Murray, 7th Earl of Dunmore, rode into Fort Garry, modern Winnipeg, at the junction of the Assiniboine and Red Rivers, determined to hunt the buffalo and elk in the surrounding plains. At twenty-one, Dunmore possessed the stamina, intelligence, and ambition that one day would place him among Britain's elite international explorers. There is a frontispiece portrait of the mature Dunmore in his 1893 account of a year's expedition

on horseback and foot through Kashmir, Western Tibet, Chinese Tartary, and Russian Central Asia. He had a handsome face, imperious stare, and a strong compact body that even a heavy fur-lined coat cannot conceal. His book also documents a talent for recording his exploits in fine watercolor sketches.

The little we know about Dunmore's hunting expedition comes from two of his own watercolors, among the Clements Library collections, and a journal kept by two other intrepid adventurers, Viscount Milton and Dr. Walter Cheadle, published in 1865 as *The North-West Passage by Land*. The watercolors are well-executed hunting scenes on the western plains, one of a herd of elk fleeing unseen hunters, the other picturing a single hunter riding hard in the midst of a buffalo herd, framed by rolling hills, with the bleached bones of a carcass in the foreground.

Milton and Cheadle encountered Dunmore briefly at Fort Garry in 1862 as they were preparing their expedition in search of a route across the continent to British Columbia, through a northern pass in the Rocky Mountains. Their book provides an excellent description of Fort Garry, a flourishing bastion of the Hudson's Bay Company. The fort's original high stone walls, erected in 1811, enclosed a compound of wooden buildings, the governor's residence, a jail, company warehouses, and a store "thronged from morning till night by a crowd of settlers and half-breeds, gossiping and drinking rum." Beyond the fort, the Red River settlement extended twenty miles northward into the open plains.

According to Milton and Cheadle, the most exciting annual events, locally, were the spring and fall hunts. Buffalo were still a principal source of food. The whole able-bodied population set out for the plains, men on horses followed by women and children in hundreds of carts who would turn the buffalo meat into pemmican, cakes of dried and pounded meat mixed with melted fat. As Milton and Cheadle describe the hunt, once buffalo were found, "the horsemen are formed into lines, and ride up as close as possible before the herd takes flight at full speed. Then the captain gives the word, and all charge, as hard as horses can gallop, into the middle of the herd. The fattest beasts are singled out and shot down, and often more than 1,000 carcases strew the ground."

Dunmore and a party of military officers stationed at Montreal had come to join the hunt. While Milton and Cheadle completed their preparations to winter along the Saskatchewan, the officers set off for Fort Ellice on the Assiniboine. Several days later the explorers left Fort Garry, "riding through undulating country, full of lakes and marshes thronged with wild-fowl . . . continually coming across the skulls of buffalo, whitened by age and exposure." Suddenly they were intercepted by a train of carts returning to the Red River settlement. The driver in charge carried a note from Lord Dunmore urging Dr. Cheadle to come at once, saying he was lying ill with jaundice at Fort Ellice.

Milton and Cheadle responded quickly: "We tied our blankets behind our saddles, hung a tin cup to our belts, and taking a couple of unleavened cakes a piece, set out on a forced march to the Fort, leaving the men to follow with the carts. We rode hard, and reached our destination on the evening of the third day, when we found that our exertions had been useless, as Lord Dunmore had left the day before to continue the hunt." Fortunately, he must have taken his watercolors and brushes with him.

Purchased from Sotheby's by MacManus, 1988.

⇜ 87 ⇝

A CAPTIVE AUDIENCE FOR THE NATIONAL GAME

THE CRACK OF THE BAT SIGNALS the return of spring, and at no time during our history was the sound more welcome than at Salisbury, North Carolina, during the spring of 1862. Baseball's leisured pace and its ability to consume the many hours of a long day appealed to Americans, North and South. At Salisbury Military Prison it provided relief from the tedium of confinement, and a momentary taste of life at home.

Among the inmates enjoying the game that spring was Otto Boetticher, a Prussian immigrant soldier and lithographer. In 1861 he and two of his sons enlisted in the 68th New York Infantry, recruited mainly among the German community in New York City. On March 29, 1862, less than a year into his service, Boetticher was captured at Warrenton Junction, Virginia. As frequently happened during the war, he was officially reported missing, and as a result he was dismissed from the army. In reality he had been sent to a converted cotton factory at Salisbury, North Carolina.

Fortunately for Boetticher, he was captured early in the war when prisoners were usually treated in compliance with a time-tested, "gentlemanly" code of conduct. Salisbury Prison was then one of the best places for a Union prisoner. There were only 1,500 inmates, and Boetticher found spacious accommodations, acceptable food, and baseball. While some men were roughed up dur-

ing capture or robbed of valuables, generally speaking prisoners could be assured of humane treatment. Beginning in July 1861, most could also expect a quick release on parole and could find themselves at home after swearing to remain inactive until "regularly discharged." Other parolees bided their time in "parole camps," out of the line of fire, out of action, until formal exchange was arranged. The parole system benefitted both sides by reducing the burden of guarding and caring for potentially hostile prisoners.

The first formal exchange of prisoners took place in February 1862, and from that July on, exchanges occurred nearly monthly. Soldiers could be traded straight up for soldiers of equal rank, or they could be bartered for any number of a lesser rank: a general brought 60 enlisted men, a colonel, fifteen, and a sergeant only two. In Boetticher's case, he was exchanged on September 21, 1862, for a captain in the 7th Virginia Infantry. When he returned home, Boetticher prepared this wholesome image of Salisbury, incidentally one of the best early views of our national pastime, and one of the most unusual views of a Confederate military prison.

By 1863, the unwillingness of the Confederacy to release African-American soldiers and Ulysses Grant's tactical decision to refuse exchange led to the rapid deterioration of the system. The lives of all prisoners of war dramatically deteriorated. At prisons such as Salisbury or the notorious Andersonville in Georgia, prisoners flooded in and choked the system. Maltreatment, malnourishment, disease, and even murder became routine facts of life at Andersonville. The miserable federal prison at Elmira, New York, was little better, and there were many other rivals, North and South, for Andersonville's title as most lethal hole in America. The moments of joy and recreation celebrated by Boetticher virtually disappeared.

The experiences of prisoners of war form one of the great strengths of the Schoff Civil War Collection at the Clements Library. Almost three dozen sets of soldiers' letters and diaries document the lives of imprisoned soldiers, civilians, and political prisoners.

Gift of James S. Schoff, New York, 1982.

LINCOLN ADVISES HIS COMMANDING GENERAL

DURING THE CIVIL WAR, the Presidents of neither the United States nor the Confederacy were willing to leave matters of military strategy entirely up to their commanding generals. Jefferson Davis was a West Point graduate who had served with distinction in the Mexican War. Lincoln, on the other hand, was a politician, entirely untrained in military matters. Yet historians tend to give President Lincoln fairly high marks as a military tactician, while they almost universally criticize Davis for constantly interfering with his generals.

Lincoln did not pretend to be an expert on how to fight a war, but he did have two strong beliefs that he communicated regularly to each of his commanders: never let up the pressure on the enemy, and remember that beating armies, not capturing territory, is the way to win a war.

George McClellan was appointed commander in chief of the army in November 1861 after the disastrous defeat at the first Battle of Bull Run. He was given vast manpower, and he did an excellent job of training recruits and building morale. The trouble was, he never felt that the army was quite strong enough to fight. Lincoln pushed him into action. McClellan's offensive on the Peninsula during the summer of 1862 crawled along as he constantly overestimated his opponent's strength and continually requested reinforcements. "Sending reinforcement to McClellan," Lincoln is said to have quipped, "is like shovelling flies across a barn."

McClellan's reluctance to fight led to his replacement by John Pope, who was promptly, resoundingly defeated at the Second Battle of Bull Run, setting up McClellan's return. Resuming his accustomed snail-like pace, McClellan so irritated the President that he made another change in October 1862. Ambrose Burnside only reluctantly accepted the command of the Army of the Potomac, egged on by officers who hated to see Joe Hooker, the alternate selection, at the helm. Burnside is remembered largely for ineptitude at Antietam, where he allowed Lee's army to escape, and for his even less distinguished performance at Fredericksburg and in the Falmouth "mud march" of January 1863. Burnside had the strength of character to admit to his inadequacies and resign.

Character certainly was not Hooker's qualification for succeeding to the command. He was a bawdy, hard-drinking man known for a profusion of profanity in his speech and a succession of questionable women in his tent—his moral flaws well documented by letters in the Library's collections. He was said, reliably, to prefer a dictator to a president in wartime, and he was notorious for undercutting his superiors when it worked to his advantage. But Hooker had the talent and aggression that Lincoln desired.

By June 1863, Lincoln's frustration with the Army of the Potomac was once again mounting. Aware that Lee's army was preparing for a major move, but uncertain of the intentions (Gettysburg is where it ended), Lincoln was desperate for guidance. In probing enemy defences, Hooker surmised that Lee intended to invade the North. He suggested striking Richmond, which would be left vulnerable. Robert E. Lee himself understood, and feared this strategy. Hooker communicated his thoughts to Lincoln, and the President wrote back, "If left to me, I would not go South of the Rappahannock upon Lee's moving North of it — If you had Richmond invested to-day, you would not be able to take it in twenty days; meanwhile your communications, and with them, your army, would be ruined. I think Lee's Army, and not Richmond, is your true objective point."

Was Lincoln right? Hindsight, of course, is a risk-free game to play. Lincoln replaced Hooker with George Gordon Meade on June 28. He made Lee's army his true objective point at Gettysburg, and according to many observers, he turned the tide of the war in the process. But it took almost two full years of bloody fighting to end the rebellion. One cannot help but wonder whether Hooker's plan for a quick strike to Richmond might have been effective at blunting Lee's foray to the North. This is one of thousands of Civil War letters in the Schoff Collection, which is considered by scholars to be one of the country's finest resources for studying this endlessly fascinating conflict.

Gift of James S. Schoff, New York, 1976.

ᔙ 89 ᔙ

PICTURING THE WEST

A HANDFUL OF NINETEENTH-CENTURY PHOTOGRAPHERS, among them Carleton Watkins, Timothy O'Sullivan, A. J. Russell, George Fiske, Eadweard Muybridge, and E. Jay Haynes, associated with government survey parties, created breathtaking images of the West in the 1860s through the 1880s — pictures of vast, unbounded spaces peopled sparsely, if at all, by a "backward" and "vanishing" race.

Among the more obscure photographers of the West was Rudolph d'Heureuse, a man whose diverse talents included mining engineering, metallurgy, prospecting, and surveying. He became the first person to photograph the Mojave Desert. While the Civil War raged in the East, the West struggled on its own, and the Mojave was the scene of a particularly fierce contest. In crushing the resistance of Mojave Indians to white encroachment in 1858 and 1859, the federal government constructed Fort Mojave, a crude and dusty outpost near the three-way border of California, Arizona, and Nevada, and began a systematic examination of the region, involving mapping, botanical and geological surveying, and military fortification.

Having prospected the region in 1862, d'Heureuse was available when the state embarked on pacifying and securing the Mojave. In 1863 d'Heureuse prepared a photographic survey of the

route between San Bernardino, California, and Fort Mojave, Arizona Territory, as well as the El Dorado Canyon in Nevada. Lugging his wet-plate apparatus deep into the rugged desert, he produced the first documentary views of the Southwest. The unforgiving scrub and the xerophytic flora provide a very different impression of the West than the grand landscapes of the better known surveyors, and his unromantic pictures of soldiers and surveyors posed with the Indian inhabitants, such as this view of John Moss and the Paiute chief, Tercherrum, are highly unusual. Looking at Moss's buckskinned nonchalance and the dead-on stare of Tercherrum, wrapped in his soft rabbit-skin cape and grasping a rifle, it is hard to imagine how quickly this frontier would change and the Indians disappear.

While d'Heureuse's photographs were apparently not made available commercially, their importance was recognized within the scientific community. Twelve prints found their way into the hands of Benjamin Silliman by 1865, and forty-four into the possession of William H. Brewer, head of the geological survey of California. The Clements set of thirty-three views was acquired by Harvard student Horace Mann, the eldest son of the educator of the same name, when he and a fellow student, William T. Brigham, undertook a botanizing expedition to Hawaii. En route, the two stopped in California to study the geology and collect plants and, apparently, photographs.

Purchased from Forrest Sweet, 1944.

∽ 90 ∼

BRADY OF BROADWAY

THE CIVIL WAR was a landmark in journalism, the first American war covered extensively by photographers and the first in which same-day national news was expected and delivered. The war was a media event, and photographers like Mathew Brady were the catalyst to new ways for the public to comprehend the nature of warfare.

The son of Irish immigrants, Brady moved to New York City in 1839, the same year that photography arrived in the United States. Opening his first studio in 1844, the young man displayed an unusual aptitude for photography, but an even greater aptitude for self-promotion. Fashioning

himself "Brady of Broadway," his name became synonymous with quality in photographic portraits, and by the early 1850s nearly every would-be well-known public figure could be counted on to trek to the corner of Broadway and Fulton to have a "likeness" taken. In 1858 he franchised himself, opening a studio in Washington, D.C., followed three years later by an even more important expansion when he organized a small corps of photographers to document the progress of Union armies during the Civil War.

Technical difficulties made it extremely difficult to take pictures out-of-doors prior to the late 1850s, and to take a picture of something as chaotic and active as warfare was nearly unthinkable. But a few years before the Civil War a new photographic technique—the wet plate collodion process—was introduced, featuring shorter exposure times and, most importantly, the ability to mass-produce positive prints from a single negative. From a technical perspective, wet plate negatives were still difficult to make outside of a studio setting, since the glass plate, coated with wet collodion, had to be exposed and developed before it dried. In taking pictures outside, it was necessary to cart along nearly an entire darkroom, no easy task with a hostile army bearing down. The image of Brady cradling a glass plate and dodging minié balls while hustling back and forth from his photographic van is the stuff of Civil War legend, but, in reality, poor eyesight prevented the master from taking many of the images bearing his studio's name.

Pictures like the "Confederate dead at Allsop's House, Spotsylvania," taken during the Wilderness Campaign of 1864 and illustrated here, had an electrifying impact on the American public. While death was a familiar part of Victorian existence, never before had Americans seen carnage and destruction on such a scale. However moving a written account may be, few can convey the agonies of death or the cold reality of mutilation, bloating, and decay like the photographs taken by Brady's able assistants. These images continue to haunt each new generation of observers and in large part help to explain the timeless interest of Americans in Civil War history and battlefield sites. The Schoff Collection at the Library includes an extensive collection of contemporary Civil War photographs.

Gift of James S. Schoff, New York, 1977.

ᘓ 91 ᘔ

HARDTACK AND A HARD PENCIL

THE ROMANCE OF WAR held powerful sway over American manhood during the nineteenth century, and not even a conflict as brutal and divisive as the Civil War could remove all the lustre. Edgar H. Klemroth, a bookbinder by trade and a skilled artist, was one soldier who indulged in martial romance but who learned to relate to all facets of the soldier's lot. His service is memorable in that he successfully captured the many aspects of army life with pencil and brush.

The 6th Pennsylvania Cavalry, Klemroth's regiment, was raised largely among the social elite of Philadelphia in July and August 1861. Its colonel, Richard Henry Rush (1824–1893), son of American diplomat Richard Rush and a graduate of West Point, selected officers "with reference to their social standing, soldierly qualities and experience." The unit was designated a regiment of lancers, supposedly at the suggestion of George McClellan himself, and its soldiers were issued ribbon-bedecked, nine-foot-long lances with deadly-sharp blades. The weapon had never before been used by American regular soldiers and was eventually discarded as "unsuited to use in the South." As a twenty-six year old working man originally from New York City, Corporal Klemroth was not a typical recruit for this particular unit.

Riding into the nation's capital on New Year's Day 1862, the 6th Cavalry must have presented a stirring sight, with a thousand men on horseback, lances glistening, banners fluttering, accompanied by the music of the regiment's superb mounted band. Before long they matched show with performance, participating in at least forty-two different military actions, from the Peninsula Campaign of 1862 to the last days at Appomattox. At the end of the war, Sheridan personally commended the "enviable reputation" won by the regiment in the muddy fields of Virginia.

Klemroth's early service record, however, is a bit less glorious than that of his unit. Excited and complaining of "heart palipatations" on the eve of the Battle of Antietam, Klemroth was ordered by the regimental surgeon to take to the rear wagons. The rear, however, as he chose to interpret it when he finally stopped, was in Washington, D.C.! Pleading guilty to absence without leave, he was reduced in rank to private and placed on half pay for six months. Fortunately this incident did not destroy his career. He reenlisted and, during the Shenandoah Campaign of 1864, was even as-

Head Quarters, Genl Torbert
near Winchester va. Nov. 1864

signed to work at the headquarters of General A. T. Torbert, where he apparently developed a close friendship with Captain Rudolph Ellis of Company B, the general's assistant inspector general.

Toward the end of the war, Klemroth presented the volume of forty-five sketches to Captain Ellis, depicting their life during the Shenandoah Campaign. It is now at the Clements Library. Delicately drawn with a flowing sense of line, these drawings display a soldier's wry sense of humor and an extraordinary ability to capture personality and the feel of the scene. While he sketched lifelike images of Sheridan and Custer, Klemroth's forté was portraying such things as the exhaustion of soldiers returning from a raid, the humorous indignities of camp existence, the simple but dependable servants and teamsters who performed work without the glamour of military rank. The sketch shown here, one of his more picturesque efforts, is a view of General Torbert's headquarters near Winchester, Virginia. It successfully captures some element of the distinctive beauty of the Valley of Virginia.

Klemroth and his friend Ellis both mustered out of the service in August 1865. Returning to civilian life in Philadelphia, Klemroth worked as a draftsman and later an architect, Ellis as a highly successful stockbroker. By 1885, Klemroth was listed in the *Philadelphia Blue Book* and was sufficiently affluent to "summer" in Bryn Mawr.

Purchased from Riba Auctions, 1991.

92

CAPITALIZING ON THE GREAT OIL BONANZA

On August 27, 1859, Edwin L. Drake struck oil at 69 feet in a crudely constructed oil derrick near Titusville, Pennsylvania, creating one of the industries that has transformed the world in the years since and setting in motion a prospecting mania that would eventually overshadow the California Gold Rush several times over.

The existence of mineral, or "Seneca oil," had been known in this area of Pennsylvania for years. Here and there the Indians had discovered a dark, thick, heavily-scented liquid which seeped into streams and rivers. They had found the substance beneficial for medicinal purposes, and it was skimmed off the surface and sold by the bottle. Oil Creek, running south from the Titusville area into the Allegheny River, was appropriately named well before Drake's discovery and had been a primary collecting site for both the Indians and settlers. Once the initial success was achieved, speculators vied to secure mineral rights and land for each of the forty-one farms along the fourteen mile stretch between Titusville and Oil City. By 1860 there were 74 productive wells pumping an average of 1,200 gallons of oil a day.

James Tarr had a two-hundred acre farm approximately four miles north of Oil City. The land was relatively poor, and like most of his neighbors, he had barely scratched out a living, farming in the summer, cutting and rafting timber in the winter, and supplementing the family diet by hunting rabbits and small game. He was a big, loud, rough-spoken, and uneducated man, but was particularly fortunate in the location of his property and exceptionally shrewd when it came to business. With a couple of partners, he drilled and successfully hit oil in June 1861 with the Crescent Well, but it went dry a year later. Thereafter, he specialized in selling land but keeping partial mineral rights, or selling partial rights and keeping land. The Phillips Well, at the right forefront of the picture, "struck" in August 1861, and over the following ten years it produced a million barrels of oil—a record for a single well which held for twenty-seven years. The Woodford Well, at the left of the picture, struck in December 1861 and made $600,000 for the lessee in eighteen months. The success of these two wells alone drove the price of nearby leases well beyond that of the most desirable real estate in London or New York, and the Tarr farm became a small, muddy, oil-soaked city in itself, with small refineries, underground storage tanks, a hotel, stores, rooming houses, and a post office.

The lithograph cover for *American Petroleum* (New York, 1864), which describes the composition as a "polka, schottisch, galop, waltz, march," would appear also to have doubled as a poster for the oil industry and even a real estate advertisement for what may then have been the ugliest but most valuable piece of property in the country. Although based on an actual photograph, a print of which exists in the Library's collections, the lithographer "cleaned it up," took some liberties with the composition, and added Tarr, his daughter, and business partner "Wed" Clarke (seated, presumably holding the lease!). This sheet music cover is drawn from the Library's outstanding collection. Dating from the 1790s to the twentieth century, popular songs and their illustrated covers graphically and irreverently document every aspect of American social and political history.

James Tarr himself sold out in 1865 for close to three million dollars and retired to a mansion

POLKA, SCHOTTISCH, GALOP, WALTZ, MARCH.

BY

J. J. WATSON.

NEW YORK,
Published by Wm Hall & Son, 543 Broadway.

New Haven
Skinner & Sperry.
Pittsburgh,
Wamelink & Barr.

Rochester,
W.S. Mackie & Son.

Buffalo,
Penn & Remington.
Chicago,
Alanson Reed.

5.

and a life of ease in Meadville, Pennsylvania. His timing was always nearly perfect. He died and went to claim his heavenly reward in 1871, at just about the time that oil began to "play out" on the farm.

Purchased from the Old Print Shop, 1946.

⤳ 93 ⤳

PROUD MAN OF MANY TALENTS

BORN IN VIRGINIA to an enslaved father and free mother, Martin Delany (1812–1885) was legally a slave. To make his education possible, his mother relocated to Chambersburg, Pennsylvania, and at the age of nineteen, Martin moved to Pittsburgh, where he served as an apprentice to a white doctor by day and a divinity student by night.

Gaining wide recognition for his intellectual gifts, Delany became a leader of Pittsburgh's African-American community, taking an active role in the Pittsburgh Anti-Slavery Society, the Underground Railroad, and in a number of benevolent and charitable organizations. As he would throughout his life, Delany stressed the need for African Americans to take their fate in their own hands and to rely only upon themselves to advance their cause. He thus became an enthusiastic participant in the "convention" movement of the 1840s, organized by African Americans to lobby for full civil and political rights.

After a fortunate marriage to the daughter of the wealthiest African-American man in the city, Delany entered into the publishing business. His newspaper, *The Mystery*, was devoted to the antislavery movement, and while its run was brief, he turned the experience to good advantage when he teamed up with Frederick Douglass to publish *The North Star*. Delany also became a frequent contributor to other journals, including the *Anglo-African*, establishing himself as one of the most authentically radical and intellectual voices on the American scene, committed to proclaiming the achievements of African peoples. He named each of his sons after heroes of the Haitian revolution and other Black leaders, and his only daughter was name Ethiopia Halle.

In 1850, Delany attempted to return to the study of medicine. Rejected elsewhere because of his color, he enrolled at Harvard, but after only a month white students pressured the administration to expel him, allowing him only to finish the semester. To his dismay, his white abolitionist "friends" failed to take up his case. Due to the absence of licensing laws at the time, however, he hereafter called himself "Doctor."

This snub at Harvard deeply wounded Delany, causing him to reflect further on the prospects of people of African descent in the United States. "We are a nation within a nation," he concluded, and "we must go from our oppressors." Turning the ideas of white colonizationists to Black ends, he proposed to establish "colonies" for freedmen in Africa, Haiti, or South or Central America. Only in their own communities, he argued, could African Americans find equality or justice.

Delany's activism also sought other outlets. Moving to Ontario, where as many as 10,000 fugitives from slavery had settled, he helped recruit soldiers for John Brown's planned insurrection and voiced his opinions at the Chatham Convention of 1854, ratifying Brown's constitution for a new,

Maj. Martin R. Delany, c. 1864

antislavery United States. Shortly after Chatham, Delany left to scour the African continent for a home for his colony, winning international fame in the process as an explorer.

Returning to the United States in 1861, the Civil War aflame, Delany immediately began to advocate the arming of former slaves. When military necessity eventually forced the reluctant hand of President Lincoln, Delany volunteered as recruiter, enlisting his own son, Toussaint, in the fabled 54th Massachusetts Infantry. Delany's efforts earned him a commission as Major in the United States Army, the first person of African descent to be awarded such high rank.

This portrait of Delany in uniform, one of a few copies known, shows the man at the height of his career and influence. The victory over the slaveholding South should have been the cap to Delany's years of labor, but after the war his radicalism softened and his efforts soured. An official for the Freedmen's Bureau in South Carolina, he became actively involved in that state's Republican Party, but switched allegiance to the Democratic Party in the mid-1870s, hoping pragmatically to salvage some vestige of the aims of Reconstruction.

Delany continued to harbor hopes of emigration and spent his last years writing about the cultural achievements of Africans. Looking back on nearly forty years of work, friendship, and occasional rivalry, Frederick Douglass could write, "I thank God for making me a man, but Delany thanks Him for making him a *black* man."

Purchased from Thomas T. Moebs, 1980.

ᔆᔆ 94 ᔆᔆ

"DEATH BED OF THE MOST REMARKABLE MAN OF MODERN TIMES"

JAMES TANNER, A YOUNG CORPORAL in the 87th New York Regiment, badly wounded at Second Bull Run, was forced to have both his feet amputated. Rather than let this misfortune ruin his life, he attended Ames' Business College in Syracuse, New York, and was hired as a clerk in the War

Department in Washington. On Friday evening, April 14, 1865, he joined a friend to attend a performance of "Aladdin, or The Wonderful Lamp" at Glover's Theater in Washington, D.C. While the play was in progress, at a little after 10:00 p.m., a man entered the theater and announced, "President Lincoln is assassinated in his private box at Fords!" After a moment of excitement, someone else cried out, "Sit down, it is a ruse of the pick-pockets." The audience quieted, and the performance recommenced. Shortly thereafter, the play stopped and a theater manager stepped from behind the curtain, confirming that the previous news had been correct.

Tanner happened to rent the two front rooms on the second floor of a house across the street from Ford's Theater. He returned to his lodging, only to discover that Lincoln was in the second floor apartment of the adjoining building. Tanner went up to his room and found that the balcony enabled him to look into the next door apartment and converse with its occupants. An investigation of the shooting had already begun, and General Halleck called for the services of a shorthand reporter. Tanner was the only person in the vicinity who had such skills. At about midnight he was admitted to the Petersen house, where the President was "breathing hard, and with every breath a groan." Summoned to a nearby room, which contained several generals, Chief Justice Chase of the Supreme Court, Chief Justice Carter of the District of Columbia, the entire Cabinet except for Seward, and many other distinguished men, Tanner began taking notes in shorthand of the questions and testimony of witnesses. After an hour and a half, he began transcribing his notes, finishing at 6:45 a.m.

Writing on April 17 in a lengthy shorthand letter to Henry F. Walch of Grand Rapids, Michigan, a former schoolmate at the business college, Tanner provided a vivid description of Lincoln's death:

"At 6:45 Saturday morning I finished my notes and passed into the back room where the President lay. It was very evident that he could not last long. There was a crowd in the room, which was small, but I approached quite near the bed on which so much greatness lay, fast losing its hold on this world. The head of the bed was towards the door, at the head stood Capt. Robert Lincoln, weeping on the shoulder of Senator Sumner. Gen. Halleck just behind Robt. Lincoln and I stood just to the left of Gen. Halleck, and between him and Gen. Meiggs. Stanton was there, trying every way to be calm and yet he was very much moved. The utmost silence pervaded, broken only by the sounds of strong mens tears. It was a solemn time, I assure you. The President breathed heavily until a few minutes before he breathed his last, then his breath came easily, and he passed off very quietly. As soon as he was dead, Rev. Dr. Gurley, who has been the Presidents pastor since his sojourn in this city, offered up a very impressive prayer . . . Secretary Stanton told me to take charge of the testimony I had taken, so I went to my room and took a copy of it to be delivered to him, as I wished to keep both my notes and the original copy . . . Walch, I would not regret the time and money I have spent on Phonography if it never brought me more than it did that night, for then it brought me the privilege of standing by the bed of the most remarkable man of modern times and one who will live in the annals of his Country as long as she continues to have a history."

Tanner became an ardent Republican and member of the G. A. R., and he was rewarded by appointments as commissioner of pensions by President Benjamin Harrison and register of wills for the District of Columbia by President Theodore Roosevelt. He died in 1927. His original notes for the inquest are a prized possession of the Union League of Philadelphia. This letter, probably the best contemporary eyewitness account of the scene at Lincoln's deathbed, was given by Walch to Charles H. Strawhecker, his Grand Rapids partner in a court-reporting firm.

Gift of Mrs. Nellie Strawhecker and Paul O. Strawhecker, Grand Rapids, Michigan, 1936.

⤳ 95 ⤳

THE LOST CAUSE REVIVED

IN LATE MAY 1865, William P. Lane's Texas Rangers (the Third Texas Cavalry) disbanded and returned to Harrison County in northeastern Texas. Although many histories paint a picture of ragged Confederate soldiers returning home to face years of privation and despair, such was not the case with many of the veterans of this unit. Disproportionately well-off prior to the war, many Rangers returned home to find their property entirely untouched by the war, and a number immediately set to work salvaging the system they had failed to preserve by force of arms. Using whatever social and political leverage they had at hand, and terror and force when necessary, many Rangers became self-professed "redeemers," scratching and clawing to advance states rights and white supremacy. In Harrison County, at least, they managed to make dead letters of political Reconstruction and the Fifteenth Amendment.

In a pattern repeated across the country, veterans began writing and rewriting the history of the war. To the victors go the spoils, but even the vanquished have literary license. William Heartsill sat down at home in Marshall, Texas, to celebrate his exploits, publishing his very thorough wartime journal as *Fourteen Hundred and 91 Days, in the Confederate Army*. It was no mean feat: he worked in the odd ends of the day on an Octavo Novelty Press, as he meticulously notes, printing one page at a time between December 1874 and June 1876.

"You will find this journal 'Chock full' of three things," he wrote, "first, doings of the W. P. Lane Rangers, secondly, bad orthography; and thirdly, a great deal of shocking grammar." Its unvarnished language provided an element of authenticity to the experiences described. As a final touch,

Capt. Sam. J. Richardson.

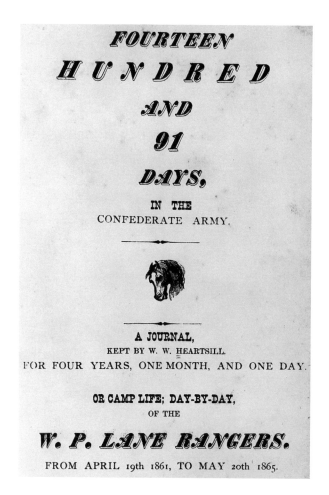

FOURTEEN
HUNDRED
AND
91
DAYS,
IN THE
CONFEDERATE ARMY.

A JOURNAL,
KEPT BY W. W. HEARTSILL.
FOR FOUR YEARS, ONE MONTH, AND ONE DAY.

OR CAMP LIFE; DAY-BY-DAY,
OF THE
W. P. LANE RANGERS.
FROM APRIL 19th 1861, TO MAY 20th 1865.

Heartsill tipped in photographs of 61 of his comrades, giving readers a chance to see for themselves what these determined Confederate heroes looked like and providing a final stamp of authenticity. The flamboyantly-dressed soldier pictured is Captain Samuel Richardson, a relative of the author.

The pages of Heartsill's book were an attempt to redeem the Confederate cause and end Reconstruction. The Library has a very extensive collection of Civil War regimental histories, and this is considered one of the greatest rarities.

Purchased from L. M. Foster, 1947.

📚 96 📚

THE UGLY FRONTIER

TODAY, WHEN TOURISTS VISIT HISTORIC SITES or one of the many quiet, restored towns and villages that exist around the country, they usually find themselves in park-like surroundings. They see old trees, manicured lawns, and a sort of charming beauty which promotes nostalgic longings for a simpler age, when there seemed to be a sense of community, when one could get a true crafts-

man who cared about quality to build a house, and when man was more in touch with nature. It is a charming and naive pipe dream.

In fact, generally speaking, early American farms, small towns, and even cities tended to be quite ugly, full of unpainted houses and stores nailed together from green lumber, trash littering the mud-choked or dusty streets, vast clouds of mosquitoes breeding in stagnant pools of water created by half-cleared forests, poor sanitation, and pigs and chickens running loose, rooting and defecating at will. Travelers from abroad constantly emphasized the unsightliness and uncleanliness of most American towns and habitations until after the Civil War.

The picture shown here probably dates from the 1870s and is most likely a scene in Michigan, Wisconsin, or Minnesota, the great lumbering frontier of that era. It would have been a pristine forest five years earlier, but now the hills have been stripped of trees, leaving stumps everywhere. A crude sawmill sits with little timber left to cut, and the land appears to have no promise for farming. The introduction of outdoor photography in the 1850s provides us priceless glimpses of frontier America "in the raw." It is not a particularly pretty sight, but it is historical reality. New Amsterdam, Williamsburg, and Charleston were probably just as rough, homely, and unsanitary in their earliest decade or two.

The Clements collections are rich in the sources that portray our land before, during, and after settlement. Although photography only records the conditions of the past century and a half, pictures such as this provide an element of hard reality, tempering the sort of nostalgia historical tourism tends to promote. If one is particularly fond of tree stumps, houses that easily burn to the ground, mud, and malaria, the good old days on the frontier might seem special. Otherwise, maybe "going back" isn't such a great idea after all. Although historical sites are an important part of preserving our history, a bit of scepticism is in order when they start to look attractive!

Purchased from Todd Wesloh, 1993.

⇎ 97 ⇎

THE SMOKESTACK ECONOMY

WHEN VICTORIAN AMERICANS looked upon a landscape of belching smokestacks and soot-stained factories, they reveled in the beauty. By 1850, the "dark, satanic mills" of the eighteenth century had become symbols of American economic supremacy and the promise of future prosperity and might. Every popular medium, from magazines and newspapers to books, music, and photographs, hailed the factory and American industrial ingenuity as a benediction. That so much of our wealth was based on extractive enterprises and the processing of raw materials made the sight all the more glorious: natural riches were our divine blessings, and the dark mills were merely the ovens for baking this heavenly manna.

One of the best known photographers of the far West, Carleton Watkins (1829–1916), is usually associated with grand views of America's scenic wonders rather than industrial panoramas. Having apprenticed in the San Francisco studio of Robert Vance, Watkins ventured out on his own in 1861, and later that year he paid a visit to Yosemite Valley, taking the first of many views that

became his signature work, not to mention his primary source of income. Like many photographers, Watkins was forced to go wherever a profitable commission beckoned, traveling from Utah to Oregon and to the homely mercury mining district of New Almaden. He went bankrupt in 1874, and in an attempt to reestablish his solvency, he took two trips to Virginia City, Nevada, and produced a number of views of that decidedly un-scenic but historically interesting mining town.

In 1876, when this picture of the interior of a pan mill was probably taken, the western economy was entering a major period of transition. The "old" gold fields of California were still productive, but the true mining excitement had shifted elsewhere, notably Nevada, Colorado, Idaho, and Montana, and silver had replaced gold as the source of greatest wealth. This mill was a typical concern in Nevada's Comstock Lode, which had been producing millionaires since at least 1859. The Comstock was a deep shaft rather than a surface operation such as those that characterized the first California Gold Rush. This sort of mining required great investment and outlay of capital. This photograph, made technically difficult by low lighting levels, gives a sense of the scale of these operations, and the extraordinary outlay of money, manpower, and resources necessary to make mineral extraction profitable.

The transition from shops and small industrial plants to large-scale factories was gradually transforming the American economy at every level in the post-Civil War era. To the first generation of mine owners, investors, and workers, the efficiency of an operation such as this must have seemed wonderful. Most nineteenth-century Americans embraced industrialization wholeheartedly. Only gradually would the public come to realize the price being paid in terms of the lives of the workers and the scars on the once-pristine wilderness.

Purchased from New York Bound Books, 1984.

⊂⊃ 98 ⊂⊃

THE COUNTY ATLAS: RURAL AMERICA
AS IT NEVER QUITE WAS

WILLIAM T. MURDOCK AND HIS WIFE, Sarah Hoover Murdock, both in their late sixties and married for forty-four years, seem to have had absolutely nothing of an extraordinary nature occur in the course of their lives, yet their vividly realistic portraits and a somewhat idealized "artistic rendering" of their farm take up an entire folio page of the 1878 Tippecanoe County, Indiana, atlas. Murdock was one of five children, born in 1811 in Ohio. His father, not unlike many western settlers of his era, seems to have had a restless streak. In 1819 he moved to Wayne County, Indiana. Before he had finished clearing the land, he moved to another farm in the same county, and three years later abandoned the new property for a homestead in the prairie region of the state, an area where he wouldn't have to clear trees! He resided in his original log cabin on this farm until his death.

William Murdock was apparently the dutiful or favored son who helped farm the homestead property until the father's demise. He married a local girl, produced six children, and inherited the

Wᴹ T. Murdock   Mrs. W. T. Murdock

Res. of William T. Murdock.
Sec. 8 Wayne Tp. Tippecanoe. Co. Indiana.

farm. He was a Democrat, a Methodist, and a long-time county commissioner. He obviously improved the property after his father's death, built a frame home to replace the log cabin, and would appear to have been a typical midwestern American farmer. How, then, did he qualify for such an extraordinary amount of space in a book which purports to be the history and record of the leading citizens of what was a very sizable, populous, and historically important county?

The answer is that he paid, and paid very well. In 1890 Bates Harrington published *How 'Tis Done. A Thorough Ventilation of the Numerous Schemes conducted by Wandering Canvassers . . . for the Swindling of the Public* (Syracuse, 1890). The author attempted, without much success, to create a scandal where there was none, but in the process he provided a great deal of useful detail about how "illustrated" county atlases were produced. Harrington portrayed their production as a swindle because he felt that the publishers were enticing customers to spend good money for something that they did not need. He missed the point entirely.

In a strictly business or geographical sense, these farmers certainly did not have any practical use for county atlases or expensive, full-page lithographs of themselves and their farms. But in an emotional sense the books satisfied a very real need — one which was even a little more satisfying in that it involved and was known to neighbors to have involved considerable extravagance. In essence, these were statements of personal success on the part of people who secretly harbored some nagging doubts as to whether they had actually "made it."

The generation which patronized these illustrated county atlases and histories was largely made up of men and women who were intensely proud of the fact that they were born in rude log cabins and had been provided few advantages. They had scraped and scratched to purchase land, had cleared forests and plowed prairie lands which never had been farmed before, and had succeeded by their declining years in achieving respectability and affluence. It wore them out physically and, in contrast to today, when people smile and emphasize whatever degree of youthful beauty remains when their photograph is taken, these survivors glorified in looking old, careworn, and ready to meet the Lord.

There were about three hundred of these illustrated or "combination" county atlases published between the late 1860s and early 1880s, the majority of them in the Midwest. Teams of canvassers would descend upon a carefully selected county, secure any previous surveys, and add simple details such as the exact location of farmhouses, orchards, and streams to emphasize their accuracy. Township maps, a few pages of historical anecdote, a list of old settlers, and a few views of public buildings were the standard features of every atlas. Everything beyond that cost extra money.

Mr. Murdock probably paid about $75 for the picture of his farm, $200 for the portraits, and $25 for a biographical sketch that appears elsewhere in the book. The finished atlas itself cost $10 to $15. For additional expenditures, the publisher would gladly have included deceased family members, prized livestock, pets, the farm as it looked twenty years earlier, a barn that hadn't even been built yet, or anything else the subscriber desired.

The Library has a sizable collection of these atlases and constantly adds those it lacks. Why, considering that they are essentially vanity publications? For one thing, they are a rich and uniquely important pictorial source for rural and small-town America, containing birdseye views of half-settled villages, domestic architecture, hotels, county fairgrounds, business and manufacturing operations of all sorts. But they are more than that. They are an unequaled graphic expression of the aspirations and ideals of average Americans, who in the nineteenth century transformed the United States from a post-colonial frontier into a powerful if provincial nation.

Purchased from Swann Auction by MacManus, 1992.

༺ 99 ༻
A SPIRITED PHOTOGRAPHER IN SAN FRANCISCO

ONE OF THE SPECIALTIES of the Clements Library's photographic collections is views of private homes, particularly interior views. They provide wonderful documentation not only of the personalities of the owners, but changing tastes in furniture and decoration. Particularly for the wealthy, who could afford the latest fashions, these photographs give a glimpse of how people viewed themselves and wanted others to see them.

In San Francisco, a new city founded on gold and commerce, the desire for elegant display may have been even more intense than in the older, more established cities of the East. In 1880, Robert and Kate Johnson hired Eadweard Muybridge (1830–1904), one the best known photographers on the West Coast, to document both their city and country homes. Their San Francisco house was on O'Farrell Street, and their country estate was in fashionable Menlo Park. The Johnsons were patrons of the arts, known publicly for their generous spending on the finest things that life had to offer, and they were considered, rightly so, to be highly unusual people. In later life, Kate Johnson became known as the "Cat Lady" and was reputed to have kept over 300 felines in her home.

Muybridge more than matched the Johnsons in eccentricity. He was just beginning to enjoy the fruits of national fame for his photographic studies of the horse and of man in motion, a precursor to moving pictures, though he was still accepting commissions to photograph private residences inside and out. The album purchased by the Johnsons, one of the Library's more interesting collections of interior photographs, is highly unusual.

At first glance, it would appear to be the typical vanity album, commissioned to prove the exquisite taste and extensive wealth of the owners of a house furnished in the latest style. Room after room is bursting with furniture and art, every space on the first floor brimming with "taste" and "decorum," and even the stairwells and hallways are lined with works of art. In the bedroom on the second floor, however, Muybridge throws a curve. Amid the lush surroundings, he posed Robert and Kate Johnson, with one as "spirit" and the other as flesh, and even more curiously he placed himself, barely visible, as a reflection in the lower right hand corner of the mirror. Other pictures in the album are equally bizarre, using the juxtaposition of small and large objects to fool the viewer's eye.

One of the most contentious issues in photography in 1880 was whether the photographic image was a true representation of nature. Some photographers insisted that photographs never lie, while others, in essence, argued that they can never tell the full truth about their subjects. Muybridge was an innovator in creating composite photographs, positive images constructed of numerous negatives, and in the Johnson album he seems to be casting his vote, showing not only that the living can be depicted as dead, but that the hand of the artist, literally, can be seen in every image. In so doing, he may also be casting his vote on the meaning of such conspicuous consumption—for if appearances can deceive, what are we to make of the appearance of such wealth and stability?

The Muybridge album is more than a simple documentary of the Johnson home. It is a conspiracy of visions of three eccentrics, a creative blend of photography and commentary on the modern world. Above all else, what Muybridge and the Johnsons seem to say is that appearance is not always reality.

Purchased from a private collector by Stephen Resnick, 1991.

❧ 100 ❧

INNOVATIVE FOX, IN A PINK DRESS

The National Police Gazette, a typical issue of which is illustrated here, was the most notorious, the most innovative, and during its heyday, one of the most profitable periodicals in the history of American journalism. The man behind the publication's success was Richard Kyle Fox, who emigrated from northern Ireland in 1874. His previous, modest career in journalism had been restricted to that of business manager of a newspaper in Belfast. He grew up in a highly respected, middle-class Presbyterian family, and in his own private life was a very quiet, conservative, proper family man who neither drank nor gambled.

Fox was a careful businessman and a brilliant promoter and publicist. *The National Police Gazette* began its long life in 1845 as an unofficial professional journal for policemen. Several of the early editors were former or even active New York law enforcement officers. By the post-Civil War era it was neither informative nor sensational, and it had lost most of its subscribers. Taking over the debt-encumbered periodical at virtually no cost, Fox transformed it, in 1878, into a large-format illustrated magazine and introduced one innovation after another. He invented the sensational headline, the "condensed" news story, the sports page, the theatrical gossip column, illustrations within columns, and prize contests—anything to get attention and name recognition. His coverage of gunfighters and train robbers helped establish America's love affair and stereotypes about the Wild West—both Jesse James and Billy the Kid were themselves avid *National Police Gazette* readers. The modern sports journal, *Variety Magazine*, and the supermarket tabloid are all to some extent descendants of the *Gazette*, but so was the "yellow" journal of the sort which Hearst perfected in the 1890s.

Fox printed the magazine on pink paper to make it distinctive on the newsstand. He produced garish, diamond-encrusted trophies and belts for every sort of competitive event, from traditional sports such as walking, sculling, and bicycle racing to exhibitionist stunts such as jumping off bridges. For a brief period in the late 1880s, Fox became the international arbiter and promoter of the sport of boxing. He built a showy Police Gazette Building at a strategically-located corner where the new Brooklyn Bridge entered Manhattan, and he invented an imaginative public personality for himself as a rakish man about town who appreciated all the finer things in life—French champagne, fast horses, and beautiful women—a "gentleman" in the world of saloon keepers, "sports," and working men. He endowed the journal itself with a worldly tone and personality of its own.

BEAUTY AT THE BILLIARD-TABLE.
HOW DAINTY BEAUTIES HANDLE THE CUE AND ARE PROVING DANGEROUS RIVALS TO THE STERNER SEX AT THE BILLIARD-TABLE.

From the beginning, Fox's *Gazette* was partly a sophisticated joke and partly a lively, cynical commentary on human nature and all the ways that men and women had come up with to make fools of themselves. There was no such thing as innocence in Fox's Calvinistic world—children and "respectable" businessmen were as capable of evil as the traditional "criminal type." Above all, he scorned hypocrisy in all forms, and he particularly delighted in pointing out the foibles and crimes of the rich, of politicians, and of clergymen. He had a soft spot for the average, honest laborer, and his attitude toward women was far in advance of his age. He was in awe of the abilities and independence of American women, and although the journal became famous for pictures of seductive, well-proportioned ladies showing a bit more flesh than was considered respectable, the "girls" of the *Police Gazette* were powerful amazons to be taken seriously, not the exploited subjects of pornographic magazines today. Within five years of Fox's takeover of the magazine, it had the largest circulation of any illustrated journal in the nation.

It soon became a victim of its own success. Richard Fox, himself, had made several million dollars from the venture by the late 1880s, and he began to lose interest. The sophisticated qualities of his social commentary had generally gone over the heads of the majority of his readers anyway—primarily working-class men and boys who hung around shoeshine parlors, barber shops, and saloons—and Fox gradually let it degenerate into a magazine of sports commentary, pictures, dime-novel stories, and formula theatrical gossip, omitting names so the news articles could never form the basis of lawsuits. It remained highly profitable until Prohibition, when it lost its basic audience. In spite of serious attempts to upgrade the quality of sports commentary in the late 20s, it went bankrupt in 1933, was later revived, and permanently went out of business in the early 1970s.

At the time the *National Police Gazette* was issued, respectable libraries would not have dared to subscribe. Only two extensive files exist. The Library of Congress has the issues deposited for copyright purposes, and this library has the publisher's own file. It is fortuitous that these have survived, because for the history of low-life New York, sports, crime, off-Broadway theater, and the elusive lifestyles and attitudes of working men and women, *The National Police Gazette* is a unique and invaluable source.

Purchased from New York Museum Auction by Patterson Smith, 1994.

EPHEMERAL VISION OF GRANDEUR
THE COLUMBIAN EXPOSITION

AS THE FOUR HUNDREDTH ANNIVERSARY of Columbus' discovery of America (1492) loomed on the horizon, Congress passed a bill authorizing a massive loan to finance an international exposition to surpass all previous efforts. Planning committees in Washington, Philadelphia, and New York competed for the role as hosts, but as of 1891, a year before the event should have opened, the whole thing was tied up in political rivalries, and it appeared that the opportunity would be lost. At that point, a committee of wealthy and determined Chicago business and civic leaders made good on a pledge of five million dollars of their own funds and began work. The actual centennial year of 1892 had already been lost, and the summer of 1893 was agreed upon for the Chicago Fair, permitting New York to save face by launching the celebration in 1892 with a dinner, parade, and naval exercise welcoming the Spanish reconstruction of the *Santa Maria*. It took a full measure of shrewd, behind-the-scenes politics, a brilliant public relations campaign, and a massive design and construction project, the likes of which had never been seen before, to meet even the new opening deadline, but in March 1893 the resplendent "White City" opened to the public.

The Columbian Exposition, in spite of a cool spring and the fact that it was held in the midst of a serious world economic depression, was a brilliant success. Built on a magnificent Lake Michigan site, the grounds and buildings of the Fair were designed by Chester Burnham and a team of outstanding architects, sculptors, and artists as a dream-like modern-day Roman capital city, only grander, cleaner, and more picturesque. The main exhibit halls and foreign and state buildings were full of remarkable natural wonders, the latest technological wizardry, and historical and artistic treasures from around the globe of a quality and diversity never before seen in this country. The Midway, a sort of side show adjunct to the Fair, proved to be immensely popular with the public. It contained living "anthropological" exhibits of authentic native peoples, shops and amusements, and the world's first Ferris Wheel. There were numerous conferences, concerts, and daily theatrical performances, and special visitor days for significant constituencies.

Previous to the Columbian Exposition, official European familiarity with the United States was largely confined to the cities on the East Coast. Chicago proved to be an exceptionally gracious host to the kings and queens, prime ministers and diplomats, and they generally left with highly favorable impressions. In the process, Chicago developed a sense of itself, not merely as a large and prosperous hub of economic activity but as a grand and sophisticated city of the world. It has been that ever since.

The invitations to diplomatic receptions, shown here, come from a unique collection of ephemeral Columbian Exposition material in the papers of Moses P. Handy, Head of Promotion and Publicity, whose brilliant efforts played a major role in the event's success. The Library makes a point of collecting invitations, menus, travel brochures, theater programs, and advertising leaflets. They are an important type of historical documentation, capturing the nuances of everyday life more effectively than formal library materials.

The Imperial Ottoman Commission
at the
World's Columbian Exposition
has the honor to invite you
to be present at the ceremony of the
Dedication of the Mosque and Bazar
at the

Chicago,
September 5th 1893.

Auditorium
Hotel.

Messieurs Frederick Douglass and
Chas. A. Preston,
Commissioners of the Republic of Häiti ,
request the pleasure of your company
at the opening of the
Häitian Pavilion,
at 3 o'clock, Saturday, June 24, 1893.

The Imperial German Commissioner
Privy Councillor Adolph Wermuth
requests the honor of your presence, with ladies,
at a reception with musical entertainment in
the
German Government Building,
Jackson Park,
on Tuesday, May twenty third,
from four to six.

Sir Richard Webster
and the Members of the
Royal British Commission
request the honor of the company
of Major Moses P. Handy and lady
at a reception at Victoria House,
Jackson Park,
Saturday, September twenty third,
from four to six o'clock.

R.S.V.P.

Invitations to Diplomatic Functions, Columbian Exposition, 1893

In many ways, the Columbian Exposition was the symbolic culmination of the nineteenth century. It displayed to the world the fact that the United States, even its heartland, had come of age and was a powerful force to be reckoned with. At the same time, it gave average Americans, isolated and provincial for decades, a glimpse of the greater world community into which they would be irrevocably drawn by the Spanish-American and First World Wars, and by the very technological innovation displayed so effectively at the Exposition.

Purchased from Handy Family Trust, 1985.

THREE THOUSAND TWO HUNDRED FIFTY COPIES OF

One Hundred and One Treasures

HAVE BEEN PRINTED IN DECEMBER OF 1997
AT THE STINEHOUR PRESS, LUNENBURG, VERMONT.
TYPE HAS BEEN SET IN ADOBE JENSON, ILLUSTRATIONS
REPRODUCED AS 300-LINE DUOTONES AND PRINTED
OFFSET ON MOHAWK SUPERFINE TEXT.

BINDING BY ACME BOOKBINDING,
CHARLESTOWN, MASSACHUSETTS.